from Motorcycle Consumer News

MORE
Proficient Motorcycling

MASTERING THE RIDE

by

David L. Hough

A Division of BowTie, Inc.

Irvine, California

Ruth Strother, Project manager
Nick Clemente, Special consultant
Karla Austin, Editor
Michelle Martinez, Assistant editor
Cover and book design by Bocu & Bocu
Gloria Klein, Indexer

Library of Congress Cataloging-in-Publication Data
Hough, David L., 1937-
  More proficient motorcycling : mastering the ride / by David L. Hough.

      p. cm.
Includes bibliographical references and index.
  ISBN 1-931993-03-3 (pbk. : alk. paper)
 1. Motorcycling. I. Road rider. II. Motorcycle consumer news. III.
Title.

TL440.5.H65 2002
629.28'475--dc21

                              2002011174

BowTie Press®
A DIVISION OF BOWTIE, INC.
3 Burroughs
Irvine, California 92618

Printed and bound in Singapore
10 9 8 7 6 5 4 3

Dedication

This book is dedicated to all the magazine editors I've worked with over the years. The editors are the ones who do all the hard work to make each issue seem fresh and interesting. Editors are the ones who remind contributors to get their work in, so they can sweat an issue together in time to ship to the printer. And the editors are the ones who take all the flak from readers when they read something they don't like.

I've learned a great deal from every editor I've worked with, but I'm especially indebted to Fred Rau, Senior Editor of *Motorcycle Consumer News*. Over the years, Fred has continued to encourage me to keep writing my skills columns long after I felt I should back out of the picture. Without his support and friendly persuasion, the "Proficient Motorcycling" column would have disappeared from *Motorcycle Consumer News*, and books such as *Proficient Motorcycling, Street Strategies,* and *More Proficient Motorcycling* might never have been published.

Contents

Foreword

get on a plane and listen to the flight attendant drone on about emergency exits and flotation devices, and I sincerely hope I never have an occasion to make actual use of this information. In my checkered motorcycling career, however, I have put helmets, jackets, pants, boots, and gloves to the test, mostly because nobody ever taught me how to ride a motorcycle. Back in those "I Like Ike" days, we pretty much taught ourselves. And the lucky survived.

My riding days began when I was fifteen, when my equally underage friend Dick bought a Harley 125. The owner delivered it to Dick's house, which, fortunately, backed onto woods and a river. Dick's father, a Corvette-driving doctor, returned home, saw the little motorcycle, muttered, *Death machine*, and never mentioned it again. Dick and I went down into the woods and learned the rudiments of riding all by ourselves. This was simple "woodsing," poking along the dirt paths, learning how not to stall the engine and not much else.

I passed my sixteenth birthday and paid a high school chum $10 to go down to the Department of Motor Vehicles (DMV) with me and let me get my license on his Whizzer. After giving me the written test, which I barely passed, the DMV inspector came out to the steps of the building and said, *Okay. Go around the block and if you're back in five minutes, you get your license.* Done.

My parents said I could have a motorcycle if I earned the money to buy one; which I did, whereupon they presented me with a helmet and the warning that if I were ever seen on the bike without the crash hat on my head, it would be the end of my motor-cycling days. Pretty smart.

But had I learned to ride a motorcycle properly? Not a chance. I had mastered the rudiments of a motorcycle's controls, but insofar as knowing what to do when some-thing unexpected happened on the road: of that I was entirely ignorant. So I went out on my used NSU 250 Max and had a series of minor accidents, all part of the learning process of the 1950s.

I thought the front brake was something to be used when waiting at a traffic light on a hill, and in my first panic stop, I locked up the rear wheel and fell down. Darn! Why did that happen? And I found that train tracks were very slippery in the rain, espe-cially if approached at an acute angle.

Learning by experience can be painful, but that is the way it was done in those years before the advent of safety consciousness and the Motorcycle Safety Foundation (MSF). A dealer thought nothing of selling a neophyte a bike, showing him where the clutch and gas and brakes were, watching him do two loops in the parking lot, and sending him on the road. More experienced riding friends would offer advice, but there was really nowhere that I knew of that I could go to acquire this knowledge beforehand.

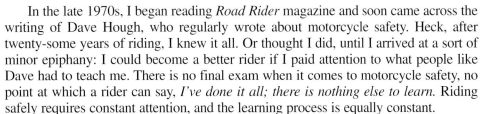

In the late 1970s, I began reading *Road Rider* magazine and soon came across the writing of Dave Hough, who regularly wrote about motorcycle safety. Heck, after twenty-some years of riding, I knew it all. Or thought I did, until I arrived at a sort of minor epiphany: I could become a better rider if I paid attention to what people like Dave had to teach me. There is no final exam when it comes to motorcycle safety, no point at which a rider can say, *I've done it all; there is nothing else to learn.* Riding safely requires constant attention, and the learning process is equally constant.

These days, I read Dave's books, I take the MSF's Experienced RiderCourse (ERC) every few years, and I listen when my riding buddies tell me that I sometimes tend to be less than overly cautious when overtaking. I intend to lead a long and happy life, riding well until I am fourscore and something. I don't like to fall down. And maybe some little bit of knowledge imparted through Hough's experience will save me from myself.

If a single thought from this book helps you avoid a spill, it is definitely worth the small money you spent on it. A simple low-speed low-side in a sand-strewn corner will cost you a great deal more in terms of repairing fiberglass and flesh—plus the substantial damage to ego, which MasterCard does not cover. Safety cannot be over-valued. Yes, it can be boring, it can be tedious, it can even be overdone, but it cannot be valued too highly.

—Clement Salvadori

Clement Salvadori is a motorcycle journalist and world traveler. Clement writes many different columns and articles for motorcycle publications in the USA but is best known for the "On Touring" column in Rider *magazine.*

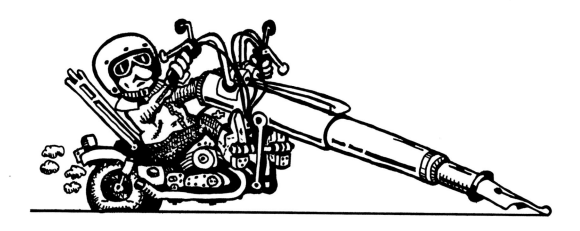

Preface

If you've already read my first book, *Proficient Motorcycling*, you'll know that I accumulated my knowledge of motorcycling firsthand from thirty years of daily commuting to work by motorcycle. And you'll know that I pronounce *Hough* like "rough" or "tough," and that I wrote for *Road Rider* magazine and kept on writing when it became *Motorcycle Consumer News (MCN)*.

But I've made some recent discoveries about my personal history that I'd like to share with you. In the process of digging up all the illustrations needed for *More Proficient Motorcycling*, I ran across a tattered, old black-and-white photograph of me as a chubby twelve-year-old sitting on a motorcycle. I'd forgotten all about it. In the photo, I'm wearing a leather aviator cap, fleece-lined leather mitts, and I'm covered by a canvas lap robe. The machine belonged to my father's friend, a mysterious Russian sailor who loved to play chess. The Russian had ridden up from the Oregon Coast in midwinter to play a game, face-to-face. The cold weather was the reason for the heavy fleece gloves, aviator cap, and lap robe.

At twelve years old, I wasn't riding the bike; I was merely posing as sort of a photographic joke for my father. The time frame was the winter of 1949–50. The location was Aberdeen, Washington. And I didn't know anything about motorcycles. It would be many years before I bought my first motorcycle.

For the first time since that photo was taken fifty-two years ago, I studied it carefully. The motorcycle appears to be a 1937 Indian Sport Scout with a 1947 front

fender light and leather saddlebags. The 45-cubic-inch Sport Scout was no slouch for its day, clocking a 111.55 mph speed record at Daytona Beach in 1938. That's pretty fast considering that wimpy little front drum brake.

Until seeing the photo, I hadn't realized that the bike and I were the same age. Then, when I thought back through my motorcycling experiences, I was jolted by some coincidences. First, I've ridden the Oregon Coast many times on different motorcycles. I suddenly realized that I've ridden sections of old Highway 101 that are almost the same today as they were fifty-two years ago when the Russian rode up to Aberdeen. Those weren't all summertime rides, either. I've also done a few wintertime transits on the Coast, and I know from personal experience what a tough ride that trip can be on a bike.

Out of curiosity, I added up the years I'd been riding motorcycles before I happened upon that faded old photo of me on the 1937 Indian. Would you believe I'd been riding for thirty-seven years? This was getting creepy. The final jolt came as I was getting ready to ride off the ferry from Seattle. I was thinking about my upcoming birthday, and for some reason glanced down at the speedometer on my vintage BMW. The odometer read 37,373. I'm not a superstitious person, but I had to stop and take a picture to prove I wasn't making this all up.

Do you suppose there was something about that wintertime trip and the 1937 Scout that planted the seed that sprouted into my interest in motorcycles and eventually the subject of riding skills? Naw, it's probably all just an odd coincidence. But if I find an Indian Scout for sale next March 7 for $3,737.37, I'll be buying it.

Whatever the start of my fascination with motorcycles, I'm still involved, and *More Proficient Motorcycling* gives me another opportunity to share my passion—and maybe a little humor—with other motorcyclists.

—David L. Hough

Introduction

The book *Proficient Motorcycling* is a collection of columns from *Road Rider* and *MCN*. That first volume was my personal selection of the columns that I felt would best explain motorcycle dynamics, control skills, and accident avoidance tactics.

Like the first book, *More Proficient Motorcycling* is mostly a selection of columns previously published in *Road Rider* and *MCN*. But this volume covers a wider variety of motorcycling topics and also includes a few articles written for other magazines, plus one or two that were written exclusively for this book.

Since the publication of *Proficient Motorcycling* in 2000, more than a few motorcyclists have asked about advanced riding skills. A common question is, *Is there a course I can take that's a notch above the ERC but not quite as intimidating as a racetrack cornering school?*

That question is a hint that some riders believe that there are some secret advanced skills we are withholding. The truth is, no one is holding back any secrets. The information is already available. The limiting factor isn't the availability of knowledge, but rather the lack of motivation to master what's being offered.

More than a few readers have admitted to me privately that they skim through my articles but don't really study the information. Others admit that they study the articles carefully but never practice the suggested skills on the bike. Obviously, not all riders are interested in changing their habits. And I'm not here to try to force you to do anything you don't want to do. But for those of you who can't seem to get enough information, this book should help you on your quest to master the ride.

If there is a secret about "advanced" skills, it's that they are mostly mental skills, not physical skills such as countersteering (push steering) or controlling the throttle or hanging off. Yes, there are additional physical skills to hone, but mostly it's a matter of observing, predicting, planning, and timing, rather than using muscle power. And it's not only a matter of controlling the motorcycle you're riding but also controlling the situation around you.

More Proficient Motorcycling is a continuation of what I started in *Proficient Motorcycling*. You'll find many of the same subjects, many of the same fictitious characters (based on real people and experiences), and even many of the same topics. But now we're going to dig a little deeper into the mysteries of motorcycling and add a few subjects that weren't covered in the first book.

Note that this book adds to the information in the first book, and we're not going to repeat all the basics in this volume. It isn't absolutely necessary to read *Proficient Motorcycling* first, but you'll probably find that *More Proficient Motorcycling* is easier to understand if you read the two books in sequence.

Learning LEARNING

Ride TO RIDE

CHAPTER 1
LEARNING TO RIDE

Biker Bill's Last Ride

Today, circumstances will conspire against Biker Bill. Down the road a few miles, his knowledge and experience will be challenged by a special situation, and the situation will beat him. This story is based upon a real crash that happened during the summer of 1991, although Biker Bill is a fictitious name. This is not an indictment of the rider but rather a potential learning experience for every touring motorcyclist.

The Ride

The day is young, the desert is cool, and the air is still. The evaporating dew leaves a heady perfume of sagebrush and juniper in the air. The sky is the light turquoise color that hints of perfect weather. The road surface is clean and dry, and the motor homes have yet to clog along. It's hard to imagine that anything could go wrong on a day as perfect as this, especially to a rider as well traveled as Biker Bill.

Bill is not a youthful rider with a need for excess. He is married with children at home, and he understands his responsibilities. He knows only too well how his family feels about the dangers of riding a motorcycle. Bill and his good riding buddy have been riding together every summer for the past eight years, gradually expanding their touring horizons. This year, they

What special circumstances had conspired to turn a great ride into a disaster in a few short seconds?

have been exploring the Southwest. Yesterday it was the Grand Canyon. Today it's off to Monument Valley.

Bill and his companion don't usually ride in formation. The attention required to pace another rider hour after hour distracts from the full attention needed for riding their own machines. So, instead of riding just a few seconds apart, they split up and ride toward a common destination at their own paces. Bill is the following rider today, perhaps ten or twenty minutes behind his companion. They have agreed to meet at the restaurant of a trading post to take a coffee break and share the discoveries of the morning.

The Road

The two-lane highway meanders east across the top of a juniper-strewn mesa. An hour into the ride, the road drops over the edge in a series of switchbacks, then straightens out at the bottom and heads like an arrow toward a distant horizon, rising and dipping slightly with the ripples of the landscape like long waves at sea. Somewhere to the right, there is a shadowy canyon where the Colorado River has cut a deep groove into the red rock. To the left is a long reef of brilliant reddish pink cliffs so awesome that the scene sends a tingle up Bill's spine.

Bill feels good to be here, riding a powerful motorcycle in the cool morning air with the pungent scent of the desert stinging his nostrils. How marvelous to be so far from the confusion and noise and pollution of the cities, and to be flying across the desert waves on a sweet-running machine. The speed limit is humorously posted at a creeping 55 mph out here in the desert, but everyone seems to drive at least 70. The big four-cylinder BMW hums along comfortably at 80 mph.

The awesome Vermillion Cliffs demand that they be appreciated, and Bill can steal about two second's worth of breathtaking scenery at this speed before the rushing road demands his attention again. He even develops a little routine, waiting until the machine tops a rise to provide a view and then stealing another two-second glance at the cliffs.

This routine goes on for another half hour. Bill considers stopping to take a picture of the cliffs. He even considers pulling the auto-focus camera out of the tank bag with his left hand and trying a shot on the fly, but he decides to keep motoring along and get a shot when he stops for coffee. Besides, he feels a need to catch up and share the excitement of the ride. Or perhaps the urgency is because he doesn't want to be thought of as a slow rider, even by his friend. The K-bike feels sweet at 80 mph, and he holds it there.

Bill can steal about two second's worth of breathtaking scenery at this speed before the rushing road demands his attention again.

The Crash

Topping a rise in the undulating road, Bill steals another glance at the cliffs. But when his eyes flick back to the road, it isn't there anymore, there's just sagebrush. He suddenly realizes the pavement has made a left turn, but the bike is heading straight into the desert at warp speed.

It is a short flight—perhaps only two seconds, maybe 200 feet. When the front tire touches down in the soft sand, bike and rider are flipped into a cartwheel. Plastic is peeled off the bike like the skin of an orange, and the saddlebags explode into a trail of clothing.

When the desert finally stops spinning, Bill finds himself lying on his back in the sand with the sun in his eyes and a terrible pain in his ribs. Fighting the urge to pass out, he tries to make sense of what happened. He remembers the mesa, the straight road, and the Vermillion Cliffs. Then slowly he remembers riding a bike, and the road curving away. Bill tries to roll over to look for his bike, but a searing pain shoots across his chest to his forehead and he almost blacks out again. He lies still, trying to ignore the pain, wondering how far he is from the road and whether he'll make it out of this disaster alive.

Fortunately for Bill, a passing motorist catches a glimpse of something shiny off the side of the road and slows to investigate. The motorist is shocked to realize that he is looking at a serious and very recent motorcycle crash, and he rushes back to the trading post to call for help. The police arrive within a few minutes, radio for a medevac, and less than an hour after the crash, Bill is in the hospital in emergency care. He survives the crash, but it is enough of a crisis to end his motorcycling career forever.

Was Bill a Dangerous Rider?

So, what do you think? Was Biker Bill an irresponsible, daredevil zoomie we would expect to crash? No. We've established that Bill was an adult touring rider with a family at home and a good sense of self-preservation. He's a lot like you or me. Does that mean you or I could have gone flying into the sagebrush if the same circumstances had ganged up on us? Maybe we had better take a closer look at Bill's unfortunate crash, and see if we can figure out what really went wrong.

What Happened?

The police wrote down "excessive speed" as the cause of the accident, but we might suspect that speed was only part of the problem. The question they didn't ask is, *Why would an apparently experienced rider miss this particular turn?* Let's consider Bill's proficiency and then see if we can figure out what went wrong.

Bill, like most of us, had absorbed some better riding skills over the years. He followed better cornering lines, maintained a leading throttle during the turns, understood the relative traction of his tires, and favored the front wheel brake. Coming down off the mesa, he practiced these skills, entering turns closer to the outside to follow the safer delayed apex line and keeping his eyes level with the horizon for better spatial orientation. He smoothly applied the front brake to keep speed in check when approaching each turn, released brake pressure just before leaning, and countersteered to accurately control his cornering lines.

Closer to the Edge

Intellectually, Bill understood the importance of keeping speed within his perceived sight distance, distance he would need to decelerate or stop should he encounter an obstruction such as an antelope or a tourist making a U-turn. But with experience, he learned that his K-bike could stop very quickly, so he became complacent about sight distance. Like many of us, Bill kept pushing the speed up more and more every year, accepting the occasional loss of sight distance without slowing down. While he used to cruise at 55 or 60 mph eight years ago, now he cruises at 70 or 80. While he might have taken a tight corner at 35 mph, he now leans over confidently at 55.

The setting for Bill's crash becomes as clear as the desert air when you look at the road from the direction in which he had come. The road runs straight as an arrow over the waves of the desert, with no hint that it doesn't just keep going straight forever. It just happens to curve left beyond the crest of that last rise.

Warp speed may seem reasonable out in the desert, but be aware that you can't see what's over that rise ahead.

Let's back up 20 miles to where Bill dropped off the mesa because that's where the crash started. Bill got into a routine of riding over each little rise without realizing that he couldn't always see the back side of most of them until he crested the top. His brain just filled in the missing road, and sure enough, when he crested each hill, the road was always there. Well, "always," except for that last rise.

Bill's machine probably could have taken this particular curve at 80 mph in the hands of a skilled rider, except that this rider wasn't prepared for a curve. More importantly, what could have been a close call was morphed into an accident by some other bad habits—habits that many of the rest of us could claim as our own:

1. Bill allowed assumptions to override his sight distance and allowed his complacency to become a routine, mile after mile. A wise rider makes predictions only on what can be seen, not on assumptions. And when the view closes up, a smart rider immediately slows down to allow full control within the roadway in view.

2. Bill allowed his attention to be distracted by the scenery. At 80 mph, Bill's bike was eating up 234 feet of road every two seconds. With his attention distracted, he missed the important clues that would have warned him about the upcoming curve. The wise rider either slows down to take in the scenery or punctuates a fast ride with frequent stops to gawk.

3. Bill was attempting to catch up to the leader. Think about that: catching up requires that you ride *faster* than the leader. It's critical to ride within your own limits, even if that means letting the other guy disappear over the horizon and making him wait for you.

David L. Hough

Managing Risk

There are a lot of riders who just go riding without much thought about managing the risks. Too many believe that motorcycling is simply a two-wheeled form of Russian roulette. Take a spin and maybe your number will come up. In other words, if it isn't your turn to crash today, then don't worry about it, and if it is your turn, then there is nothing you can do to prevent it. But was it just chance that Bill's companion managed to keep the rubber side down riding the same road on an almost identical motorcycle?

The moral of this sad tale is that to a considerable extent we make our own luck. A rider's skill, knowledge, and attitude help control the relative risk. Some veteran riders have traveled hundreds of thousands of miles without an accident by being constantly aware of the situation and staying well within the limits of their bikes and riding skills. That's not easy, but it's possible.

How to Become a Better Rider

You learn to ride when you first get a bike. Then about the time you think you've learned it all, you get another opportunity to learn to ride. Punching through the envelope and cartwheeling off into the landscape is a harsh wake-up call to the risks of motorcycling. I've drawn the short straw a couple of times in 800,000 or so miles of riding. And I can tell you that crashes look a lot like close calls, right up to the point where you hit or miss. So, whether you have an accident or a near miss, it should be motivation to improve your knowledge and skills. Let's back up a bit here and think about how we learned to ride.

Trial and Error

When I learned to ride back in 1965, there weren't any rider training courses available. I just got on the bike, rode off into traffic, and learned by trial and error. I looked to my buddy Ricochet Red for sage advice about motorcycling. After all, Red started riding a couple of years before I did and had moved up to a powerful Marusho 500 while I was still learning on my Suzuki 150, so by comparison he was the "experienced" rider.

My first bike was a little Suzuki 150, which I learned to ride by trial and error with a little help from my buddy, Ricochet Red.

Red's collective wisdom was summed up in one serious statement: *There's only two kinds of bikers, Hough. There's them who have crashed and them who are gonna crash.* But Ken and Donna, a couple who had ridden motorcycles for many years, offered a different philosophy: *If you ever stop being afraid of a motorcycle, it's time to park it.* Sure, Red's folk wisdom was true. Just about every motorcyclist gets the turn to crash once or twice in a lifetime of riding. Ken and Donna had a point, too, about not getting too cocky on a bike. But I didn't find those sage statements particularly helpful. They are a lot like saying, *Be careful,* or, *If you can't run with the big dogs, stay on the porch.*

The question is what do I need to do to survive today? What are the right tactics for managing the risks? For instance, is it better to ride at the same speed as other traffic, at the speed limit, or faster than traffic? Should I lean the bike by counter-steering, by bodysteering (shifting my weight on the bike), or both? Should I brake just short of a skid during a quick stop, or should I slide the rear tire? Should I wear bright hi-viz (visibility) yellow, or camouflage? And during a desert ride, would a nice cool beer help stave off dehydration or make the situation worse?

You've probably heard the expression, "Experience is the best teacher." That theory when applied to motorcycling means that you just get on the bike and ride. And after you've ridden long enough and under a wide enough variety of conditions, cultures, and climates, eventually you should have absorbed most of the needed lessons.

The trouble with learning about motorcycles by trial and error is that a lot of motorcycle hazards aren't obvious. For instance, you might not appreciate how dangerous an edge trap is until the bike topples over and throws you down the road. What's more, not all control skills are easy to master. Let's say you suddenly need to pull off a quick swerve around a left-turning car. Do you think you can resist the urge to snap off the throttle?

The point is that learning by trial and error can be painful and expensive. Learning to become a proficient rider is hard work, and it takes a humble attitude. Many riders don't seem to be willing to take their learning seriously. Slithering through mud washes is nothing compared to the way many riders slither around the subject of riding skills.

A few years ago, a local rider smacked into a deer on his way home and neither survived. The rider's fellow club members wanted to do something to make everyone feel better about the situation. One of the officers called me to get the address of a

David L. Hough

national motorcycle safety organization so the club could make a donation in the rider's memory. I suggested that rather than send the money off somewhere else, perhaps the donation would be better spent subsidizing rider training for the local club members. The officer bristled, *Do you really think rider training would help anyone else avoid an accident like that one? Just give me the address where we can send the money!*

Yes, I do believe that rider training could potentially help the other club members avoid accidents, including deer strikes. But of course spending the money on local riders would have been an admission that the "experienced" motorcyclists in the club didn't know it all. The club's way to slither through the situation was to cough up some money and keep on riding the same as always. It's a modern-day version of Roman soldiers throwing coins into the baths to help ward off evil spirits before they rocket down the road on their chariots.

Cutting Through the BS

A big part of getting smarter about motorcycling is cutting through all the misinformation. "Everyone" seems to know that motorcycles are dangerous. Just ask your coworkers, your mother-in-law, your family doctor, or your local newspaper columnist. If you don't believe them, look at the scary statistics from the National Center for Statistics and Analysis, the Insurance Institute for Highway Safety, or the National Safety Council. "Everyone" knows that motorcycles are ten times (or twenty times or whatever) more dangerous than automobiles.

Basing your riding strategies on the opinions of nonriders, newspaper articles, or statistics is unreliable. First, friendly advice may not be very friendly. Second, being a professional in some field doesn't make that professional an expert in motorcycle safety. Third, there is no such thing as an average rider. Finally, is it really worthwhile to look at what crashees did wrong, or should we be figuring out what successful riders do right?

Ignore Friendly Advice

The chances are your nonriding doctor (or coworker or helpful neighbor) is probably less interested in helping you improve your odds and more interested in feeling superior to you. One day I had a coworker put his hand on my shoulder, and with a disparaging glance at my helmet plead sympathetically, *I sure wouldn't want my son to ride one of those things.* This paternalistic coworker might actually have been interested in helping me avoid injury, but he certainly didn't have the foggiest idea of where to start.

What's more, there are a lot of people who have a secret desire to ride motorcycles but can't overcome their fears. Putting you down is a way of justifying their fears and jealousy. The point is you can safely ignore "sympathetic" advice from people who don't know anything about motorcycles.

Ignore the Professional Experts

Let's say you finally get a few minutes with your family doctor, and he spots your riding jacket and mumbles something about "donor-cycles." Doc may think he knows something about motorcycle safety, but most medical doctors only see the results of accidents, not the successful riders. From their viewpoint, it's obvious: swing a leg over a motorcycle and BAM! It's your turn to be an organ donor.

But consider that being a doctor, lawyer, or engineer doesn't automatically make that professional an expert on motorcycling. After all, motorcycle safety isn't taught in medical school. So just thank Doc for any opinions he offers about bikes, and then refocus the conversation on his specialty. If Doc can't let it go, you can always remind him that statistically a human is more likely to die from a hospital error than from a motorcycle ride.

Forget the Movie Stars

You should also ignore what the movie star biker wannabes do. It's tempting to think that Cher or Arnold Schwarzenegger or Gary Busey are good role models for your own riding tactics, but wealthy actors are some of the world's worst riders. They have plenty of bucks to buy into the biker image but don't seem to understand that motorcycling is real life, not show business. Riding a bike is not a movie stunt where the director can call *cut* and do the scene over if something goes wrong. Don't pattern your riding gear or riding tactics after what the movie stars do.

I bring up all these examples of bad advice because they contribute to considerable misinformation about how to manage the risks of motorcycling. The opinions of nonmotorcyclists and biker wannabes are a frequent distraction and a waste of time and energy.

Statistics

On the other hand, wouldn't it be helpful to know the truth about motorcycle accidents? Well, there are a lot of statistics floating around, but the last good motorcycle accident study conducted in the U.S. was the Motorcycle Accident Factors Study (the Hurt Report) released by the National Highway Traffic Safety Administration (NHTSA) back in 1980. There have been some excellent motorcycle accident studies elsewhere in the world but not in the U.S.

Certainly there are some valuable lessons we can draw from the Hurt Report, but times have changed quite a bit since and the research was limited to the Los Angeles area. One current source of motor vehicle accident data is from the NHTSA. The NHTSA tries to collect good data, but it has never been much interested in motorcycles. There aren't many motorcycle experts at NHTSA who would appreciate the subtleties of motorcycle trends, such as an increase in fatalities during a time frame in which motorcycle registrations are increasing.

Still, the NHTSA does collect a lot of data, and it's worth looking at. The National Center for Statistics and Analysis (NCSA) has considerable information available on-line. Just be aware that a nonmotorcyclist tends to sort the numbers based on the bias of an automobile driver. For instance, the researchers may note an increase in the average engine size of motorcycles involved in fatal accidents and theorize that big motorcycles are overrepresented in accidents. Well, gee, guys. If you were aware of what was happening in motorcycling, you'd know that American motorcyclists are in love with big engines. If there are more engines over 1500 cubic centimeters (cc) on the road today, wouldn't you expect more accidents and fatalities involving engines over 1500 cc?

Television and newspaper reports are usually less than helpful. The report under the headline "Local Biker Dies" will probably note whether or not Zoomie Zed was wearing a helmet but not whether Zed was drunk or sober, licensed or not, whether he had taken rider training or learned from a friend, or how long he had been riding. More to the point, you won't hear anything about Able Al (the guy who didn't crash), because riding a motorcycle safely isn't exciting enough for today's news media.

The big mistake with statistics is making them personal. Even if you think you've discovered some reliable statistics, remember that hardly any of us are "average" riders. When novice rider Zoomie Zed smacks into a Ready-Mix concrete truck a mile away from the showroom floor, his personal averages are one fatality per mile. By comparison, Able Al may enjoy 500,000 miles of accident-free riding. For Al, accidents and fatalities average out to zero per 500,000 miles. So, unless you're close to the profile of an "average" rider, the statistics are likely to be way off for you. My actual risk or your actual risk depends on a number of important variables.

David L. Hough

Motorcycle Accident/Fatality Statistics

While there hasn't been a comprehensive North American motorcycle accident study since the 1980 Hurt Report, motor vehicle statistics are being gathered by the NCSA, an office of the NHTSA.

The NCSA not only gathers statistics but also analyzes and attempts to make sense out of the data. As Hugh H. (Harry) Hurt pointed out a couple of years ago, the problem with allowing nonmotorcyclists to analyze motorcycle data is that they often don't have the background knowledge about what the numbers might be indicating. For instance, fatality rates in NCSA charts may be in "rate per 100,000 population." That might make sense for automobile occupants, but it wouldn't be as helpful for motorcyclists, who have widely different riding seasons based on weather. For motorcycles, it would probably be more informative to show the rate in terms of "fatalities per 100,000 registered motorcycles," or better yet, "fatalities per 100,000 licensed riders," or perhaps "fatalities per 100,000 licensed riders per million miles traveled." We have to remember that some motorcyclists own more than one machine, some riders borrow machines they don't own, and riding mileage varies significantly from one rider to another, unlike automobile drivers.

As reported by the American Motorcyclist Association (AMA) in June 2002, figures released by the NHTSA indicate that 3,067 motorcyclists were killed on the nation's roads in 2001, up from 2,862 the previous year. The preliminary estimate represents a 7.2 percent increase over the rate in 2000.

The recent upward trend followed seventeen consecutive years of decline. From 1990 through 1999 alone, motorcycling-related fatalities dropped by 48 percent. The AMA noted that one significant reason for the increase in motorcycling-related fatalities is that motorcycling has seen an enormous increase in popularity, with sales of new street bikes up more than 100 percent over the previous five years, from about 243,000 in 1997 to more than 500,000 in 2001. So if registrations approximately doubled between 1997 and 2001 but fatalities only increased slightly, we're still seeing a significant decrease in fatalities per registered motorcycle.

There seems to be an increase in accidents and fatalities whenever bike sales are on the rise. That hasn't been investigated, but it would be logical that a new rider would have an increased accident potential for two or three years and that with experience, the accident potential would decrease. If that's true, then we should expect to see an increase in accidents and fatalities during any increase in motorcycle sales. However, we have to recognize that new motorcycle sales are not limited to novice riders.

The 2001 NHTSA figures indicate that although motorcycle-related fatalities were up for the fourth straight year, the 2001 increase was half that of 2000. Could the tapering off of the fatality rate be a result of novice riders gaining experience? Limited statistics are available, but we need to think very carefully about how the numbers are portrayed, and what they really mean.

The NCSA statistics are crunched into every conceivable connection, from age vs. blood alcohol concentration (BAC) levels, to engine size vs. rider age. There are different breakdowns for non fatal accidents and for fatal accidents by age, motorcycle displacement, license compliance, helmet use, speeding, highway type, and BAC level. Scanning through the fatality charts, there are some clues that different age groups have different priorities. For instance, older riders apparently tend to drink more, and therefore alcohol is more involved in accidents for older riders. For riders in the age group of thirty to thirty-nine, a higher percentage than younger riders die while intoxicated. Younger riders tend to ride sober but closer to the limits of performance, so younger riders seem to die more from speeding than from drinking.

The statistics are complex enough that no simple charts can provide much real insight. The National Agenda for Motorcycle Safety recognized the need for a new comprehensive nationwide study of motorcycle safety, but no federal agency has indicated any desire to back such a study. Motorcycle accident studies are being conducted in foreign countries, but any resulting data is not likely to be accurate if applied to motorcycling in the U.S.

If you want to access the data, it's important to recognize that the federal government is a huge bureaucracy with many offices. The NHTSA is an office of the United States Department of Transportation (DOT). The NCSA is an office of NHTSA. And, there are many other agencies, including the Bureau of Transportation Statistics (BTS) that collect, analyze, and distribute statistical information. A good place to start is the NHTSA Web site at www.nhtsa.dot.gov by selecting "Crash Statistics."

Who to Measure?

We should also remember that while the Hurt Report was a milestone in researching how and why motorcycle accidents occurred in Southern California, it doesn't say how other riders managed to avoid crashing. The assumption by rider training developers has been that the key to motorcycle safety is learning to avoid what the crashees did. The problem that researchers can't solve is how to measure the successful riders to figure out what they do right.

Back around 1979, the late Roger Hull, then editor-publisher of *Road Rider* magazine, asked the MSF why they based training programs on accident numbers rather than on the techniques veteran riders used to ride successfully. Roger convinced the MSF to hold a conference at which the safety experts could listen to veteran motorcyclists describing their individual approaches to motorcycling and accident avoidance. The MSF finally relented and agreed to hold a conference.

The 1980 "Bikers' Roundtable," in Missouri, was a unique, weeklong gathering of motorcycling veterans. The MSF tried to focus the seminars on skill tactics such as swerving and braking. But the veterans kept suggesting that evasive maneuvers aren't really important. Instead, they kept suggesting that the key is to avoid riding blindly into dangerous situations. They brought up mysterious stuff such as a sixth sense that warns them of an impending accident situation that is not yet in view. The MSF didn't really know what to do with the feedback.

Back in 1980, a group of motorcycling veterans tried to explain to the safety experts how they avoid accidents.

I suggest that the pearl of wisdom hidden in all those Roundtable seminars is that motorcycling is primarily a thinking game. The veteran rider seldom has to pull off sudden evasive maneuvers because he (or she) knows what trouble looks like and makes small adjustments to stay out of harm's way. That sixth sense is not magic but simply being aware of clues that less experienced riders don't observe, such as a flash of light reflected from the windshield of a car about to exit an alley, or a waft of spilled diesel oil.

To think of this another way, veteran riders focus on doing things right to avoid problems, not on sudden evasive maneuvers at the last second. They maintain their awareness of the situation and make small corrections early to avoid riding into hazards.

David L. Hough

A large part of my working career was as a graphics specialist in flight crew training for The Boeing Company. Way back when my daily ride was a Moto Guzzi Ambassador, I realized that airplane pilots have a lot in common with motorcyclists.

Using my Moto Guzzi 750 Ambassador for company errands in the 1970s, I could see parallels between flying and motorcycling.

It's not just a matter of both airplanes and motorcycles banking into turns but the whole approach to managing the risks. Motorcyclists, like pilots, put the priority on *avoiding* accidents rather than attempting to *survive* accidents. The energy is focused on doing everything right, rather than on surviving the crash. That's a significant difference that motor vehicle safety experts in the U.S. seem unable to grasp. The NHTSA approach has always focused on crash padding, rather than on driver skill.

Flying within the Envelope

Pilots often describe their tactics as *flying within the envelope.* The envelope is an imaginary balloon representing the physical limits of the situation at any moment in time. For example, let's say a particular airplane needs a minimum takeoff speed of 140 knots for the weight, temperature, and airport altitude. If speed doesn't exceed 140, the airplane simply won't fly.

Motorcyclists also have an ever-changing envelope. For example, let's say your bike can lean over to 45 degrees on a clean, dry, positive camber curve. If the pavement changes camber, or spilled oil reduces traction, or you increase speed until the bike touches down and levers the tires off the pavement, the motorcycle will go squirting off on a tangent. What's most important to remember about the envelope is that it is ever changing and mostly invisible. So, how do we learn to predict our envelope? And can we increase our own personal skill limits to expand that envelope?

Considering that the risk management tactics of motorcyclists are similar to that of pilots, we might take a lesson from the airplane drivers. Pilots take high-quality training in ground school classes, study their operations manuals frequently, and take recurrent training on a regular schedule to keep their skills and knowledge up-to-date. Commercial and military pilots also spend a lot of time in flight simulators, increasing and testing their skills in a realistic but risk-free environment.

Rider Training

Rider training courses can quickly help you improve both your knowledge and your riding skills. Think of it as the motorcycle equivalent of ground school. It's a low-risk way to cram a lot of trial-and-error learning into a few hours. If you haven't taken the MSF's ERC yet, that ought to be a high priority. Yes, the ERC is based on accident statistics, but it's still an excellent way to learn more about the physical limits involved in cornering and braking, as well as accident avoidance tactics.

If you think of yourself as an advanced rider with too much experience to get anything out of a parking lot course, there are track schools that focus on high-speed cornering. Track schools will certainly help you improve your cornering skills. Just remember that cornering schools don't deal with accident avoidance strategies for riding in traffic. So, regardless of your experience level, my suggestion is to take the ERC first, and then think about a track school.

Pilots spend a lot of time in training, with every move being scrutinized by a check pilot before they are approved to fly a specific airplane on their own.

Three-Wheeler Training

You should be aware that sidecar and trike training is managed by an organization separate from the MSF. Three-wheelers such as sidecar outfits and trikes require considerably different skills than two-wheelers. If you have physical limitations that make it difficult to ride a two-wheeler, or if you just want to expand your motorcycling horizons, consider taking a sidecar/trike course. The national Sidecar/Trike Education Program is administered by the Evergreen Safety Council, in Seattle, Washington.

Advanced Riding Clinic

Former *MCN* editor Lee Parks has developed a course that focuses on cornering techniques for the street rider. Lee's Advanced Riding Clinic is for experienced rider who wants to increase skills above the ERC level but in a less intimidating environment than the track schools. Lee offers his Advanced Riding Clinic at different locations around the country.

What About Simulators?

The aviation industry is big on flight simulators. The big advantage of a simulator is that you can make a big mistake without anyone getting hurt. Commercial jet pilots must prove that they can fly the simulator even with abnormal situations such as an engine failure before they are allowed to fly an airplane.

David L. Hough

The big flight simulators used in the airline industry act just like airplanes, complete with real-time motion and a matching computer-generated visual display out the cockpit windows. All the controls and instruments function just like an airplane's would under the same conditions, with both feel and sound. Flight simulators are so sophisticated that the industry talks about "zero flight time" training. In other words, if you can fly a simulator, you can fly an airplane.

Wouldn't it be great if motorcyclists could practice and test their skills in a riding simulator before taking to the streets? You could get learning experiences such as handling left-turning cars, edge traps, corners with a decreasing radius, or rain-slick streets—knowing that you couldn't get injured. You could try different cornering lines and throttle techniques, and if you "took a tumble," you could just reset the simulator and try again.

Sorry, but there aren't any motorcycle simulators. Years ago, there were a few bikes on rollers. There are rumors that Honda has been working on a riding simulator. And there have been some computer games. But at the moment there aren't any realistic motorcycle simulators. That means you'll have to explore the envelope on a real bike on real streets. So, you'll need to be much more careful about punching through the envelope while you're exploring the limits.

Wouldn't it be great if motorcyclists could practice and test their skills in a riding simulator before taking to the streets?

Keep Reading

If motorcycling is primarily a thinking game, you can understand how reading can make you a better rider. Motorcycles usually come with an owner's manual to tell you how the bike works, but they don't come with an operations manual to tell you specifically how to ride them. The *Motorcycle Operator Manual* (MOM) used by most state licensing departments is intended for raw novices, not experienced riders, so it's not very helpful once you have your endorsement (license).

Skills columns in motorcycle magazines can be useful, helping you expand your knowledge and filling in those little details that training courses or the MOM don't have time or space to include. The sad truth is that most motorcycle magazines ignore riding skills. One of the few magazines that publish a monthly skills column is *MCN*.

You can think of the book *Proficient Motorcycling* as a general operations manual for a wide variety of bikes and riders, and its companion *Street Strategies* as a refresher on common street hazards. *More Proficient Motorcycling* expands on that knowledge base. Three other books worth studying are *Motorcycle Touring & Travel* by Bill Stermer, *The MSF's Guide to Motorcycling Excellence: Skills, Knowledge, and Strategies for Riding Right* by the MSF, and *A Twist of the Wrist* by Keith Code. Reading can also help you keep your knowledge fresh. As time goes by, we forget what we've learned. If you've ever wondered what airplane pilots carry in those heavy black suitcases, much of the load is a full set of operations manuals for the airplane so they can study the details whenever there is a question. If you're serious about your riding, don't be bashful about rereading a book such as this one next winter or pulling a copy of *Street Strategies* out of your tank bag to scan while you're waiting for your buddies to catch up.

THE PROFESSIONAL

ATTITUDE

CHAPTER 2

THE PROFESSIONAL ATTITUDE

Motorcycling as a Combat Mission

My image of a good ride would be cranking up the throttle and motoring around my favorite twisty back road or cruising down a lonely highway through little towns with strange-sounding names or arriving at a big motorcycle event to rub elbows and gawk at the machinery.

That's a common problem in motorcycling: we tend to daydream about what it will be like when we get there and don't focus enough on what we need to do before the ride to make it happen successfully.

Keep your mind on your ride.

Traffic

We might not think of riding in traffic as "combat," but that's a pretty good description of what goes on. Car drivers tend to ignore motorcycles and run right into us. Motorcyclists have always been at risk among other vehicles, and it's getting worse. On top of the usual transgressions such as drivers running stop signs and failing to signal, more people today are frustrated and angry, and it shows in their driving.

Being in combat is a pretty accurate description of riding a motorcycle in traffic.

I submit that riding a motorcycle is just as serious as flying an airplane. A motorcyclist can't afford to make mistakes any more than a military fighter pilot can. Some statistics might help us put things in perspective.

According to the NCSA, a lot of motorcyclists get injured and killed in car/bike and truck/bike collisions. Here's how it stacked up for a recent year in the U.S.:

Bike-only accidents:
    motorcyclist injuries: 14,000   fatalities: 214
Car/bike collisions:
    car occupant injuries: 4,000   fatalities: 17
    motorcyclist injuries: 21,000   fatalities: 596
Light truck/bike collisions:
    Truck driver injuries: 1,000   fatalities: 0
    Motorcyclist injuries: 7,000   fatalities: 386
Heavy truck/bike collisions
    Truck driver injuries: 400   fatalities: 0
    Motorcyclist injuries: 1,000   fatalities: 114

It's pretty obvious that when bikes and cars try to occupy the same space at the same time, the motorcyclist gets hurt a lot more seriously and more often than the driver. And when bikes and trucks collide, motorcyclists are often injured fatally. The point is if you want to survive traffic combat, you need to be smarter than the average motorist or truck driver and a lot more skillful than the majority of motorcyclists seem to be.

One rider I know is a military fighter instructor—one of those top gun pilots. We'll call him Phantom Phil to disguise his identity. Phantom Phil treats each motorcycle ride with the same seriousness as a military combat mission. He chooses his "weapon" for the ride at hand, perhaps taking his Ducati for a mountain ride with the boys, or his BMW K-bike for a cross-country journey.

David L. Hough

Riding Attire

Phil points out that our protection is not only what we've learned from our training (skills and knowledge) but also what we wear. Phil chooses his riding gear for the "mission." If he is taking an easy ride downtown to the club meeting, he may wear reinforced jeans and a heavy fabric jacket. If he is heading out for a mountain run with some buddies, he dresses in full "combat" gear, including track leathers and boots, armored gloves, a full-coverage helmet, and a flawless face shield.

The Checklist

Phil also makes sure that all bike squawks (mechanical problems) have been resolved before he leaves home. Before each ride, Phil actually goes through a pre-departure bike checklist for the motorcycle and for the ride. As Phil points out, when your mission takes you into "enemy territory," there is no excuse for mechanical failures, forgotten gear, or an incomplete plan. A written checklist helps to avoid overlooking some important detail, such as packing the reflective vest and clear face shield for a ride that's likely to end after dark, or making sure you've got the water bladder for a mission into the desert.

Phil describes this in military terms: *A mission through the mountains at slightly higher speeds requires a "weapon system" that has no squawks that will cause you to go down. A detailed "preflight" check of the bike and riding gear allows you to correct any discrepancies before you "clear" the garage.*

Most of us would chuckle at the image of a motorcyclist extracting an airplane-style laminated checklist from a jacket pocket. But every serious rider runs through some sort of checklist, even if it's just a pause to mentally recall what he or she has packed. Consider your own routine for checking engine oil level and tire pressure before the ride. How do you recall what tools are on the bike, and whether up-to-date registration and insurance papers are on board? Do you always check your fuel load before "departing the fix?"

Personally, I don't use a written checklist for local rides, but I do make a list for cross-country trips to make sure I don't forget my address file, maps, the electric vest I might need for higher altitudes, business cards, slides for a rally presentation, emergency directory, or that T-shirt I intend to give as a gift.

For longer rides, I typically fuss with bike maintenance the week before the ride, looking for loose fasteners, lubricating cable ends, topping off fluid levels, and scrutinizing the tires. The day before a ride I turn on the headlight to be sure the battery is up, and then make sure I switch the ignition off so the battery is still up the next morning.

I choose my riding gear for the trip and then do a pat-down check while I'm getting suited up. I actually feel for my wallet, spare keys, neck cooler, multitool, compass, and air gauge, which should be in my jacket and pants pockets. To avoid forgetting my neck bandanna and gloves, I stow them inside my helmet. I keep several pairs of earplugs in an inside jacket pocket. I also carry a small bottle of eyewash, a tube of lip ointment, and a tube of sunscreen in an outside jacket pocket. I often stash a $10 bill in a sleeve pocket to avoid having to dig down through the gear to extricate my wallet for fuel or tolls. After I put the key in the ignition, I feel my jacket to make sure all pocket zippers are closed and then put on my gloves.

I don't use a written checklist before firing up the bike each morning on a long trip, but I do check tire pressure and engine oil before I pack it up and then listen for abnormalities as I ride along. At rest stops, I check for abnormal situations such as leaking fluids or loose tie-down straps, and I also monitor the tire treads for cuts or nails.

Pilots consider checklists to be a tool to help avoid mistakes. If you use a mental recall system to prepare for your rides and you never forget anything, there's no reason to change. But if you often find during rides that you have missed something, consider making a written checklist. Using a written checklist is not a sign of low skill but rather an indication of how serious you are about your motorcycling.

The Mission Plan

It's easy enough to just hop on the bike and head off on a ride without a plan. But note that a lot of motorcyclists have accidents within a few miles of home in familiar territory. If you don't have a definite plan for where you are going, it's more likely you will make impulsive decisions that put you at risk.

Phil thinks through each ride carefully and follows a military model for his encounters with traffic. For "combat missions" in city traffic, Phil keeps his head "on a swivel" and his eyes on "long-range scan." He treats every unknown vehicle as a "bandit" (enemy) until he can "VID" (visually identify) it to be nonhostile.

For "fast combat missions" in the mountains, Phil prefers to ride with a "wing man" because of the increased risk of unseen hazards. If you have an accident on a lonely road while riding solo, it's tough to save yourself. A riding buddy provides some backup in case of potential problems.

Whatever the mission, part of Phil's tactic is to build up to it progressively, not suddenly jump out of the garage into a traffic dogfight. Leaving home base, he runs lightly traveled secondary streets for a few minutes, allowing some time to get familiar with the bike and see how it is performing before "entering combat."

Combat Tactics

Phantom Phil agrees that motorcycling, like flying, is mostly mental. You need to turn your attention well ahead of the bike, plan what is going to happen next, and be ready for it. If you see a potential hazard and prepare to avoid it but then nothing happens, it was a nonevent because you were ready for it. You may have heard of SIPDE (search, identify, predict, decide, execute). Phil uses the military version, OODA (observe, orient, decide, act).

Observe

If you want to avoid riding into a problem, it's critical to observe what is happening well before you get there. By *observe* we're not talking about just peering out through a scratched face shield with glazed eyes, but actively searching the situation ahead. Phil points out that many riders don't seem to know how to look for a threat, don't know how to determine whether something really is a threat, and waste time staring at things that are not threats.

For instance, let's say you find yourself on a rough, ground-away surface in a repaving operation. That rough surface may attract your attention, but that's not the threat. The real threat is the curblike edge of the pavement at either side of the lane being resurfaced. That steep pavement edge forms a trap that can quickly drop the bike if you attempt to ease over it. Even veteran riders have been brought down by edge traps. It's important to be aware of the real threat—the steep edge, not the rough surface.

Orient

It's also important to mentally and physically orient yourself to be able to observe all the threats that might affect your mission. Phantom Phil points out that this may mean slowing down to give yourself more time to see what's happening and reacting to multiple threats. Or it may mean changing position—say getting out from behind a truck that's blocking your view. Or you may need to accelerate to separate yourself from merging traffic. There are no hard and fast rules for this. Rather, you need to orient yourself constantly to what's happening, both in your thinking and in where you position the bike.

Decide

You'd think it would be easy to make a simple decision about a hazard such as a left-turning car by quickly choosing whether to brake, swerve, or accelerate. But that decision depends on a lot of variables such as weather, skill, habits, and training. Deciding how to handle a situation is difficult when you're not quite sure what the bike is likely to do because you've never really practiced evasive maneuvers. Making decisions is easy for Phil because he is proficient at a number of survival tactics and can even switch to a secondary response if the situation quickly changes. As Phil points out, our riding environment is dynamic. You need to be prepared for a variety of evasive actions and be familiar with all of them.

Act

The whole point of observing, orienting, and deciding is to take whatever evasive actions are needed to avoid the threat. For instance, let's say Phil is approaching an intersection with two opposing vehicles waiting in a left turn lane. He has the green light but suspects that the first driver might attempt a quick left turn in front of him. He watches the top of the car's left front wheel for the first clue of movement and prepares to either brake or swerve. Sure enough, he observes the top of the front wheel starting to rotate: a warning sign the driver is attempting to turn left. Phil decides to swerve around behind him, so he eases off the brakes and swerves to the left side of his lane.

What Phil hadn't planned for in this skirmish is the second vehicle also turning in front of him at the last moment. But he knows how to convert a swerve to a quick stop, instantly getting the bike straight and squeezing on the front brakes to the limit. Braking provides enough separation to avoid a collision.

Our riding environment is dynamic. Be prepared for multiple hazards requiring a variety of evasive actions, and be familiar with all of them.

It's also important not to waste any energy on things you can't do anything about. It is common for secondary accidents to be caused by drivers who are gawking at the first accident rather than focusing on their own situation. Instead of being distracted by problems, it is important to focus on where you need to put the bike to avoid the crash.

How Are You Feeling Today?

One other issue: motorcycling requires both good judgment and quick reflexes. If you are not mentally or physically up to a ride, scrub the mission. It should be obvious that alcohol or drugs don't mix well with motorcycles. But it's equally important to be aware of your mental attitude. If you've just had a knock-down-drag-out argument with a family member, it's a poor time to jump on your bike and head off into enemy territory. It would be a lot less risky to take a slow, angry walk than a fast, angry ride.

Training

As Phil points out, a fighter pilot wouldn't survive long trying to dodge missiles in combat without first learning how to do it on a practice range. It's the same with motorcycles. Why should anyone expect to negotiate diesel-lubricated pavement in a curve if he hasn't learned to read the surface or doesn't have a good feel for what his tires are doing on dry pavement?

Phil frequently takes his bikes to track schools to learn their capabilities so that when the need arises he feels comfortable taking them to the limits. Do yourself a favor and take the time to actually practice different skills on your bike, whether it's on your own or in a training course.

Riding Practice

The standard accident avoidance school is the MSF's ERC, which you do on your own bike. The ERC is about half classroom theory and half skill practice. For

Each track school is independent with different training philosophies.

Riding Instruction

Experienced RiderCourse

The ERC is offered by rider training sites nationwide. This one-day course includes both classroom study and riding practice, with the emphasis on accident avoidance strategies for riding in traffic. To locate your nearest rider training site call the MSF hotline: (800) 446-9227.

Advanced Riding Clinic (Lee Parks)

P.O. Box 1838
Victorville, CA 92393
(800) 943-5638
Web site:
www.leeparksdesign.com
Lee Park's Advanced Riding Clinic (ARC) is for street riders wishing to take their skills to a higher level than the ERC but in a less intimidating environment. The ARC focuses on the specific techniques needed to improve control skills for riding on public roads. Relatively inexpensive.

California Superbike School (Keith Code)

940 San Fernando Road
Los Angeles, CA 90065
(323) 224-2734
Web site:
www.superbikeschool.com
This is arguably the oldest and most comprehensive of the track schools. Focus is on better motorcycle control, not racing techniques or accident avoidance strategies. Motorcycles and riding gear available. Midrange cost.

CLASS Motorcycle Schools (Reg Pridmore)

320 E. Santa Maria Street,
Suite M
Santa Paula, CA 93060-3800
(805) 933-9936
Web site:
www.classrides.com
This street-oriented course focuses on smooth control at speed and practical cornering tactics for public roads. It has large classes and is the most street-oriented of the track schools but also the most expensive.

Dennis Pegelow's dp Safety School

P.O. Box 1551
Morro Bay, CA 93443-1551
(805) 772-8301
Web site:
www.dpsafetyschool.com
This loosely organized, race-oriented track program focuses on fast riding but allows for a variety of skills and machines by dividing each class into groups.

Fastrack Riders

P.O. Box 129
San Juan Capistrano,
CA 92693-0129
(877) 560-2233
Web site:
www.fastrackriders.com
Basically, this course is an opportunity for graduates of other track schools to continue honing their fast-riding skills with minimal instruction or interference. Track days are separated into different skill levels and experience.

Sponsored by Yamaha Motor Corporation. Economical tuition.

Freddie Spencer's High Performance Riding School (Freddie Spencer)

7055 Speedway Boulevard,
Suite E106
Las Vegas, NV 89115
(888) 672-7219
Web site:
www.fastfreddie.com
This detailed course focuses on specific control skills. It includes comprehensive classroom instruction, student workbook, and demonstrations of the right and wrong techniques by Spencer himself prior to student practice, plus coaching by veteran instructors. Limited class size allows personal attention but results in higher price.

Willow Springs Motorcycle Club New Racer School

P.O. Box 911
Rosamond, CA 93560-0911
(661) 256-1234
Web site:
www.willowspringsraceway.com
This serious, high-performance racing school focuses on racetrack techniques, taught by instructors from the Willow Springs Motorcycle Club. The school provides corner workers, safety and track personnel, and two ambulances on duty at all events.

higher speed practice, there are different track schools offered around the country. Some schools coach you through cornering techniques or provide sessions on specially equipped training bikes; others simply let you wring out your own bike in controlled conditions away from traffic and radar traps. Some are just track time for racers thinly disguised as a school.

Bear in mind that each track school is independent with different training methods and philosophies. Most of the track school instructors come from a background in professional road racing. Track schools typically cost $900 and up per day, and you'll need to prepare your bike to racing standards. While most of the track schools are located in the Southwest, a few are taken to different racetracks around the U.S. and even to foreign countries. For specific course information, access the school's Internet site or contact the school directly.

Wimp-o-phobia

I always get excited about motorcycle events, whether they are big structured gatherings such as Americade, Honda Hoot, and the BMW Motorcycle Owners of America (BMWMOA) International; or small rallies such as the Brotherhood of Motorcycle Campers; or even local club meetings. I've been to all sorts of rallies, races, shows, rides, and tours over the years, and the excitement never seems to wear off. As I get close to a rally site and begin to see other motorcyclists arriving from other distant locations, my blood begins to stir.

The continuous stream of exotic motorcycles is a feast for the eyes, and for me, "kicking tires" around the campground with other riders is socially enjoyable and often educational. Even after the field events are over, the vendors have packed up their displays, the last door prize ticket has been drawn, and the participants begin to pack up their tents, I'm still hyped.

On the other hand, big gatherings of motorcyclists tend to bring out some strange riding tactics, both at the event and on the way to and from. For example, imagine my wife and me on our touring bike, climbing up over a Colorado mountain pass: two-up, camping gear, extra clothing, steep grade, thin air, and continuous traffic. In my mirrors

Big motorcycle events can be entertaining and educational.

I spot two solo riders moving up fast. Are they someone I know? Will we share a moment's understanding with a quick glance and a wave of the gloved hand, or perhaps a barely perceptible nod of the helmet? The two riders are slicing through traffic aggressively, zipping around cars and motor homes with little regard for social conventions such as speed limits or double yellow lines. The duo tuck in behind us for a moment, then immediately sense that I'm only cruising at traffic speed and blast by us in a blind curve without so much as a nod.

Hey, wait a minute, big dogs! I feel insulted, betrayed, ignored. *Do you slimeballs think I'm some sort of motorcycle wimp? I'll show you I am a rider worthy of respect!*

Wimp-o-phobia Takes Control

Suddenly, wimp-o-phobia takes over my brain. My right hand rolls on more throttle. I weave around Ma and Pa Kettle in their motor home, cheating the no passing zone a few yards, leaning harder into turns, riding closer to the edge of the envelope. My wife tenses at the suddenly frantic pace, tucking her knees more tightly under my thighs, gripping my waist more firmly. She says nothing, because she's been through this before.

Of course, the overloaded old touring bike complains immediately. The engine tries to accelerate the heavy load uphill at more rapid velocities, but it's down on power in the thin air. The frame flexes, the front end weaves, and the centerstand leaves a trail of sparks. When the rear shocks bottom hard, whomping into another dip, it's a wake-up call for common sense to overrule my fear of being seen as a motorcycle wimp. The scary view over the edge of the cliff also provides a helpful reality check. The worst part of it all is that those other riders didn't even notice my attempt to catch up.

The cold truth is those other riders can do it to me. First off, those other guys might just happen to be skillful riders. Even if they aren't better riders, I'd have to be awfully skillful to stuff an overloaded tourer through the twisties as quickly as a rider on an unladen sportbike. Maybe they didn't wave because they were snobbish squids. Or, maybe they didn't wave because they were focusing intently on what they were doing.

It doesn't really matter, does it? This wasn't a group ride.

What matters for me is that riding over my head on a treacherous mountain pass is a good way to punch through the envelope with disastrous results. And, while crashing is bad enough, crashing a thousand miles from home is even more of a nightmare.

Do many riders actually crash during big events? Yes, there are a lot of accidents at bike events, both here and abroad. During a typical Tourist Trophy (TT) race week on the Isle of Man, an average of one rider per day expires in a nasty crash—not just racers but spectators zooming around the course between races, trying to dodge through island traffic. Wimp-o-phobia is rampant at the TT not only because of so many riders but also because national pride is on the line.

Consider the political implications of a Frenchman passing a German, who is passing a Brit, who is passing an Italian.

Big biker events in the U.S. such as Sturgis, Daytona, and Laughlin typically produce a number of nasty accidents and fatalities as riders mix up a cocktail of traffic, wimp-o-phobia, and alcohol.

A veteran rider and well-known author friend of mine once explained his reluctance to go on any rides during big motorcycle events. Too many times he had seen a cloud of dust ahead around some modestly difficult corner and then encountered a rider extricating himself from the bushes opposite the apex. The first time this happened, my friend stopped to help, only to hear a litany of complaints about the road engineers, the tire manufacturer, the local dealer, and the bike's ill handling.

Then, before the first bent bike could be dragged out of the underbrush, he would hear the sound of screeching tires, there would be a SLAM-KEBAM, and everyone would scatter as another bike plowed a furrow into the landscape (followed by more blathering excuses and complaints, then the sound of yet another bike approaching fast). Once my friend had stopped to help, he could be there all day dodging stray bikes and listening to irresponsible blather. Worse yet, if anyone recognized him as a journalist, they would pencil his name down as a potential expert witness in a frivolous lawsuit.

Every weekend, favorite biker roads yield several crashes and even fatalities.

Not Just a Big Rally Problem

Of course, you don't have to be one of fifty thousand rally participants to experience the wimpy image syndrome. Let's say you go for a ride early in the morning with six friends. It's a nice day, traffic is light, and everyone is feeling his or her oats. It just feels natural to pick up the pace a bit. No one really announces, *We're going to ride over our heads.* Everyone just starts pushing on the envelope, and the pace increases toward warp speeds.

The guy at the back of the pack may be thinking, *Wow, those gals leading this ride sure are fast—I'd better ride a little faster to keep up, or they'll think I'm a wimp.* Well, guess what the leader at the front of the pack is thinking? *Wow, those guys behind me sure are fast—I'd better stay on the gas, or they'll think I'm a wimp.* Sometimes the reality check comes as a close call—or a traffic ticket. Sometimes

David L. Hough

Don't let other riders slicker you into dangerous stunts.

the overenthusiasm ends in an accident. Often, everyone admits later that they were all over their heads in one big adrenaline rush. At the time, few were willing to admit their concern about riding faster than was comfortable.

Fast riding is exhilarating and addictive, and it's especially exciting for those who get high on adrenaline or enjoy snubbing the authorities. The problem with riding over your head is that the laws of physics are self-enforcing. Officer Friendly may not catch you, but you can't escape the laws of gravity, inertia, and traction. Stir up a mix of poor cornering skills, unpredictable traffic, and wimp-o-phobia, and it shouldn't be surprising that accidents are common on group rides.

There are also a few well-known roads in every region that local bikers turn into racecourses on Saturday and Sunday mornings. Since the twistiest roads are often in canyons leading through mountains, rides through them are often called canyon rides. Sometimes they become a strange intertwining of high speeds, police patrols, getaways, impounded bikes, and spectacular crashes. And of course the canyon antics are a source of tall tales at various eateries that have gained notoriety as canyon-rider hangouts.

Popular canyon roads such as Deals Gap, in the Great Smoky Mountains between Tennessee and North Carolina; the Ortega Highway, in Southern California; and the web of county roads in Marin County north of San Francisco generate many accidents per weekend and more than a few fatalities each year. While many of the canyon crashees are novices, there are more than a few serious accidents involving veteran motorcyclists, as reported in biker newspapers such as San Francisco's *City Bike*.

Controlling Your Wimp-o-phobia

Whether you're heading for a big motorcycle event such as Sturgis or Americade, or you simply like to take a fast ride with a few friends, or you need your adrenaline fix every Sunday in the canyons, it's essential to keep your wimp-o-phobia under control. Here are some suggestions:

Ride Your Own Machine

Bike magazines like to show test motorcycles all bunched up in a photogenic group, riding inches apart in a tight formation at warp speed. That makes a great cover shot for a multibike comparison. But remember, the shot was staged for the photographer to get the maximum amount of machinery in a minimum amount of space.

That's not the way you want to ride. The fast riders I know separate themselves from each other. It's important to ride your own machine, even when there are a lot of other bikes on the road. It's not too clever to think you're in some sort of group ride, especially when you don't have a clue about the riding skills of those in front of you and behind you.

If the rider ahead of you is skilled, he or she will be looking far ahead, following good cornering lines and sometimes getting on the brakes hard to reduce speed to sight distance or to avoid hazards. If the rider is not so skilled, he or she will be apexing early, running wide, barely staying on the pavement, and jamming on the rear brake out of panic. The point is that other rider might be more or less skillful than you are. If the person is a better rider, you'll be tempted to ride over your head to keep up. And if the person is less than clever, he or she will be pulling dumb stunts and suckering you into problems. Either way, you don't want to be trying to ride in formation with someone you don't know. It's smarter to drop back far enough behind the next rider that you don't get a target fixation on his or her taillight.

Dropping back is also helpful to the rider ahead of you, since he or she can quit squandering attention on you, wondering if you are going to run up the bike's pipes if he or she brakes hard for that tight corner ahead, or if you'll try to pass while he or she is swerving around that car pulling out of a hidden driveway. With the other riders a few seconds away, you'll have to scrutinize the road for yourself, spot the surface hazards, choose your own cornering lines, and adjust speed for your own skill level and risk acceptance.

You may be thinking, *Yeah, but what about that squid who comes up behind me and sticks on my tail?* Okay, that's predictable. There will be riders more willing to take

It's smart to drop back far enough behind the rider in front of you so that you don't get a target fixation on his or her taillight.

David L. Hough

Hand Signals

So, you're tooling down the road and some biker coming the other way stares at you and swats the top of his helmet like he's trying to smash an invisible fly. What's he doing? Is he making some obscene gesture? Or is he trying to communicate something important?

Over the years, motorcyclists have figured out that hand signals are a much better way to communicate than trying to shout into the wind through a face shield. Of course, some riders use CB radio's, but hand signals are still a cheap, reliable way for motorcyclists to communicate with each other. Tapping the top of your helmet is a signal that the other rider's headlight is not illuminated. Get it?

As you might expect, hand signals aren't standardized. Different clubs uses different signals, or different signals mean different things in other parts of the world. Some hand signals, such as the one for okay, should never be used outside of the U.S. since they may have different—even insulting—meanings in other countries.

Sometimes well-meaning clubs create problems with hand signals. For instance, if you point your finger at a pothole or broken glass, does that mean, *observe the problem and avoid riding into it,* or does it mean, *put your tires where I am pointing?* A better way of calling attention to a surface problem is to tap the brake two or three times, and let the following rider find the hazard and make his or her own decision on how to handle it.

Your fellow motorcyclists in North America will generally understand the following hand signals:

GO AHEAD AND PASS ME (or **YOU LEAD**)	**SINGLE FILE** (arm vertical)	**STAY IN THIS LANE** (or form double file)	**TURN ON HEADLIGHT** (tap top of head)	**RIGHT TURN**
I NEED A PIT STOP	**SLOW DOWN**	**HOLD IT! DON'T PASS**	**CHANGE LANE TO RIGHT**	**TURN ON YOUR CB RADIO** (hold mic up high)
HELLO, FELLOW SIDECAR (OR TRIKE) ENTHUSIAST	**YOU LEFT YOUR TURN SIGNAL ON**	**OKAY (I understand, or I don't need help)** note: do not use this outside of USA	**HELLO, FELLOW MOTORCYCLIST** (note: palm out)	**I COULD USE SOME HELP** (hitchhiker signal)

risks than you are and a few who are truly arrogant or unskilled. Any rider who tailgates you is a potential risk. Here's where we separate the seasoned rider from the wimp-o-phobe. The seasoned rider takes charge of the situation to force a separation. For example, you could pull to the right side of the lane in a straight, and wave the squid on by. Remember? Ride your own bike. Don't let someone else set the pace for you or join you in a ride unless you agree to it.

Single File in the Twisties

Sometimes it's fun to participate in a group ride with a ride captain setting the pace and everyone riding in formation. Or perhaps there are so many riders at an event you just find yourself surrounded by others. On a straight road in traffic, it's better for everyone to position in a staggered (left-right-left) formation. The staggered lane placement gives each rider a better view and provides more space for evasive maneuvers.

But when the road narrows and starts twisting around corners, a staggered position is awkward. So, on a twisty road, forget the stagger. Open up some space between riders, and use your whole lane. This single file tactic allows each rider to follow cornering lines that maximize traction, improve the view, and maintain separation from opposing traffic. *But how will the other riders know I'm going to use the whole lane?* you may wonder. If it's a group ride in formation, you should follow the ride captain's lead. A clever ride captain will give a signal to single file. If it's just an informal gaggle, use your whole lane, starting with the first curve, and the other riders around you will quickly get the idea. When the road straightens out again, resume the staggered position based on the riders ahead of you.

Riding Skills

If you're participating in a big rally or poker run in which there are hundreds of other riders on the road, you're likely to come up behind gaggles of skill-challenged riders. It's easy to spot the unskilled. Leaving a stop sign, they paddle walk for the first 100 feet. They focus on the road 5 feet ahead of their front tires, enter turns too fast, and then slam on their rear brakes while leaned over. Trying to make right-angled turns from a stop, they wobble over the centerline. Their front brake discs are rusty from being unused. And their disinterest

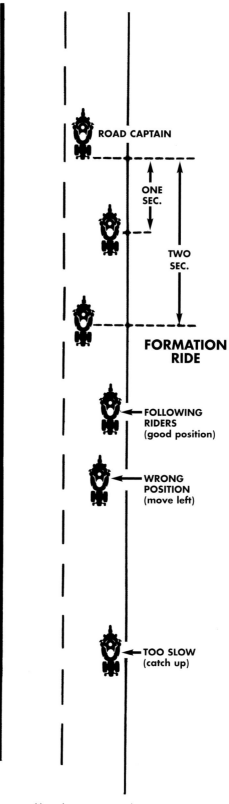

The staggered lane placement gives each rider a better view and provides more space for evasive maneuvers.

A poorly maintained motorcycle hints of a skill-challenged rider.

in riding skills is often reflected in their nonchalance about riding gear and bike maintenance.

You'll have to decide for yourself whether to pass skill-challenged riders or creep along behind, trying to keep from laughing. It can be entertaining to hang back and watch the strange maneuvers and odd gyrations that impede their progress, but give 'em a lot of room. If you do decide to pass a gaggle of less-than-proficient riders, choose a location where you can get by them without having to elbow your way through the pack. Smile and wave as you go by to defuse the put-down.

If you recognize any of those give-away symptoms in your own riding, it's a clue you could benefit from training and skill practice. Proficiency is not just a matter of miles or years. I've met a lot of 100,000-mile riders who have been balancing their bikes by "just doing it," never having figured out common skills such as countersteering, rolling on the throttle in curves, delayed apexing, slow-speed balancing, or quick stopping.

Avoiding Wimp-o-phobia

I'd like to say that I've cured myself of wimp-o-phobia; that I have learned to control my urge to do stupid things with my throttle hand when some aggressive squid jerks my chain. Without getting into embarrassing specifics, let's just say I've pulled a few stunts in the past that had the potential for serious monetary and physical damages. While I'm not completely cured of the urge to show 'em, the passing years have made me much mellower. Perhaps the key is to decide what's really important, and what's not.

For example, it's pretty important to me to complete the ride without crashing, whether I'm on one of my own bikes or on a test machine. I can't afford the expense of fixing serious bike damage. I also know that my aging bones are more brittle than they used to be. My riding priorities are now skewed more toward enjoying the ride and less toward proving I'm a big dog to someone who probably doesn't care anyway.

Most importantly, absolute speed is not a very good indicator of either riding skill or self-worth; if you really want to go fast, buy a ticket to fly on United or Delta. Realize that there will always be riders faster than you and slower, too. If you are confident of your skills, your speed at the moment should be your own decision based on your judgment of the situation, your skill level, and your acceptance of relative risk. In simpler terms, it's okay to ride at your own pace, and it's not okay to ride at someone else's pace if you're uncomfortable with that.

Now, start making plans for one of the big motorcycle events this year.

Road Rules

Road Rules

CHAPTER 3
ROAD RULES

To Speed or Not to Speed

So the phone rings the other day, and some motorcyclist from the other end of the country wants to bend my ear. He admits he's not even an *MCN* subscriber, but my name was on a copy of an article someone had passed to him, so he tracked me down for a talk. I momentarily wondered how I got to be America's motorcycling psychologist but decided to listen to his sad story anyway. Seems that Big Ticket Ted had been caught in a radar trap and nabbed for 1,200 big ones. Of course it took Ted a while to ramble through a long-winded explanation, so my ear was getting sore by the time he got to the point.

Ted claimed that he was normally a law-abiding motorcyclist. But he'd found himself behind a line of slow-moving cars on a twisty secondary road, and none of the other drivers behind the creep-

er car were willing to pass. Then several other cars began to jam up behind Ted, so he decided he'd better get out of the gaggle before someone did something stupid. So, when the parade rounded a corner and Ted saw a long straight without any opposing traffic, he put the spurs to the big V4 and rocketed on by. It was only at the point where he was zipping by the leading creeper car at warp speed that he spotted a snake patrol radar car coiled at the bottom of a dip in the road ahead, and, uh-oh, blue lights.

Big Ted was bothered by the price tag for that ticket. But what really ticked him off was getting nabbed at all, because up to that point he had seen himself as a sensible, law-abiding rider. The reason for his telephone call finally became apparent: he needed some assurance that he hadn't done something dangerous as well as illegal. In terms of risk management, was passing the smart move, or should he have stayed in line and risked a rear-ender?

I suggested that there is seldom one answer to fit all situations. We must constantly make decisions about our relative risks and take whatever actions we feel are necessary, including passing. I also suggested some alternatives to passing, such as pulling over and letting the gaggle of frustrated drivers get on down the road. Ted didn't take kindly to the suggestion that he might have had other options.

Well, I'll tell you one thing, snarled Ted, before he slammed down the phone. *I'll never ever pass anyone again, no matter how many cars are backed up behind me!*

Risk vs. Scofflaw Behavior

I suspect that Big Ticket Ted's real frustration stemmed from his failure to put traffic laws in perspective with accident avoidance tactics. We'd like to believe that we can ride sensibly and also stay within the law, but the deck is stacked against us. Sometimes we have to choose between remaining legal and reducing the risks.

For example, let's say I find myself following Ma and Pa Kettle in their motor home on the one and only highway that goes from point A to point B. The posted speed limit is 55 mph. Pa manages to get the old Winnie wound up to 54 in the straights, but he slows down to 40 through the curves and brakes to 30 whenever he encounters a bridge.

To pass or not to pass?

Look, creeping along behind a slow-moving motor home or farm truck means I'm not only sucking up diesel fumes and restricting my view ahead, I'm exposing myself to becoming a motorcycle sandwich when the creeper driver suddenly slows for no obvious reason. And I'm more likely to be sideswiped by a driver who attempts to pass us both and then has to pull back in line. Unless I'm willing to pull over for a break, I'm faced with three bad choices:

1. **Stay behind the creeper and try not to get rear-ended or sideswiped by some other impatient motorist.**
2. **Try to pass without exceeding the speed limit.**

3. Drop down a gear and get around Ma and Pa as quickly as possible—without getting caught speeding.

For me, the choice is obvious: I'll get on by the creeper as soon and as quickly as possible before the driver tows me into trouble. But before you make up your own mind, let's think about the potential hazards of passing, and then consider how to play the cops-and-robbers game.

To Pass or Not to Pass?

Would it have been "safer" for Ted to stay in line, knowing that the drivers behind him were getting more frustrated? Or, assuming that passing was a good idea, would it have been "safer" to hop around one car at a time, rather than passing the whole gaggle at once? And when Ted decided to pull out to pass, was it better to accelerate quickly to minimize his time hanging out in the opposing lane, or should he have crept on by just a bit faster than the other cars?

If you do decide to pass, scrutinize the road ahead before you commit, and never ever pass where the shape of the road limits your view, such as when approaching the crest of a hill or in a curve with limited sight distance. It's also smart to signal early and take one last glance in the mirror before you pull out to avoid getting crunched by someone passing you.

Even if it's a legal passing zone and you can't see any oncoming traffic, be aware of side roads. You need to be ready to abort the pass if you sense a problem.

Before you zip out to pass that farm tractor, are you sure there isn't a car about to pull out from that side road?

For instance, it should be an easy pass around that slow-moving hay wagon, right? Well, before you zip out to pass, notice that intersecting road on the right. Are you sure there isn't a car about to pull onto the road in front of you?

In Big Ticket Ted's situation, he wasn't being very clever about sight distance. Since he couldn't see that radar cop hiding at the bottom of the dip ahead, he couldn't have seen oncoming traffic, either. If you can't see ahead well enough to spot a cop, you probably shouldn't be hanging out in the wrong lane at warp speed.

No Passing Zones

One big problem with getting around slower moving vehicles is that there are fewer and fewer passing zones. It used to be that highway departments painted the double-yellow no passing lines at zones where it really was unsafe to pass, such as approaching the crests of hills or on bridges. But over the years, those no passing zones have been spreading like dandelions. Now some roads have the double yellow for miles, even through areas where a motorcyclist clearly has adequate space and sight distance to make a safe pass.

The Speeding Dilemma

Many states have quietly passed laws making it more difficult to pass legally. It used to be that many states allowed a motorist to temporarily exceed the speed limit while passing. But that loophole was apparently too big for the legal eagles, so the laws in many states have been revised to make it illegal to exceed the speed limit when passing. Now, if that's not the way it is in your home state, beware the laws in neighboring states.

I'm already on record as suggesting that if you're going to pass, put the spurs to it and reduce your exposure time in the wrong lane. So, my dilemma is whether to exceed the limit to reduce my time in the wrong lane or hang out there trying to creep on by without speeding.

Okay, there are jokes about it being legal to pass on a motorcycle so long as you keep your tires between the two yellow "motorcycle passing lines," but the reality is that we're often faced with several bad choices, not the least of which is the threat of snagging a ticket.

Slow Trucks

Long-haul trucks tend to bog down on steep upgrades when climbing over mountain passes. So, truck drivers put the pedal to the metal on downgrades to build forward energy for the next climb. If you pass a slow-moving truck on the upgrade, and then maintain just the speed limit, the driver will be pulling out to pass you on

Dancing the truck tango can be unnerving.

the next downgrade, then pulling back in front of you and slowing down as the road pitches up again. The majority of truck drivers I've encountered are reasonably polite to motorcyclists, but I know they have a limited view from their side mirrors, and it is easy for them to lose track of an itty-bitty motorcycle alongside a trailer.

If it isn't obvious, doing the highway tango with trucks increases both the risk of getting a ticket and the risk of a collision. When sharing the road with trucks, it makes sense to maintain a speed that allows as much separation as possible. Speeding up to stay ahead of a truck on a downgrade may reduce the risk of getting run over, but it increases the risk of being exposed to Officer Friendly's radar gun.

If you dance the truck tango for a while, you'll observe that not all the drivers speed. There is often just one hot dog trying to pass everyone. Let him on by, and you may discover a quieter space between the other trucks— and you're not as obvious to Officer Friendly.

It's easy for a driver to lose track of an itty-bitty motorcycle 60 or 80 feet back from the mirrors.

Fast Traffic

Freeway speeds also present a dilemma. On a recent transit from Chicago to Seattle, I noticed that posted speed limits and actual traffic speeds varied dramatically from state to state. Westbound from Chicago, Interstate 90 has the speed limit posted at 55 mph, and traffic was moving at about 60. I had been warned by other bikers about unmarked patrol cars and heavy-handed enforcement in Illinois, so I maintained speeds between 55 and 60.

In Minnesota, the speed limit increased to 75, and traffic was moving at about 80. In South Dakota, drivers were doing 85 in a 75 zone. In Wyoming, traffic was up to 90, with some cowboys cruising at 100. In Montana, traffic speed was down to 80, and in Idaho and Washington traffic had slowed down to about 78. Yet it was basically the same highway design through all those states. Is there any real correlation between traffic speed and risk?

The Speed Enforcement Game

For whatever reason, speed enforcement in the U.S. is a bigger deal than elsewhere in the world. In Europe, police seem to be more concerned about preventing accidents and less consumed with the passion to write speeding tickets. The speed limits and traffic fines tend to reflect this difference. In England, even narrow secondary highways have 70 mph speed limits, but the big fines are for truly dangerous stunts such as not slowing down in villages or not stopping for a pedestrian in a "zebra crossing." In Germany, a fine for 20 mph over the limit on a secondary road might be the equivalent of $10 or $20, but passing on the right on the autobahn could result in confiscation of your vehicle and license.

It's frustrating being put in a position of having to juggle accident risk against the risk of arrest. In my opinion, it's more important to reduce the risks of an accident than to be strictly legal. What that means is that here in the good old U.S. of A., we need to be smarter about playing the speed enforcement game.

Before we move on, let's note that increasing speed above the "reasonable and safe" speed of traffic dramatically increases our risks. Even 20 mph over the average speed of traffic appears to jack up the accident risk about 300 percent. I know some riders who get a real thrill out of cruising across the landscape at warp speeds. It's a big adrenaline rush and it's addictive, but higher speeds demand greater rider skill to avoid getting arrested by either physics or Officer Friendly.

If you choose to cruise at high speeds, it's important to get your looking and thinking up to bike speed. Bad stuff happens quickly as the speedometer needle climbs up the dial. Even if you do find a straight stretch of road with no traffic and an unlimited view, there are hazards such as wild deer, armadillos, edge traps, spilled diesel oil, and flooded washes waiting for you. Remember, forward energy increases four times faster than miles per hour.

Look, I'd prefer to avoid being an anarchist. It's in our best interests for people to obey the laws. I think someone who steals my bike should be tracked down, arrested, and locked away. People who intentionally run red lights deserve to lose their licenses. When I can obey the laws without compromising my safety, I do so. I try to signal well before lane changes, I keep my exhaust system quiet, and I come to a complete stop for stop signs.

Bad stuff can happen quickly as the speedometer needle climbs up the dial.

And I don't hate cops. They have their job to do, and it's a difficult task, considering the pay scale and the risks. I know that an officer doesn't write the laws, and that today's enforcement focus is determined by the chief back in the office. I also know that each officer has a different attitude about bikes. For an officer with no motorcycling experience, it might seem appropriate to pick off the bike and ignore the automobiles cruising at the same speed. However we've gotten into the speed paranoia in the U.S., we need to be clever enough to play the game well.

Speed Traps

To avoid getting nabbed, it helps to think like a cop. If you were a patrol officer out looking for speeders, where would you hide? Who would you be looking for? When would you be there?

In Washington, the state patrol often sets up a radar trap at the end of a passing lane, preferably just over the top of a hill. With one radar car spotting and three or four catchers, it's a gold mine on Sunday evenings. If the situation looks like a good place for you to nip over the double yellow and zip around the slow movers, remember that Officer Friendly knows that location, too. Don't you think the officer who nabbed Big Ted knew exactly where to hide to take advantage of the situation? You don't want to be the tail-end Charlie in a fast-moving group either. If you were a cop, why would you elbow up through traffic to arrest the pack leader when you could easily pick off that bike at the tail end?

It's not smart to pass anywhere in a work zone. First off, there are a lot of surface hazards in construction zones, and you don't need the angry driver you just passed on your tail just as you hit a patch of deep gravel. Second, the fines are often much stiffer if you get nabbed.

On secondary highways out West, it's common for police to park off the road just around a curve on the outskirts of small towns, right where drivers would normally be increasing speed. Remember, the posted speed takes effect at the sign, not before. So when leaving small towns, which have a lot of locations for cops to hide, it's smart to keep creeping along at the 25 limit until you pass the 55 sign, and then hold right at 55 until you get out of radar range.

It's not smart to be passing anywhere in a work zone.

If you were a cop, wouldn't those trees provide a good place to hide and wait?

In southeastern states, it's expected that cops hide behind billboards or trees right after the speed change sign. If you were a cop, wouldn't you be hiding behind those trees right after the speed sign?

You also need to be clever about what the speed signs say. For instance, you might think the 25 mph speed limit sign is the limit through this village, but that small 15 mph sign a hundred feet later also applies. If you cause a problem rounding that corner faster than 15, you could be cited for speeding.

On freeways, the best place to zap traffic is at the top of an entrance ramp. A cop can sit at the top and zap traffic emerging from beneath the overpass. That's why it's

Yes, the posted speed here is 25 mph all the way to that 15 mph limit on the turn sign.

smarter to stay out of the passing lane and keep your speed in check when cruising under overpasses. Some riders also adjust their right mirror up and more to the right to see more of the on-ramp as they pass by so they can brake if a patrol car is spotted.

Radar Detectors

If you're going to play the speed game, think carefully about using a radar detector. In some states, detectors are illegal. And even if detectors are legal, having a detector in plain sight on your bike is an advertisement that you're playing the speeding game. The officer who does catch you speeding is much more likely to give you a ticket if he sees a radar detector. He wins this round, you lose. If you do choose to run a detector, it's smarter to mount it out of view, or at least camouflage it.

Some radar or laser guns are left in standby mode until the officer pulls the trigger, so the radar detector can't detect a signal except in the instant the officer shoots. Even with such "instant on" guns, a multichannel detector often generates a blip or two from the cop shooting vehicles a mile or so ahead, giving you some warning in advance. I know some big-dog riders who brake hard whenever they get a warning on their detectors. The theory is that braking hard changes your speed so quickly that the cop's gun can't get a stable reading. Obviously, that's another good reason to avoid tailgaters.

A radar detector won't protect you from speed cops in the sky, of course. When you're cruising across a wide-open landscape way out in the country, keep an eye out for the spy in the sky. Watch for airplanes flying parallel to the highway or circling over the same stretch of road.

Big Ticket Ted clearly wasn't playing the game well. He wasn't thinking clearly about either the laws of physics or the laws of the state. Successful motorcycling requires that you be just as clever at playing cops and robbers as you are at avoiding collisions.

If You're Going to Ride Fast, Get Serious About Your Riding

A few years ago, one of my Canadian friends was blitzing the back roads of British Columbia on his BMW. The pavement had given way to gravel, but Beemer Bob was still trying to maintain a fast pace, even with the front end slip-sliding in nervous twitches. Beemer had the throttle cranked on to the point of scaring himself, and he was getting quite a rush from stretching the traction enve-lope to his limit. But after a few miles of this, a following rider on a tatty old R75 turned up the wick and roared by Beemer Bob at warp speed. As the other machine rocketed by, Bob recognized the legendary Fearless Phil, a Canadian rider well known for his take-no-prisoners riding style. Phil went by so fast, Beemer was completely demoralized.

Been there yourself? Done that? Got a T-shirt? Speed is so intertwined with our images of motorcycling that most of us can't help but evaluate our self-worth based on who is the faster rider. My old friend Bob Carpenter once summed it up nicely. I'll have to paraphrase, since I don't have the exact quote in front of me, but I'm sure you will get the idea: If you are riding as fast as you can and come up behind a slower rider who doesn't get out of your way, he's a stupid, unskilled jerk who ought to be arrest-ed and thrown in jail. But if you're riding as fast as you can and another rider zooms around you, he's an arrogant, reckless fool who ought to be arrested and thrown in jail.

How do we learn to ride fast, anyway? Well, you could sign up for a riding school that provides some track time and instructor coaching. A lot of riders have studied under instructors such as Reg Pridmore, Keith Code, Freddie Spencer, and Dennis Pegelow. But most of us who go out riding learn by trial and error. We just gradually increase our speed to the limit, where we either scare ourselves badly or

The rules are completely different for riding on public roads than on the track.

crash. Somewhere along the line, most of us figure out that skills and techniques are more important than horsepower.

Cornering schools at the racetracks are a good way to learn fast-riding techniques, but when we're trying to acquire high-speed skills, here's the rub: the rules are completely different for riding on the public roads than on the track.

Consider that on a closed track everyone is riding in the same direction, has qualified to be there, and are all riding well-prepared and inspected machines. The racetrack surface is kept in good condition. Corner workers are available to warn of problems such as spilled oil around the corner, and there's usually an ambulance nearby. There are no grated bridge decks, railroad crossings, patches of loose gravel, pools of diesel oil, or plops of cow poop. Nor does the racer have to contend with aggressive Labradors, wild deer, alligators, wandering bicyclists, or farm tractors.

Let's put things in perspective. The consensus among road racers is that public roads are more dangerous than racetracks. A number of famous racers have died trying to go fast in events such as La Carrera, held on public roads rather than closed race circuits. Mike Hailwood was a master of road racing on the Isle of Man, but he died in a traffic accident on his way to work in Birmingham.

The important lesson in all of this is that when any of us start poking at the speed envelope on public roads, we may have to pay dearly for the consequences. If one of your goals is to still be riding five or ten years from now, you'll want to be a little more clever about your riding.

Speed vs. Risk

If you compare vehicle miles traveled to the fatality rate over the past seventy years, the miles traveled have been rapidly increasing while the fatality rate has been steadily dropping. The fatality rate was higher during World War II when the recommended speed was 35 mph. The fatality rate continued to drop after the national 55 mph speed law was enacted in 1974 and even after the limit was raised to 65 mph in 1987. The national speed limit was repealed in 1995. The point is that increasing maximum speeds doesn't cause an increase in the fatality rate.

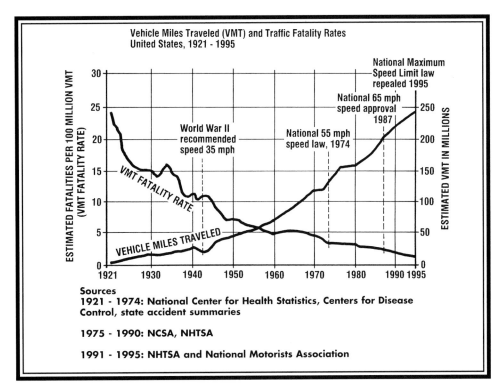

Vehicle Miles Traveled (VMT) and Traffic Fatality Rates
United States, 1921 - 1995

Sources
1921 - 1974: National Center for Health Statistics, Centers for Disease Control, state accident summaries

1975 - 1990: NCSA, NHTSA

1991 - 1995: NHTSA and National Motorists Association

Highway bureaucrats want to believe that risk is proportional to speed. The U.S. DOT did a study a few years ago on the effects of raising and lowering speed limits. They expected to prove that the higher the speed limit, the greater the accident risk. That would justify speed enforcement as a safety tactic rather than a money-grabbing game. The shock for the DOT was that reducing posted speed limits increased the accident rate. Below is a chart of accident risk compared to traffic speeds, based on the DOT research. As you might guess, the DOT didn't like the results and would probably not appreciate any mention of the report.

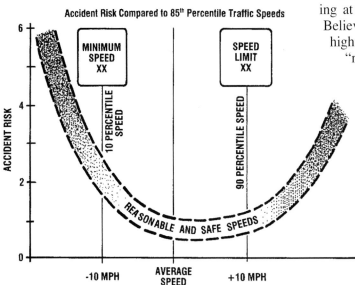

based on U. S. DOT Report no FHWA/RD-85/096

Fewer accidents occur when all drivers are moving at the same speed, whatever the posted limit. Believe it or not, the safest situation is when the highway engineers let drivers determine their own "reasonable and safe" speed for a given stretch of highway, then post a maximum limit that's about 10 mph faster than the average speed of traffic and a minimum speed that's about 10 mph slower than average.

If you find yourself on a busy freeway with most vehicles doing 75 to 85 mph, your "safest" speed is around 80 mph, even if the signs say 55. That's a dilemma for motorcyclists who would prefer to stay within the posted speed limit. A riding acquaintance swears he will never break the law. If the sign says 55, he'll ride at 55. But if traffic in that zone is moving at 80, he'll be jacking up his risks approximately 400 percent by motoring along on a bike in freeway traffic at 55.

Distance Divided by Time

When we're thinking about speed, it's useful to remember that speed is simply distance divided by time. If you could sustain 120 mph for two hours, your average speed would be 120 mph. But if you drop your bike on a dribble of diesel oil at the end of mile 238, and spend the next two hours putting an epoxy patch on the crankcase, your speed drops to 59.5 mph. And if you have to spend another two hours getting your clavicle x-rayed before you can ride again, your speed drops to 39.7 mph. A rider who drones along the same road at 55 for that same two hours will have averaged 55 mph, a lot faster than you managed. So, the first rule of riding swiftly is to know how to avoid crashes.

Avoiding Crashes

Riding on public roads obviously involves skillful control of the bike to make it do what we need it to do. A fast rider must be a master at maximizing traction. We can't afford to go wide in a corner with decreasing radius and make an unplanned excursion into the forest. But avoiding crashes is more than just good control of the bike. We've also got to be masters at avoiding collisions with obstructions such as farm tractors, left-turning cars, and wild deer. And that's more a matter of mental skill.

All right, enough sermonizing about risks. Is it possible to ride swiftly in public and still avoid serious accidents? Think about this: although Fearless Phil is a Canadian, he learned a lot of his tactics from zipping around on motorcycles in Great Britain, Europe, and the Middle East. We might also note that many of those big doggies we hear about have also honed their skills in Europe. And European motorcyclists have a lower accident rate than American motorcyclists. Perhaps it would be worthwhile to look to the Europeans for clever fast-riding techniques.

The Europeans

It's true that European motorcyclists tend to ride at higher velocities than we would under similar conditions in the U.S. It's also true that Europe is much more compact than the U.S., so most of that fast riding takes place on narrow, twisty public roads. And those twisty mountain roads in the Alps will automatically teach a rider a lot about cornering. You must accelerate and decelerate quickly, pushing the tach needle farther up the dial to jump around tour coaches, between switchbacks, and then brake hard to slow for a tight corner surfaced in wet cobblestones.

Of course, our images of European riding tend to be of tantalizing roads snaking up the side of a breathtaking Alpine pass through a hundred switchbacks. You know, just like those Edelweiss Bike Travel ads in the magazines. So, when we think of high-speed motorcycle accidents, the image that pops to mind is a single motorcyclist leaned over into a corner and splattering into the granite.

But the reality of European riding is that the roads carry a lot of traffic other than motorcycles. And when you get down off the pass, you have to navigate through a dozen congested villages with webs of intersections, and compete for space with cars, long-haul trucks, motor coaches, bicyclists, and foreign tourists. So, the most likely "high-speed" accident would be a collision with an automobile, usually at one of those boring old urban intersections down in the valley, at motorcycle speeds of merely 35 or 40 mph.

So, Is European Riding Dangerous?

Considering the spectacular passes, crush of traffic, and high speeds, you'd think riding in congested Europe would be a lot more dangerous than motorcycling in the U.S., right? Well, let's take a brief look at some statistics released at the 1991

The most likely "high-speed" accident is a collision with an automobile at one of those boring old urban intersections down in the village.

International Motorcycle Conference. Back in 1970, fatalities averaged 6.4 per 10,000 motorcycles for all of Western Europe. At the same time, fatalities averaged 8.1 per 10,000 motorcycles in the U.S. So even back in the hippie era of the 1960s, riding in the U.S. was more likely to be fatal than in most of Europe. What's really interesting is that by 1987, European motorcyclist fatalities had dropped to 3.4 per 10,000 bikes. By comparison, U.S. fatalities had also decreased but at 5.2 per 10,000 they were still higher than Europe fatalities.

The European numbers are even more impressive when you consider that the Federal Republic of Germany (our BMW heroes?) was the second most dangerous nation in Europe in 1970, with 11.9 motorcyclist fatalities per 10,000 bikes. Sweden was the worst, with a staggering (as in *Let's have one more for the road, Lars*) 40.3 fatalities per 10,000 in 1970.

But by 1987, Germany had reduced that to 4.3, and Sweden had reduced motorcyclist fatality rates to 4.2. By 1987; Great Britain was still a more dangerous place to ride than the U.S. or western Europe, with 6.2 fatalities per 10,000 motorcycles. The point is that by 1987, the U.S. was a more hazardous motorcycling environment than any western European nation, except for Great Britain.

What's the purpose in showing me these numbers? you may be wondering. The lesson is that although we have had a gradual decline in motorcycle accidents in the U.S., European riders significantly reduced their accident and fatality numbers over two decades. In other words, fast riding doesn't have to be more life threatening.

Attitude

In the U.S., many people have too much of an *it wasn't my fault* attitude. After a crash, the suddenly indignant rider crawls out from under the broken plastic, sniveling, *It wasn't my fault. It happened because the* (circle your favorite villain) *dealer/manufacturer/salesman/mechanic/tire/lubricant/cow/road crew/license department/ helmet/farmer/stupid driver/loose gravel/other did it to me.*

The European attitude is more, *If I do something dumb and crash, it's my own fault.* That "I'm responsible" attitude is quite evident in both road construction and riding gear. European road engineers don't waste money putting up expensive signs and safety barriers. It's up to the individual rider to scrutinize the corner ahead, spot the wandering cow, observe the wet cobblestones, make room for downhill traffic, and select an appropriate speed and lean angle to avoid going off the cliff.

European riders also seem to understand that even with good tactics, there is always the risk of taking a tumble. So, most European riders wear racing-weight leathers, abrasion-resistant boots and gloves, and a high-quality helmet. By comparison, you'll see many Americans wearing denim or even shorts and a T-shirt. If you look around at race spectators in Europe, it's easy to spot the Germans in their

Expensive riding gear doesn't make you a better rider, but it certainly says something about your attitude toward the risks.

heavy leathers. Buying expensive riding gear doesn't make you a better rider, but it certainly says something about your attitude toward the risks.

The lower accident and fatality rates in Europe are not only a result of more serious licensing tests and driving while intoxicated (DWI) enforcement but also rider attitude, riding gear, and driving discipline. In most European countries, drivers follow very strict lane positions based on speed. In Germany, you may throttle up to wide open in the left lane of the autobahn to pass slower traffic, but you n*ever ever* pass on the right. The left lane is for passing, not cruising. In England, the lanes are reversed, but the rules follow the same concept. You might ride at the national speed limit of 70 mph along a narrow English "A" road, inches from a thorny hedgerow, but you never ever even *think* about passing on the left. Separation of traffic according to vehicle speed is one excellent way of avoiding collisions.

By comparison, here in the U.S. we have drivers cruising in the passing lane, passing willy-nilly on left or right, changing lanes without looking or signaling. We have "wolf packs" weaving at warp speed through superslab traffic and drivers making sudden turns at intersections. More than a few good foreign riders have been scrunched here in silly smashos they would never have expected back home. And our traffic seems to be getting worse, not better.

Why Are U.S. Fatality Rates Higher?

Why would you suppose our motorcycle fatality numbers are worse than Europe's? Given that motorcycles are at the bottom of the food chain in traffic, you'd think U.S. motorcyclists would be getting smarter and more skillful. Well, we are, but not as rapidly as the Europeans are. For one thing, it's a lot easier to get a motorcycle license in the U.S. Even so, we still have a significant percentage of motorcyclists riding without licenses. The NHTSA calculated that for 1995, more than one out of five motorcyclists in fatal crashes was operating without a valid license.

American riders also seem to have an ongoing problem with alcohol. In 1995, 30 percent of all fatally injured motorcycle operators in the U.S. were intoxicated. For weekend nights, the numbers soared: 61 percent of those killed were intoxicated. In Europe, DWI enforcement is much more serious, and it shows in the numbers for certain countries. For instance, Sweden and the Federal Republic of Germany both enacted tougher DWI laws. Remember, Germany reduced its fatality rate from 11.9 to 4.3, and Sweden reduced it's rate from 40.3 to 4.2. The AMA and NHTSA have initiated a campaign to address this issue, but we're a long way from solving the problem.

Too many American riders seem to have an ongoing problem with alcohol.

The overall lesson we can take from the Europeans is that fast riding doesn't have to increase the risks if we treat our motorcycling seriously. *Fast*, as my friend Beemer Bob discovered, is a relative term. The good news for Americans is that you can significantly tilt the odds in your favor by getting serious about your riding. Take training courses, get a license endorsement, wear crash-resistant riding gear, and separate booze from bikes. Most importantly, take responsibility for your riding.

And by the way, the absolutely positively best way to learn fast-riding tactics is to spend a few days in the Alps, bagging as many passes as possible. So, if you're really serious about fast riding, start making plans for a trip to Europe.

Sources of Statistics:

Institut fur Zweiradsicherheit GmbH. "Safety Environment Future Nr. 7." Proceedings of the International Motorcycle Conference, Orlando, Fla., October 31 to November 3, 1990. (Institute Address: Westenfelder Str. 58, 4630 Bochum 6, Germany)

U.S. DOT, National Highway Traffic Safety Administration, National Center for Statistics and Analysis. "Motorcycles Traffic Safety Facts." 2000. (Reports are updated annually. Address: NRD-31, 400 Seventh Street, SW, Washington, D.C. 20590. For motorcycle traffic safety facts on-line: www.nhtsa.dot.gov/people/ncsa/FactPref/mcyfacts.html.)

Alcohol

Uh-Oh, "Preacher Dave"

Uh-oh, here's old Preacher Dave up on the pulpit again, banging his fist, thumping the Hurt Report, and giving us another boring sermon about devil rum. Well, okay, I've been accused of being a little preachy, but my job is to help you reduce the risks. I don't dream up the hazards out of thin air; I become aware of them through personal experience, accident reports, motorcycling war stories, conversations with accident victims, and, yes, statistics. According to the numbers, motorcycling has gradually been getting safer over the years, except for one big problem that isn't going away: the involvement of alcohol in fatal accidents. It's a serious enough problem that I'd be doing you a disservice if I didn't mention it from time to time. It's time.

The Assistant Coroner

I got my rude awakening to the booze problem when I bumped into the Assistant Coroner (AC) at a helmet law hearing at the Washington capitol. He described his job as *scraping up the remains of the victims Medic One couldn't save.* In other words, after the emergency medical technicians (EMTs) have determined that they can't save an injured motorist at the scene of an accident, the Coroner's office sends out a crew with a van to pick up the cadaver and determine the cause of death. Since I seldom get to talk face-to-face with someone who "scrapes up" dead motorcyclists, I pumped him for details.

Up to that conversation, I had assumed that the typical accident scenario involving alcohol and bikes was a drunk driver running into a sober motorcyclist. The AC set me straight. He figured that about two of every three dead motorcyclists they bring in have alcohol in the blood. What's more, the AC informed me, they could pretty well predict which cadavers would have a significant amount of alcohol in the blood, based on the crash scenario.

In addition to hauling away the corpse, the crew from the coroner's office analyzes the scene and takes measurements. Sober riders tend to leave skid marks; drunk riders tend to smash into immovable objects such as bridge abutments and power poles without any attempts to take evasive action. The drunks also usually crash at speeds roughly twice the posted limit. So if the speed limit is 35, the crash results often indicate a 70-mph impact, and if there aren't any skid marks, the motorcyclist/cadaver is likely to have a high blood alcohol content (BAC) of perhaps 0.17 or 0.20—well above the legal limit.

Would a mandatory helmet law reduce the number of fatalities? I asked.

The AC looked me straight in the eye as he composed his response. *A good helmet would certainly protect the brain,* he said, *but that won't help the rider much when the head comes off the body.* He was serious. I got a little queasy thinking about times I had ridden after a drink or two.

A Second Opinion

Knowing that "safetycrats" are often prejudiced against motorcycles, I thought maybe the AC was feeding me a political agenda rather than honest statistics. So, I started digging into the numbers. According to the Hurt Report, drunken riders accounted for 10 percent of accidents and 41 percent of fatalities. But haven't the motorcycle fatality rates dropped a lot since the Hurt Report came out in 1980?

Yes, the U.S. fatality rates have dropped. According to NHTSA Traffic Safety Facts, the average U.S. motorcyclist fatality rate in 1985 was 8.4 per 10,000 registered bikes. By 1998, the rate had been reduced to 5.9. That sounds pretty good, until you compare motorcycles to cars and trucks.

Fatality Rate, 1998

	Passenger Cars	Light Trucks	Motorcycles
per 10,000 registered vehicles	1.7	1.5	5.9
per 100 million vehicle miles	1.4	1.2	22.4

Many motorcycle fatalities involve riding after drinking.

Well, the motorcycle fatality rates look pretty bad, but what role does alcohol play in the numbers? Are we talking drunk drivers running into sober riders, or drunk riders doing it to themselves?

According to the 1995 NHTSA Traffic Safety Facts, motorcycle operators involved in fatal crashes had higher intoxication rates than any other type of motor vehicle driver.

Of the fatally injured motorcycle operators, 30 percent were legally intoxicated. An additional 11.5 percent had been drinking but weren't legally intoxicated.

We could go on and on about which states have the greatest fatality rates, what time of day is worst, and how the rates compare for single-vehicle crashes vs. collisions, but the important message in all this is that a big share of motorcycle fatalities involve riding after drinking.

The Effects of Alcohol

Down the Hatch

Once alcohol gets into the stomach, it quickly enters the bloodstream and gets pumped throughout the body, from head to toes. Alcohol first acts as a sedative in the brain, relaxing mental functions such as inhibition, concentration, and judgment. The first effect is a happy feeling, caused by loss of inhibitions. It also degrades physical functions such as speech, hearing, pain, coordination, and balance. As more alcohol is absorbed, there is a degradation of judgment, self-control, and muscle coordination. If the concentration of alcohol in the blood continues to increase, the person will experience confusion then fall into a stupor. (right)

HAPPY
Reduced Inhibitions
Reduced Judgement

IMPAIRED
Reduced Self-Control
Impaired Muscle Control
Blurred Vision
Difficulty Hearing

CONFUSED
Degraded Mental Functions
Loss of Automatic Functions
(reflexes, pain, visual focus, bladder control)
Degraded Muscle Control
(Difficulty with Balancing, Walking)

Down the Drain

The body eliminates alcohol by oxidizing or burning it in the liver, so the amount of alcohol in the body at any moment depends upon how much was ingested and when. The percentage of alcohol in the bloodstream also depends upon body weight. Bigger people have a larger blood volume. One final point: not everyone is affected the same by the same concentration of alcohol. Alcohol's effect on any individual depends upon that person's sensitivity to booze. In other words, after four drinks one rider may be almost fully functional, while another rider may be falling on his lips.

STUPOR
Mental Blackout
Loss of Muscle Control

I should mention that drugs other than alcohol, including both illegal drugs and over-the-counter medications such as cold and allergy pills, are also implicated in accidents. Drugs and medications often interact with alcohol to multiply its effects. When you're taking any medications that cause drowsiness, it's not smart to get on a bike. And you should especially avoid combining alcohol with other medications.

I'm Not Too Ride to Drunk!

Alcohol may be a social advantage for people trying to overcome shyness at parties, but it does all the wrong things to someone trying to operate a motorcycle. I often underscore the need for motorcyclists to make good decisions and be able to maneuver a motorcycle accurately. It should be obvious that alcohol degrades both judgment and skills. After one or two drinks, is a rider capable of judging his or her own condition to operate a motorcycle? Even if control skills have not yet been affected, would a rider have sufficient perception and awareness to adjust speed for conditions or to choose the correct evasive maneuver to avoid a collision? The sober conclusion is that even one or two drinks probably skew a rider's opinion of his or her ability to handle a motorcycle.

Alcohol Content of Drinks

Okay, so maybe you're "just drinking beer." How much alcohol can there be in a beer, anyway? Let's dabble in some typical drinks. There is slightly less than 0.5 oz of pure alcohol in one shot of whiskey, one mixed cocktail, one glass of wine, or one can of beer. Specifically, a 1 oz shot of 90 proof bourbon contains 0.45 oz of alcohol. A 4-oz glass of Burgundy at 11 percent contains 0.44 oz of alcohol. And a 12 oz lager beer at 3.2 percent actually contains 0.384 oz of alcohol. So, okay, the 3.2 percent beer has slightly less alcohol. But whether it's two beers or two shots of bourbon straight up, two drinks add up to almost 1 oz of alcohol.

Come on, Dave, How Serious Can It Be?

Is alcohol really a serious problem? A lot of riders have stopped off for a few drinks during a ride and managed to wobble on to the finish without crashing. I've been to motorcycle club meetings held at taverns at which almost everyone sucked down a few beers before the ride home. I've seen bikers fortify soda with a shot of whiskey right out of the saddlebag and then continue a poker run without a wobble. I can't remember any BMW rally that didn't have a beer garden or at least a keg on tap. So, if all these folks can complete the ride after a few beers or maybe a couple nips of Jim B., is there really a problem mixing alcohol and motorcycles? Fair enough. Let's see if my personal knowledge parallels the statistics.

A few years ago, I attended a presentation by "Slider" Gilmore, a hard-core biker who is also an EMT. Slider was teaching a seminar in handling a motorcycle accident. He forewarned us that his presentation would include some photographs of gory accidents, both to educate us to the types of injuries to expect and also to expose us to the shock and revulsion we would have to suppress at the scene of a bad accident.

12 oz. Beer

4 oz. Cocktail

"ONE DRINK"

5 oz. Wine

1 1/2 oz. Whiskey

3 oz. Sherry

While the main point of Slider's class was the importance of getting EMTs to the scene quickly, one background theme kept repeating itself throughout the presentation: booze. Slider ticked off one biker brother after another now lying underground "pushing up daisies," as a result of riding after partying. Slider even showed us a number of "before" photos of proud owners of customized bikes and "after" photos taken later, after the drunken riders had crashed.

The loss of so many friends moved Slider to give up alcohol entirely. For me, the message was clear that riding after drinking does jack up the risks of a nasty accident. Those riders who had managed to wobble home after a club meeting at the tavern were lucky. Following that presentation, I adhered to a strict rule of never drinking before or during a ride.

There have been a great many studies around the world comparing BAC to actual impairment.

For example, The British Columbia Medical Association (BCMA) conducted a study that suggests impairment begins at a BAC of 0.035 percent, or about two drinks. The BCMA further suggests that many people would lose enough sufficient driving skill to be a "menace on the highway" at a BAC of 0.05 percent, or about three drinks within one hour.

Burning It Off

Although different people react differently to alcohol, most folks burn off about 0.015 percent per hour per 150 pounds of body weight, say one drink per hour. Nothing speeds up the process of burning off alcohol. Coffee might help you pee more, but it won't help you see more. A cold shower might make you shiver, but it won't speed up the liver. All you can do to sober up is to wait for the liver to do its thing.

So, What's My Safe Limit?

What all this stuff about percentages and ounces and BACs and hours boils down to is this: keeping BAC within safe limits means no more than one drink per hour. It's best if you can avoid alcohol during a ride; but if you're addicted, at least limit your BAC. Remember that biker who fortified his soda pop with whiskey during a ride? Well, it may have been poor judgment, it was probably illegal, and it certainly sustains a bad image, but one shot of whiskey is within the "safe" BAC limit.

So, What Are We Going to Do About Booze?

But I Don't Drink

Let's assume for a moment that you and I are smart enough to separate the demon rum from motorcycling, but our friend Buddy Biker can't hold his booze. Does it matter to us that Buddy has lost his license, nips from a flask during a ride, and occasionally wanders down the wrong side of the road? Well, it should matter. Even if we don't know the guy personally, the accident and fatality statistics have a direct effect on our wallets through motorcycle insurance rates and health insurance premiums. If we ride with him, Buddy could involve us in a crash. And if he's a friend, we ought to care about him enough to help prevent a fatal accident.

Let's Make It Taboo

The trouble is that booze has been such an integral part of many biker events that we're going to have to get really pushy to change old attitudes. The old attitudes are: *I can handle it. A real biker can corner faster after a few beers; I'll sober up when I get a little wind in my face. I've had a few accidents, but being drunk kept me from getting injured. If we can't have an open keg at the rally, why bother to go?*

If we want to reduce motorcycle fatalities, the single most important issue is to make riding after drinking a motorcycling taboo. What's important to remember is that the decision not to ride while under the influence needs to be made before the first drink goes down the hatch.

Wise riders who want more than one drink per hour choose either an alcohol-free drink or to hand their bike keys to a sober friend. Smart group leaders avoid stopping at cocktail lounges during a ride. Clever rally organizers do not allow an unattended beer keg. Responsible party hosts monitor the booze being consumed and make arrangements for alternate transportation for those who can't control their urge to get plastered.

David L. Hough

The decision not to ride while drunk needs to be made before the first drink goes down the hatch.

Riding Straight

The MSF has a videotape titled *Riding Straight* for use in MSF courses. The tape is also available to anyone else for showing to motorcycle groups. The twelve-minute video is an excellent overview of the hazards of riding while under the influence, and the presentation is entertaining enough to help keep the subject from becoming another boring sermon.

The Long Arm of the Law

The concentration of alcohol in a person's system is usually measured as a percentage of blood known, or blood alcohol concentration (BAC). Drunk driving laws used to specify driving while intoxicated (DWI) or driving under the influence (DUI) at 0.10 percent, or one part alcohol for every thousand parts of blood. But NHTSA has been encouraging states to reduce their DWI limits. Today in most states the limit is 0.08 percent. Many states have stricter laws for minors, with limits at a mere 0.02 percent.

For example, in Washington State the DUI limit for adults is currently 0.08 percent, with fines starting at $350, plus twenty-four hours in the slammer, plus license suspension for up to 90 days. The fine, jail time, and license suspension escalate for higher BAC levels and repeat offenders. A BAC of 0.15 or more can net a fine up to $5,000, plus up to twelve months in jail. If it's a third offense within seven years, the minimum fine is $1,500, plus a mandatory 120 days in the slammer. And it's even more severe for minors. A rider under age twenty-one loses his license for 90 days if nabbed with a BAC of only 0.02 percent (maybe two beers) and faces the possibility of heavy fines, plus jail time.

None of the above costs include court fees, expenses of a lawyer or counselor, huge insurance increases, damage to the bike during towing and storage, or bus fare. If the DUI occurs on top of a suspended license, the bike may be seized.

Risky
R I S K Y

CROWNED
ROAD

RIGHT TURN

Business
B U S I N E S S

OWNED
ROAD

CHAPTER 4
RISKY BUSINESS

Navigating the Road

I was standing around in front of a Honda dealership the other day, waiting for the doors to open. Several other motorcyclists were also waiting, and we struck up a conversation. One of the riders (we'll call him Faultless Frank) was in need of a new machine, having recently crashed his sportbike. According to his sad tale, road crews had seal-coated a corner of one of his favorite back roads; he'd spotted the gravel too late and crashed big time. Oh, yeah, Frank also admitted he was riding at his usual outstanding speed and it was nighttime.

It wasn't my fault. The stupid road crew spread gravel all over the road. They should have put up a sign or something. I came around the corner and suddenly there was loose gravel. There wasn't even a warning sign. There wasn't anything I could do. I'm gonna sue 'em! Frank said.

I suggested that a crash was probably some indication that there was more to learn.

What do you mean? The slideout wasn't MY fault. Frank quickly pointed out that he'd been riding for years in the dirt before he took to the street, and his pavement riding even included some track time. It was obvious that from Frank's side of the eyeballs he was an outstanding rider who knew everything there was to know about motorcycling—before he was twenty years old.

Even though we'd prefer it wasn't used, seal coating is a fact of life every summer.

I wasn't quite willing to give up. I countered that this type of situation could have been avoided if he had taken a training course, such as the one the ERC teaches. He answered, *What could I possibly get out of a stupid training class? I could roast any of you guys any day!*

The conversation ended abruptly at that point. Yes, it's a true story. I relate it to you because Faultless Frank typifies the no-fault attitude so prevalent among younger riders today, aggressively pushing on the envelope until the laws of physics are exceeded, then searching frantically for someone else to blame for the resulting smasho.

Hopefully, one of these days a few tiny electrons will zap in Frank's brain, and he'll suddenly realize that riding a motorcycle on public roads is much different from riding on the dirt or on a racetrack. Yes, there are a lot of booby traps out there on the back roads, as well as on city streets. The point is that the person responsible for what happens next is whoever is hanging on to the grips at the moment.

Loose gravel is only one of the many hazards we must learn to negotiate. Every road has a different set of hazards. To think about the challenges, let's separate them into surface contaminants, road geometry, and other users.

Surface Contaminants

Faultless Frank had already set the scene for disaster by assuming the road surface would be consistently good from corner to corner, the same today as it was yesterday. The real world situation is that the surface conditions change dramatically from one patch of pavement to the next and also from one day to another. It's not realistic to assume the road department is going to rush out and erect a sign for every possible motorcycle problem. Yes, loose gravel on a paved road is a big summertime hazard I wish we'd never have to face, but it's a fact of life on a lot of country roads and even a few state highways.

Loose sand (which would normally decrease traction on a dry road) might actually improve traction in the rain. Dirt blown across the road by wind gusts might decrease traction only slightly on a dry day but will quickly turn to slippery mud with only a little moisture. We must keep in mind that traction is a changing commodity that we need to monitor continuously.

Two basic tactics for negotiating surface contaminants are to learn to read the surface ahead and to adjust speed and line to keep a lot of reserve traction available. You'll have a good idea of the available traction under your tires at a given moment because you are getting instant feedback. If you feel your tires gripping the road, you can predict that as long as the road ahead continues to have the same appearance, the surface ahead will continue to have good traction.

The trick is to look for changes in surface color or texture.

When I'm riding the back roads, I probably devote half my attention to the road surface. If I'm going to avoid the common hazards, I need to observe them in time to do something about the situation. The trick is to look for changes in the appearance of the surface that indicate a possible change in available traction. A puddle of water typically appears darker than the surrounding pavement. Oil on a wet road beads up and also provides a rainbow-colored sheen. Loose gravel may be the same color as the pavement, but I should be able to detect a rougher texture.

When I observe a change in color or texture of the surface ahead, I reduce speed and lean angle until I can determine whether the traction is better or worse. And if I must ride through a hazardous area such as gravel or wet mud, I also make a point of keeping my tires perpendicular to the road surface and holding a steady throttle.

Some surface hazards are sneakier than they appear. For example, is that dark puddle ahead just water (which will quickly evaporate off my tires) or oil (which will lubricate my tires for several miles)? And weather can affect the hazards. What's the temperature? Has it been raining recently? If the weather is hot and dry, I am extremely suspicious of any dark puddles or liquid streaks. What does that different texture on the bridge mean? Is it smooth concrete or the dreaded steel grates that make tires wiggle around?

If you're riding through an agricultural area, scrutinize the surface for colored arcs, indicating farm equipment has tracked dirt or mud onto the pavement. Where there are no ditches, dirt and sand can drift onto the road surface from uphill banks.

Is that different texture on the bridge surface smooth concrete or steel grating?

Dungeness Dave's Slithering Blooper

A few years ago, Dungeness Dave was zipping along some back roads in northern Oregon. There had been thundershowers the previous night, and even though it was still wet in places, the paving had decent traction. Cresting a hill, Dave observed freshly plowed farm fields on both sides of the highway and what appeared to be a stream of water crossing the pavement from one field to the other. But as he got closer, Dave suddenly realized the "stream" was really a river of muddy clay that was oozing across the road.

Surprise! That "water" ahead is really slippery clay oozing across the road.

Instinctively, Dave snapped the throttle closed but had enough presence of mind to stay off the brakes as the bike fishtailed like a swamp buggy through 50 feet of slippery goo. Miraculously, he didn't drop the bike, but the experience was a wake-up call to be more aware of mud washed out of freshly worked farm fields. The lesson is to expect mud and debris in low spots after a storm.

Dave's throttle technique didn't help the situation. A trailing throttle has a similar effect as a dragging rear brake. He would have been better off to stabilize the power as well as stay off the brakes while slithering through the mud.

Ducati Dan's Can Blooper

Even when we can easily see small flat objects on the pavement, it may not be apparent that they are dangerous to motorcycles. What's the big deal about riding over a flattened soda pop can or ice cream carton? Well, Ducati Dan found out the hard way.

Dan had just fueled up his 916 at a country store and was heading back onto the road. He saw a flattened soda pop can on the road and figured he would further mash it flat with his Pirelli. But a car suddenly pulled out of a driveway across the road and Dan squeezed the brakes at exactly the moment his front tire rolled over the can. The Pirelli grabbed the can, the can suddenly became a ski, and the front end slid out, providing an excellent (although expensive) lesson in the importance of avoiding loose, slippery objects.

The clever rider keeps his tires away from flattened debris.

Negotiating Surface Hazards

The tactics for avoiding such surface hazard bloopers are to understand what hazards look like, think far ahead, and reduce traction demands. If possible, put your tires over the best surface. If you have to cross a surface hazard, reduce speed before your tires get there. Then get off the brakes, hold a steady throttle, and select a path of travel that reduces side loads on the tires.

Had Faultless Frank braked hard before reaching the loose gravel, he could probably have made the curve without sliding out. If Dungeness Dave had been thinking, he would have expected a mud wash downhill from a plowed field. If Ducati Dan had been a little more clever about the traction situation, he would have kept his tires on the pavement and away from the flattened can.

Road Geometry

The twisting, turning, up, down unpredictability of a road is what makes it so challenging for motorcycling. Even on familiar roads free of surface hazards, it's not likely we can remember every curve exactly. And on a road we haven't ridden before, there are bound to be a lot of surprises. Small errors in judgment can quickly turn into major bloopers.

Biker Billy's Hilly Blooper

Biker Billy was cruising the back roads on his V-twin one Sunday afternoon. Billy wasn't in a hurry, but he was enjoying the road, which wound through hilly farm country. It felt good to crank on a little throttle to accelerate through corners and hear the exhaust reverberating off the trees. The road disappeared over the crest of a hill, but Billy could see the power poles marching straight ahead, and he assumed that the road continued straight ahead, too.

Surprise! When Billy crested the hill, he discovered the road dove into a sharp left turn just over the top. The power lines stretched over a swamp and off across a farmer's field. Billy attempted a quick slowdown, but the physics of the situation were loaded against him. The big V-twin plowed off the road and looped end over end into the swamp. Sadder but wiser,

Are you willing to bet your life that the road follows the power lines?

Billy learned the importance of keeping speed within sight distance and never assuming anything about what's around the curve or over the hill.

Twisty Roads

A lot of country roads gradually came into being following wandering cows or old wagon paths. Corners that were barely adequate for horseback speeds can be

Off-camber turns can be a big shock if you aren't following good lines.

David L. Hough

challenging for motorcyclists. We need to be prepared for whatever combinations of dips and turns the pavement has in store. Frankly, most of us prefer that the road engineers don't "improve" such roads.

The slant, or camber, of the road affects both cornering clearance and available traction. If the pavement is cambered nicely into the turn, we have better traction and leanover clearance. But if the road slants off the wrong way, we may suddenly feel the front tire sliding or something touching down and levering the rear tire into a step-out, and then (hopefully) regain traction.

Consider that the right lane of a typical back road slants off toward the right. That's fine for a right turn, but not ideal for a left turn. In a left turn, the road crown decreases both leanover clearance and available traction in the right lane. By adjusting your line to arc closer to the centerline in a left turn, you can avoid most of the off-camber effect.

Even right turns can be off-camber, with the pavement slanting away from the turn. In an off-camber right turn, a line that arcs closer to the right edge of the pavement at mid turn maximizes both leanover clearance and traction.

Curves that don't follow a constant radius are a special challenge. Of course, curves that follow steady, predictable arcs are easiest to ride. But roads with a lot of odd turns are more challenging. A curve that tightens up halfway around (a decreasing radius) is a special challenge. If you allow yourself to get slickered into assuming it's a normal turn, there isn't much you can do halfway around, unless you have some way to momentarily repeal the laws of physics.

The worst-case scenario is an off-camber, decreasing radius, downhill left turn, perhaps with a touch of loose gravel. When you're riding an unfamiliar road, the only way to improve your odds of surviving such abnormal corners is to approach every blind curve as if it is one of those worst-case situations.

It's also worthwhile to practice that "slow, look, lean, and roll" technique taught in rider training courses. Slow down before you lean the bike. Remember, your target entry speed before you lean over into a curve is whatever speed will allow you to ease on more throttle continuously through the rest of the curve. An entry line farther toward the outside (i.e., close to the centerline in a right-hander) provides a better view. If you're going to hang off, get your weight shifted before the turn-in, look where you want to be five or six seconds from that point, lean the bike by countersteering, and ease on the gas all the way around the curve.

CROWNED ROAD

RIGHT TURN

CROWNED ROAD

LEFT TURN

Cruiser Carl's Camber Blooper

Cruiser Carl was enjoying a nice twisty back road one day. Carl liked to maintain a steady pace that kept his engine in a power band where he didn't have to shift up and down. He liked to just motor along without too much concern for braking, cornering lines, apexes, and all that zoomie bike stuff. Carl was doing all right until the camber rolled right in a left-handed turn.

The cruiser's sidestand suddenly started making sparks, and Carl reacted by jerking the bike more upright. Of course, that steered the machine wide, off the road, and into the ditch, where it came to rest with the front wheel customized into a new culvert pipe shape. With his new bike on order, Carl is now thinking a bit more about cornering skills—especially road camber.

Other Users

All of the riders we've mentioned made another potentially fatal error: they weren't planning on anyone else to be using the road at the moment. If Faultless Frank knew there was a possibility of sliding out across the opposing lane, he might have realized that sliding under an oncoming freight truck might hurt a lot more than just sliding out on gravel. Had a farm tractor pulled out onto the road ahead of Dungeness Dave, he would have had little chance of bringing his bike to a stop on slippery mud. Ducati Dan's slideout was partly caused because he wasn't watching for another vehicle. When we're riding on public roads, we must be aware of other users and be prepared to get out of their way, even if we have the legal right-of-way.

Motorhead Mary's Passing Blooper

Motorhead Mary was heading back to the farm on her 650 one afternoon. A slow-moving logging truck held her up in the curves, but a short straight with no oncoming traffic looked like a good place to snort on by. Mary rolled on the gas and was accelerating past the back wheels of the truck when she realized the truck driver was turning left onto a side road. Faced with the choice of going under the wheels or off the road, Mary banked the 650 toward the ditch. When the dust settled, the truck driver didn't have a scratch, the 650 was totaled, and Mary got a trip to the hospital.

Yes, Mary made the right decision to get out of the way once she realized she was on a collision course, but the decision to pass had failed to take into consideration the possibility of the truck turning onto the side road. Okay, the electrical plug to the trailer lights was broken, so Mary didn't have a clue that the driver had signaled. But you can't depend upon signs and signals to caution you to every potential problem.

All of the same automotive blunders you find in the city occur on the back roads, plus a few more. In addition to left-turning vehicles, folks turning off without signaling, and sleepy drivers crossing the centerline, we must also expect locals to suddenly stop for a driver-to-driver chat maybe even in the middle of the road. Farm vehicles often use the public road to get from one part of a spread to the other, and some implements have serious weapons mounted on them. The point is that you need to be aware of what those other road users are up to.

When you're sharing a public road, you need to be aware of what the other users are doing.

Take these lessons from Faultless Frank, Dungeness Dave, Ducati Dan, Biker Billy, Cruiser Carl, and Motorhead Mary. Maybe you won't have to learn it all the hard way and add your name to our list of back road bloopers.

Construction Ahead

Rider Ralph is touring the West and enjoying every minute of it. That is, until he stumbles into a work zone. The road crew is doing a little repaving and fixing a culvert. It isn't a serious project, but the road is full of construction equipment, and one lane is completely blocked off. Ralph's first warning of a potential problem is a big diamond-shaped orange sign: Construction Ahead.

Of course, Ralph isn't familiar with the area, and he doesn't know what to expect. He slows his bike from 60 mph down to 50 mph. Then the road curves around toward the morning sun, and suddenly he's enveloped in a cloud of dust. Ralph can barely see where the road goes, let alone the bump sign in the shade. He frantically rolls off the gas and hits the brakes.

It's a shock when the front wheel plows into loose gravel. Fighting for balance, Ralph slams his boots out to help keep the bike upright while the front wheel darts from side to side. Ralph is relieved to see pavement ahead. But at the instant his front wheel strikes the edge of the new pavement, the handlebars are wrenched from his grasp, and the big touring bike topples over on its side, leaving a trail of shattered plastic.

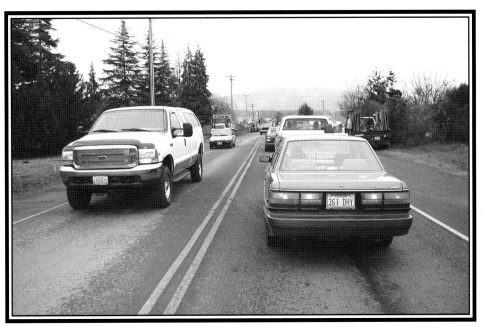

You should expect a lot of motorcycle hazards in work zones.

A bump sign can cover a lot of hazards, including loose gravel.

Every year, thousands of motorcyclists drop their bikes in work zone accidents. But it's hard to find any meaningful statistics about motorcycle accidents and fatalities in work zones. Motorcycles are such a small a minority of vehicles on the road that highway departments and contractors don't seem to have much interest in how work zone hazards affect two-wheelers.

Let's see if we can figure out how to negotiate typical work zone hazards that we are likely to encounter while traveling.

Speed

Ralph braked hard when he suddenly couldn't see, but he didn't slow down soon enough, and he didn't slow to an appropriate speed. As soon as he saw the construction ahead sign, he should have slowed and also increased his awareness of what was going on. That's a common error for all motorists, whether it's an orange sign, a flagman, or giant blinking arrows. People tend to keep motoring along into problems without slowing.

Work zone warning signs often include a speed recommendation. You shouldn't ignore those speed recommendations. First, reducing speed increases your time to react. Second, you may suddenly encounter limited visibility. Third, you may need to negotiate a surface problem that creates a special hazard for two-wheelers.

You should also remember that those temporary speed signs are more than recommendations. In most states, the speed indicated on a construction sign takes precedence over the posted speed limits. You might not be arrested for failing to slow down to the construction speed, but if you should be involved in an accident, you could be ticketed for excessive speed.

In some states, traffic fines are doubled in work zones (or in special safety corridors) as an added incentive for drivers to slow down. You may feel incensed at the concept, but it's in your best interests as a motorcyclist to have everyone slowed down in areas where there have been too many accidents.

In addition to scrubbing off some speed in work zones, you also need to get your head into what's happening. It's more important for a two-wheeler to get lined up for hazards such as loose gravel or edge traps, and other drivers aren't likely to understand what you're doing. For instance, if two lanes merge into one, you may need to cross a pavement edge while also trying to squeeze between two cars. Don't be embarrassed to pull over and wait for the hot dogs to get on by.

That 20 mph sign is more than a recommendation.

The somewhat high viewpoint of being on a motorcycle gives you the advantage of observing the situation up ahead, assuming you're not stuck behind a truck. You can prepare yourself for stopped traffic, potholes, steel plates, loose gravel, raised manhole covers, edge traps, tar snakes, and other common work zone hazards. If possible, separate the hazards. For instance, if you're facing a lane change, merging traffic, and steel construction plates, change lanes early, pick a slow car to merge in front of, and then set yourself up to cross the steel plates.

It's more important for a motorcyclist to scrutinize the surface because single-track vehicles are susceptible to certain hazards that might be only an inconvenience to four-wheelers. For example, a truck or car might slide around on loose gravel, but a motorcycle is more likely to lose balance. While we don't have any statistics on the

Doubling fines is a desperate attempt to get drivers to slow down in hazardous areas.

David L. Hough

causes of motorcycle accidents in work zones, the warning signs are a good clue about what's happening. It must be more than a coincidence that there are so many signs such as Motorcycles Use Extreme Caution, warning motorcyclists specifically.

Follow Me

If you arrive at a line of stopped traffic waiting for a one-way detour, you might consider working your way up to the head of the line and asking the flagman if you can go first or holding back and riding at the end of the line. You can't depend on other motorists to understand about slippery surfaces, flying stones, or your need to get lined up to bounce over edge traps. The flagman may not understand about hazards specific to a motorcycle but may be sympathetic to allowing you to separate yourself from the line of cars to avoid damaging your paint.

Reading the Signs

The big construction sign at the beginning of a work zone won't give you much specific information. It's just a warning that you should expect a variety of hazards. As you see other, more specific signs, you may need to read between the lines.

For example, you may see signs that read Abrupt Lane Edge or Motorcycles Do Not Change Lanes. What such signs usually mean is that there is a repaving operation ahead. The signs often go up after a few motorcycle crashes. You can't assume the construction crew understands motorcycle hazards, only that they've had enough motorcycle crashes to be concerned about liability. You shouldn't be surprised to discover a layer of new paving angling across your lane, requiring you to bounce over the edge.

A bump sign indicates a change in elevation from one section of road to another, such as the end of new paving laid on top of old pavement. But you should be aware that a bump sign can also be used for pavement edges that cross the lane at odd angles or where there is hard paving on one side of the bump and soft gravel on the other. So, you need to watch carefully to see what sort of hazards the signs are warning you about.

You can usually translate this sign to mean Watch for Edge Traps.

Surface Hazards

Edge Traps

What brought Rider Ralph down wasn't the loose gravel. Ralph lost balance when the raised pavement edge trapped his front wheel. The wheels of a car or truck can straddle the edge. On a motorcycle, you can easily make the mistake of riding into an edge trap while you're focused on traffic or trying to follow the temporary lane.

Based on the signs and resulting lawsuits, motorcycle edge trap accidents appear to be common in work zones. Construction crews don't automatically understand

It may be unnerving to ride on the grooved surface, but it's less risky than trying to cross over that edge trap to get onto the smooth pavement.

If the lane straddles a pavement joint, ride to one side or the other.

how pavement edges can instantly drop a two-wheeler, so they aren't always careful about setting up temporary lanes to avoid crossing pavement edges at narrow angles. It's not uncommon to see pavement edges rambling down the middle of the lane in a work zone with no warning signs.

It's essential to keep your tires away from raised pavement edges. If you find yourself in a lane in which the old paving has been ground away, it can be unnerving to have your bike wiggling around on the grooved pavement. It's tempting to think about easing over onto that smoother pavement in the other lane, but that's a trap. A lot of riders have fallen trying to ease over a raised pavement edge. You're better off riding out the rough surface.

If you are directed to cross an edge trap by traffic cones or a flagman, it's critical to bounce over the edge at maximum angle. The risks of dropping your bike increase when your line of attack over a raised pavement edge is less than 45 degrees. At an approach angle that is less than about 30 degrees, the front wheel tends to slide along the edge. Once you lose control of steering, it's difficult to maintain balance.

If you must cross a raised edge, treat it like a curb. Swerve away from the edge and attack it at a 45-degree angle. Roll on a little throttle to bounce the front wheel up and over the edge, then straighten the bike after you're on the higher surface.

Steel Construction Plates

Steel construction plates are often used in work zones to temporarily cover deep holes. If it isn't obvious, a smooth steel plate is slippery, especially when wet or coated with mud. Sometimes a construction plate isn't quite large enough or isn't quite the right shape to cover the hole, which can be 6 or 8 feet deep. To avoid dropping in for a quick visit, make a point of avoiding any narrow grooves between steel plates. If you can, ride around the plate to one side.

Less obvious is that the edges at the sides of a heavy plate form edge traps. The plate may be only 3/4 inch thick, but the edges are sharp, shiny, and capable of caus-

When crossing slippery steel construction plates, get the bike vertical, stabilize speed, and pick a path that avoids the sharp edges.

ing your front tire to slide out. When crossing a steel plate, get your bike vertical and stable and pick a straight line across the middle of the plate. When multiple plates are piled on top of each other, they create a lot of nasty edges to avoid.

Loose Gravel

You can expect loose gravel where a road is torn up, but you must also expect loose gravel on paved roads. When a road or highway needs a new surface, a cheap, quick alternative to repaving is to seal coat the old pavement by squirting sticky tar on the surface and then spreading loose gravel on top. The idea is that the gravel will stick to the tar, and passing vehicles will eventually roll everything down flat, sealing the surface. Seal coating is bad news for motorcyclists because the sticky goo makes a mess on bikes, and the loose gravel dings the paint and reduces traction. The loss of traction may not be a problem for the dual sport crowd, but it can be a real panic for riders with limited off-pavement skills.

Expect loose gravel on a freshly sealed road.

The gravel is obvious on a freshly sealed road. Riding in the wheel tracks may help because the gravel there will be compacted. The loose gravel outside of the wheel tracks may be soft and deep. Street riders are so dependent upon good traction that the feel of loose gravel or sand can be unnerving. Yes, the feeling that your front wheel is about to slide out is because your front wheel is about to slide out. On loose surfaces, countersteering doesn't produce an immediate result, so we don't get the expected feedback that the motorcycle really is responding.

When negotiating a two-lane gravel road, stay well away from the center to avoid the spray of stones from the tires of oncoming vehicles. Choose a path that keeps your tires out of the really deep stuff, load more of your weight on the pegs, counterbalance the bike to hold it vertical, stay off the brakes, and steer with the throttle. You'll discover that riding too slow causes more wobbles than moving along a little faster and that it also encourages faster drivers to tailgate or pass and shower you with loose rocks. Ease up on your death grip and let the bike wiggle around under you. And as the dirt donks say, "When in doubt, gas it!"

And when you do arrive back on smooth pavement at the end of a stretch of loose gravel, don't be too quick to wick it back up to speed. There may be another unmarked section of gravel around the next turn. When construction crews are working several miles of road, they don't always move the signs.

Slippery Oil

While the loose gravel on a seal-coated road will get your attention, don't ignore the sticky oil sprayed on the surface to glue the gravel in place. Sometimes the road

The overspray on the gravel at the edge of the lane is a clue that the surface is coated with slippery oil.

crew will spray down a coating of oil and then require traffic to drive over the oil while they are waiting for the gravel trucks to catch up.

The oil may not be obvious if the entire lane is coated, and it may look like new asphalt paving. But fresh oil can be slippery. If you're required to ride on fresh oil, keep the wheels perpendicular to the surface and maintain a slow but steady speed.

Tar Snakes

Another variation of slick stuff called tar snakes are hatched by road crews dribbling liquid sealer into cracks in the pavement. If the crew overfills the cracks, the slippery tar spreads out into a wide patch that's a serious hazard for motorcyclists. This varmint has bitten a lot of unsuspect-

Tar snakes are slipperier than they appear. Pick a line that keeps your rubber off the big blobs and reduce your lean angle.

ing motorcyclists. Some states apply sand to the fresh tar or use a compound that's less slippery. But it can be a big shock for riders who travel to a state in which they still use the cheaper, slipperier stuff.

The first step to prevent being bitten by a tar snake is simply to understand that tar compounds can be extremely slippery. The crack sealer is a much darker color, or perhaps reflects a shinier texture, than the surrounding pavement. If possible, pick a path that keeps your tires off the slippery guck. If you have to ride through a snake pit of dribbled tar, slow down and keep the bike more vertical, just as you would on loose gravel, wet bricks, or shiny steel.

Potholes

Potholes are common in northern climates where the pavement freezes in the winter and then thaws and crumbles in the spring. Potholes can bend rims, break spokes, or yank the handlebars out of your grasp. If you haven't yet slammed into a pothole, count yourself lucky.

You can predict that potholes will appear more frequently after a heavy winter, particularly on routes used by heavy commercial traffic. You can also predict that holes will be in the wheel tracks where truck tires pound the pavement. Often, it's possible to pick a line that misses the worst damage.

Potholes can bend a rim or yank the bars out of your grasp.

Slippery Goo

In some parts of the country, the earth contains a high percentage of clay, which can be extremely slippery when wet. Dump trucks track the slippery mud through a detour or from a detour onto the adjacent pavement. It's also common for work crews to water down the temporary surface to help control dust. So, even if it hasn't been raining for a week and you aren't off the pavement yet, watch carefully for a slippery surface.

Riding Tactics

On loose or slippery surfaces, it's important to conserve traction by choosing a line that puts your tires on the most tractable surface. Maintain a steady throttle, make only gradual changes of direction, and keep the bike wheels perpendicular to the surface.

It doesn't help to stick your legs out, because that allows your body weight to waggle from side to side, upsetting balance. Take a hint from the dirt riders, who not only keep their feet on the pegs but actually stand up to load their weight down low on the bike. And, rather than trying to balance and steer with just the handlebars, dirt riders shift weight from one peg to the other and also use short bursts of throttle to slide the rear end around.

If the thought of negotiating deep gravel or slippery mud in a work zone makes you break out in a cold sweat, the best advice is to borrow a dual sport bike and spend some time off-pavement to gain some skill and confidence. Sure, you can just wait for your next lesson whenever you happen to encounter a work zone, but that could be on a dark, rainy night in heavy traffic. Some dual sport saddle time now can make your work zone encounters less of a shock later.

No matter what direction you're headed or what route you choose, you can expect to encounter construction projects every summer. But with a good idea of what to expect, and a little off-pavement practice under your belt, there's a good chance you'll get through the hazards unscathed.

Avoiding the Elephant

If you understand what's likely to occur in traffic and continuously scan the situation around you, you can usually make some small adjustment when needed and avoid riding into a problem. But once in a while a problem just can't be avoided. Something happens that you didn't expect and couldn't see, and suddenly you are faced with a disaster.

Sooner or later, most of us will encounter some weird situation we couldn't have predicted, and we'll either take the right evasive action or bite the elephant, so to speak.

When I used to teach rider training courses, I'd pull ridiculous situations out of the air just to get students thinking about strange hazards popping up suddenly. Here are some examples: You're riding down the street minding your own business, when suddenly an oil tanker crashes into a produce truck loaded with bananas. Or you're riding down the freeway, when suddenly a row of portable toilets falls off the truck ahead. Or you're cruising across town, when suddenly you see an escaped zoo elephant trumpeting through freeway traffic ahead. What's your best option? Brake? Swerve? Accelerate? Maintain speed? Break out the peanuts?

The point is that we must keep focused on what's happening, because unpredictable hazards sometimes appear suddenly, and we may need to pull off a quick evasive maneuver. What surprised me over the years is that all of my ridiculous situations turned out to be nonfiction. One day in class, I used the old analogy of a banana peel in a puddle of gear lube to illustrate how traction can change so dramatically. Later when we walked out to the practice range, I almost slipped on a banana peel floating in a puddle of oil. Honest. And after a seminar in Minnesota, a participant came up to say, *You're not going to believe this, but once in Minneapolis I did have an escaped elephant come charging across the street.* Sooner or later, most of us will encounter some weird situation we couldn't have predicted, and we'll either take the right evasive action or bite the elephant, so to speak.

Battle Stations!

When you are faced with an impending collision with that elephant, left-turning car, or stalled truck, there are four evasive actions you can take with a motorcycle: speed up, swerve, brake, or maintain direction and speed. The trouble is, the first three evasive maneuvers all demand traction, and traction is a limited commodity. If you attempt to swerve while braking hard, the bike tends to slide, flip, or snap into a barrel roll. To pull off a successful evasive maneuver, you have only a split second to make a decision and maybe a couple of seconds to make it happen.

Of course, the logic behind the latest braking systems, such as BMW's EVO integrated antilock power braking system, is that the black box will help you avoid accidents. Theoretically, you grab the front brake or stomp down on the rear pedal, and the bike brings itself to a stop in the minimum distance without falling down. The trouble with that theory is that you may need to swerve or accelerate rather than brake. Or you may be leaned over into a fast corner when you realize there's an immovable object in your way. So, it's still important for the rider to make the best decision in emergency situations. To help prepare for that split-second decision, let's think through the advantages and disadvantages of those four evasive actions.

When you are faced with an impending collision, there are only four evasive actions you can take with a motorcycle: speed up, swerve, brake, or do nothing.

Accelerating

Let's say you observe a car approaching an intersection from the other direction, and suddenly the driver swerves left across your path without slowing or signaling. Maybe you could gas it and accelerate around the front of the car. The big advantage of accelerating is that motorcycles typically have a lot of power. It's fast and easy to accelerate—all you have to do is roll the throttle open, hang on, and keep the front wheel on the deck.

The big disadvantage of accelerating is that increasing speed increases forward energy. As a little experiment in kinetic energy, try punching a fist into the palm of your other hand. First, punch it easily, then harder and harder. Your fist weighs the same, but punching at a higher speed results in much greater impact. How that relates to motorcycling is that if you do smash your bike into something, it's going to hurt a lot more at a faster speed. The impact force at 60 mph is about four times greater than at 30 mph.

The increase in forward energy from speeding up also makes it all the harder to change direction, say if you decide to swerve around the left-turner while accelerating. You might be able to swerve around the car at 30 mph but not at 50 mph. And even if you do manage to accelerate and then swerve around the car (or the elephant), you may be faced with other motorists in the way.

So, the decision to accelerate pretty much cancels out the options of swerving or braking. Acceleration is a better option for situations such as a car approaching too rapidly behind you, or a truck merging onto the freeway beside you, but it's seldom the best evasive action for a left-turning or red-light-running car.

Swerving might be a better option if all the other guys weren't moving around.

Swerving

Maybe you could swerve around behind the offending motorist without slowing down. The big advantage of swerving is that it doesn't increase forward energy, so it is possible to swerve and then straighten up and brake hard, without increasing stopping distance.

The big disadvantages of swerving are predicting what the other guy is going to do and being able to push forcefully on the grips without rolling off the throttle. If you choose to swerve, it would be helpful to know whether the other driver is going to continue or panic and stop halfway across your lane. Swerving would be a lot more predictable if all the other vehicles were anchored in position, but they are usually moving targets.

Swerving can eat up all of the available traction, even at modest street speeds, and high-tech brake systems won't prevent a slideout caused by overenthusiastic swerving. If you're trying to do a maximum-effort swerve, you really can't afford to squander any traction on accelerating or braking. You could brake first to scrub off some forward energy, then get off the brakes and swerve. Or you could swerve first and then brake. But braking and swerving at the same time is likely to result in a slideout.

A successful swerve requires that you control your urge to roll off the gas or hit the brakes until the bike is straightened out again. Unfortunately, the natural survival reaction to an impending collision is to snap off the throttle, jam on the brakes, and freeze on the grips. It's important to realize that snapping the throttle off eats rear wheel traction as the engine tries to slow the rear wheel. Frankly, when faced with the probability of getting crushed or splattered, most of us are going to panic and roll off the throttle before we can resist the urge. It's not impossible, just very difficult.

Braking

Hard braking is the most reliable evasive maneuver, especially for avoiding collisions with moving objects such as left-turning cars, jaywalkers, skateboarders, red-light runners, and stampeding animals.

Hard braking is the most reliable evasive maneuver for typical street hazards.

One reason a quick stop (sometimes called a panic stop) is so useful is because of the amount of power the brakes can muster. On today's motorcycles, the front brakes are typically more powerful than the engine. With the correct technique, it's possible to bring the bike to a stop in less distance than it took the engine to accelerate up to that speed.

Power brakes may or may not shorten the stop, because the limiting factor is tire traction, not brake efficiency. But ABS can really help here, because if you squeeze too hard for available traction in a straight-line stop, the ABS computer will ease off the brakes just enough to keep the tires from skidding. Integrated or linked brakes do help the unskilled rider who is in the bad habit of using only the rear brake pedal.

The wheelbase, center of gravity (CoG) of the bike, and the load also affect stopping distance. A heavyweight bike with a long wheelbase tends to be more stable in a quick stop than a lightweight sportbike with a short wheelbase. Back a few years ago, the possibility of lifting the rear end and doing a cartwheel over the front was more fear than a real concern. It was much more likely that the front tire would slide out before the rear tire would lift off, or that the front brake wasn't powerful enough to do a stoppie.

Today, double floating disk systems, multiple piston calipers, metal reinforced brake hoses, integrated or linked brake systems, and sticky tire compounds add up to awesome braking power that can stand a sportbike on its nose with a modest two-finger squeeze on the brake lever. On such machines, the brake lever must be modulated short of available traction just to keep the rear wheel on the ground. That means your technique needs to be modified for the type of machine you are riding. On a cruiser with a long wheelbase, it's more important to control front wheel skids.

Doing Nothing

Yes, there are some situations in which the best choice is to keep the bike stable and do nothing. For instance, if you're faced with a 4 x 4 piece of wood that drops off the truck ahead of you on the freeway or clay washed across the road from an uphill field, you don't want to upset the bike by accelerating, braking, or swerving.

In such situations, you need to overcome your survival instincts to snap off the throttle or jam on the brakes.

The big disadvantage of doing nothing to avoid a traffic accident is that you may need to accelerate, swerve, or brake to save yourself. Although deciding to "do nothing" might be appropriate in some circumstances, in the majority of accident scenarios investigated by the Hurt team way too many riders froze on the grips and failed to take evasive action that would have helped them avoid the accident.

Speed vs. Stopping Distance

Here's a little quiz for you go-fasters. If you could stop your favorite road burner from 50 mph in 90 feet, what's the minimum distance it would take you to stop from twice that speed (100 mph) under the same circumstances?

a. 180 feet
b. 270 feet
c. 360 feet

We hope it doesn't come as a big shock to you that the answer isn't "a" or "b." Doubling your speed quadruples forward energy. And even if your machine has power brakes or ABS, the black boxes can't increase available traction or change the physics of the situation. You'll eat up maybe 270 feet just slowing from 100 mph down to 50.

It gets a little scarier once you realize that these numbers are for stopping distances after you get on the brakes. During the split second you are deciding to brake and reaching for the lever, the bike is still rocketing along at the same speed. If you're not prepared to squeeze the lever, it's going to take a lot more pavement to stop. Reaction time of only an extra half second stretches the 50 mph stop from 90 to 127 feet, and pushes the 100 mph stop from 360 to 407 feet. If you want the formula, multiply mph x 1.467 to get the number of feet per second.

Your stopping distances might be shorter than these numbers on clean, dry pavement with high-quality, warmed-up tires. But remember, those quick-stop distances in the published bike reviews are scored by experienced testers under ideal conditions, knowing when and where they would initiate the stop.

Emergency Maneuvers

Earlier, I suggested that to pull off a successful evasive maneuver you must first make a split-second decision about what to do and then have the skills to pull it off. Is there some way to practice emergency maneuvers, so that you're more likely to do them correctly when you're faced with a sudden hazard?

Rider training courses developed by the MSF are based to a great extent on the results of the Hurt Report. The philosophy is to provide the knowledge and skills that were missing among the riders who had crashed. The assumption is that practicing emergency maneuvers prepares you for those occasions when you've got only two or three seconds to get out of the way.

But some of us question whether there is such a thing as an emergency maneuver that is different from what we do in day-to-day riding. There's a lot of evidence that in emergencies we revert to our habits. A car suddenly turns left, the rider reacts (I believe the person reacts instinctively), and after the dust settles, the rider thinks about it. If you're not in the habit of covering the front brake lever when approaching a busy intersection, the probability is that you won't reach for the lever until after the WHUMP! If you are nervous about aggressive countersteering in daily riding, it's not likely you'll be able to pull a successful emergency swerve out of your helmet when that taxi cuts in front of you.

Practice Makes Perfect

We might suggest that the real reasons for taking a rider training course are to learn how to avoid riding into traffic hazards and to practice your cornering skills while there is a trained instructor to help correct any bad habits. When you are practicing swerves during a rider training course at parking lot speeds, you'll affirm it's pushing on the handlebar grips that makes the bike lean quickly. You'll also discover how difficult it is not to roll off the gas when swerving.

Practice exercises help put the right techniques in the right sequence, but after class, you need to consciously practice the right techniques in your daily riding to make them habits. My suggestion for developing proficient swerving, braking, and traction management skills is to ride twisty roads frequently and aggressively. If you tend to ride cautiously, favor the superslab over the back roads, and rarely attack twisty roads, then it is unlikely you'll do more than a gentle swerve when faced with that elephant or whatever suddenly plods out in front of you. If you always use the front brake when stopping, and squeeze on a bit of front brake as part of your cornering sequence, you're a lot more likely to be on the brakes immediately during an emergency—and you'll probably think about it after you don't have the collision.

And if you're used to quickly leaning the bike over to steep lean angles in tight curves, you'll probably swerve when it's called for without having to think about it. If you're nervous about steep lean angles, one way to calm your nerves is to put in some practice in a parking lot.

One big difference between braking on the road and braking to avoid collisions is that when faced with an immovable object, you'll probably need to brake to a complete stop. A lot of riders believe that if they can slow from a very fast speed to a fast speed without dropping the bike, they should be able to do a quick stop at street

If you're nervous about steep lean angles, consider some cornering practice.

speeds, even if they haven't practiced going from 40 to 0. When we say *quick stop*, we're talking maximum-effort stops from 30 to 0 or 40 to 0 in the shortest distance, without sliding out, falling down, or flipping the bike. Yes, hard braking at higher road speeds helps build braking skill, but bringing the bike to a complete stop from street speeds involves some additional techniques that you can only learn through practice.

The point of all this is that when you're faced with the proverbial escaped elephant or that banana peel floating in a puddle of gear lube, your habits will probably choose the evasive maneuver, and your skill practice will determine whether or not you can pull it off successfully.

TUNING UP

YOUR SKILLS

CHAPTER 5

TUNING UP YOUR SKILLS

Spring Training

There are some parts of the country where motorcyclists ride throughout the year, but many of us put the bike away during the winter months. If your motorcycle has been sitting in a garage all winter, it probably needs a little attention before it's ready to go. But don't forget that if you haven't been riding for a while, your skills probably need some attention, too. Skills and habits tend to get rusty if you don't use them. And even if you have been riding all winter, you may have gotten sloppy about some basic habits. Let's think about some spring training for your riding skills.

Put Your Brain in Gear Before You Ease out the Clutch

It doesn't take long for your motorcycling tactics to lose that edge when you're driving a four-wheeler every day. In a car, you're just part of the vehicular herd,

If you haven't been riding for a few months, your riding skills probably need a tune up.

jostling for position in traffic. But that also means other drivers are more likely to see you, since your vehicle is more or less the same size as theirs. And if your vehicle of choice has been an aggressive-looking sport utility vehicle or pickup truck, other drivers have probably given you more space. The point is that driving a four-wheeler has a way of dulling your motorcycling survival instincts.

On a motorcycle, you need to keep your brain in traffic-survival mode. Motorcycles are shorter, narrower, and harder to see in traffic. Many drivers don't think of motorcycles as real vehicles worthy of road space, and others just aren't looking for a bike. It's much more likely that drivers will change lanes on top of you, pull out of a parking lot right in front of you, or make a quick swerve across your path when you're riding a motorcycle.

If you haven't been challenged for road space recently, the first transgression may get you hot under the helmet. But before you react stupidly, remember that it may not be driver-to-driver aggression but just a lack of respect for a motorcyclist. Remember, might makes right. Bigger vehicles can push smaller vehicles off the road. Sure, your VTX might be able to knock the door off a Geo if the driver stupidly opens it into your lane. But in the traffic stream, even a heavyweight motorcycle is going to come out second best in a collision with a big car or truck.

So, before you head out into traffic on your next ride, take a few moments to shift your mental gears back to riding a motorcycle again. Remember, motorcyclists are at the bottom of the heap. Some drivers are not going to give you your road space, even if you have the legal right-of-way. You'll either move out of the way or lose it.

**SQUEEZE CLUTCH
SHIFT BRAIN INTO GEAR**

Remember: shift your brain into "motorcycle" before you ease out the clutch.

David L. Hough

Countersteering

I constantly remind everyone that two-wheelers are balanced by countersteering, but I continue to get questions about this. I get letters from people who deny that it works and from others who agree intellectually that it must work but aren't sure they want to try it yet.

Let's note that the driver of a four-wheeler changes direction just by turning the steering wheel. A four-wheeler starts to change direction instantly, just as soon as the front wheels steer toward the turn. And the driver doesn't have to maintain balance.

On a two-wheeler, you need to lean the bike over before it begins to turn. And the way you do that is to steer the contact patch out from under the bike, forcing it into a lean. In a nutshell, to initiate a left turn, push on the left grip; to make the bike lean right, push on the right grip. You have to get the motorcycle leaned over before it starts to turn, and the primary way to control lean angle is by momentarily steering the front wheel counter to the way you want to go (countersteering). Every rider of a two-wheeler countersteers, whether he or she realizes it or not. If you don't consciously countersteer, it's time you get in tune with the bike.

To remind yourself about countersteering on your next ride, focus on what you are doing to balance and steer. Before you head out into traffic, get the bike in a straight line at about 30 mph and push alternately on the left and right grips to steer from one side of your lane to the other. If you are riding a cruiser-style machine with "laid back" ergonomics, try pulling both grips toward the direction you want to go. To turn left, pull both grips toward the left. To turn right, pull both grips toward the right. Practice controlling direction by countersteering rather than just by thinking *lean the bike.*

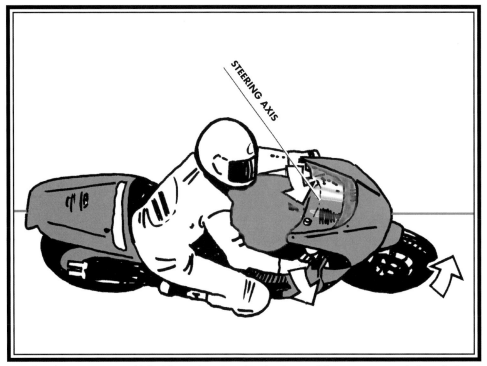

Since the grips are positioned behind the steering axis, pushing the grips toward the turn countersteers the front wheel.

Braking

While driving a four-wheeler, you've probably had to jam on the brakes once or twice to avoid collisions. If your car has ABS, you didn't even slide the tires. If it has an automatic transmission, you didn't have to squeeze the clutch or shift to neutral. You probably brought the vehicle to a stop without rolling it, catapulting it into a forward flip, or falling out the door and sliding down the pavement on your chin. All you had to do was jam down the power brake pedal with your foot and hang on.

Back on a motorcycle, you need to remind yourself that braking is much more involved. You have both the front lever and rear pedal to manipulate, as well as the throttle and clutch. And you need to maintain balance while you're braking. You need to feel what the tires are doing and progressively apply more front brake as the weight pitches forward, but not so much that the tires slide.

If you intend to pull off a panic stop successfully, whether in a straight line or in a curve, you need proficient braking skills, and that means developing the right habits. First, make a point of covering the front brake lever during your next ride. If you aren't covering the front brake, you may forget to use it or not get on the brake in time to avoid a smasho. Consciously use the front brake during every stop and as part of your cornering sequence. When slowing for a turn, squeeze the front brake lightly to help make that a habit. Approaching a busy intersection, squeeze the front brake enough to slow the bike a bit and get the discs heated up.

Second, get in some serious quick-stop practices now and again. Braking is a fine art, and you can't expect to be good at it if you don't practice or if your last practice was three years ago during a training course. Find a vacant strip of clean, level pavement away from traffic, and practice quick stops for an hour or two at least once each year.

How About Laying It Down?

There are still a few vintage riders around who believe that the quickest way to stop is to toss the bike on its side and grind to a stop on the nuts and bolts. But throwing the bike down isn't without risk and can be shockingly expensive with today's plastic-covered bikes. For most situations, a quicker stop on pavement can usually be made on the rubber, which has much more traction than plastic, steel, or aluminum.

What's more, remember that forward energy? It might sound a little macabre, but if you realize that you're going to crash into something, wouldn't it be best to reduce the impact forces? If I know I can't avoid smacking my body into the side of a pick-up truck, wouldn't it be a lot better to stay on the brakes and bang into it at 5 mph rather than slam into it at 25 mph?

In my opinion, the best option for avoiding pain is to keep the bike on the rubber and concentrate on a maximum energy quick stop. If it happens that the other guy manages to get out of my way, I can always get back up to speed after easing off the brakes.

Ride the Twisties

Aggressive riders need no encouragement to find a twisty road. Conservative riders may need a little push. Even if you see yourself as a conservative rider, it is worthwhile to spend some time on twisty roads because that's an excellent way to get skillful at changing direction quickly. Sure, you can practice emergency swerves in a parking lot, but in a crisis such as a left-turning car making a quick turn in front of you, you'll probably resort to habits. And the most practical way to develop swerving habits is to ride a twisty road that requires you to change direction quickly and frequently.

It's important, though, to practice the right habits. During your next ride on a twisty road, ride at a slow pace well within your perceived limit, and concentrate on specific cornering techniques. For instance, first concentrate on achieving an entry speed that allows you to roll on the throttle all the way around the turn, then concentrate on a better line, then on keeping your eyes level, and so on. Use your front brake to help slow the bike to cornering speed, look as far through the turn as you can to plan a delayed apex line, and then ease on the throttle as you counter-steer the bike into the turn. Keep your head up, your eyes level with the horizon, and your nose pointed in the direction you want the bike to go.

The point is to get more familiar with leaning the bike over and to gain some confidence in your tires. If you can also smooth out your braking, throttle control, counter-steering, and cornering lines, those are additional payoffs that you can use for either more enjoyment or keeping more traction "in the bank" for emergencies.

As you lean the bike into the turn, keep your head up, your eyes level with the horizon, and your nose pointed toward where you want to go.

The most practical way to develop swerving habits is to ride a twisty road.

Reading the Surface

One big concern about riding two-wheelers is maintaining balance, and that depends upon traction. A four-wheeler or sidecar rig can slide the tires without falling down. Sliding the front tire on a two-wheeler can quickly result in a fall down. Remember, a motorcycle is balanced mostly by steering the front wheel contact patch, whether the front-end geometry automatically does it or the rider does it. Either way, some traction is required to keep the bike up. If there isn't sufficient traction, the contact patches can slide sideways, allowing gravity to pull the bike onto its side. So while a car's tires can lose

Riding into a blind corner is just as hazardous as riding into a fog bank.

traction in a tight turn, the car will just drift toward the outside. But if a bike's tires lose traction in a tight turn, the bike falls down as it slides out. All motorcyclists understand this, but not all of us are expert at reading the surface. Nor do we all seem to understand the skills required to negotiate surface hazards.

To become expert at reading the surface, first, continue to monitor the road surface far enough ahead to have time to take evasive action. The primary technique is to look for changes in surface color or texture, indicating a probable change in traction.

Second, practice techniques for managing traction. Next time you're out for a ride on a curvy road, practice smooth cornering lines and smooth throttle/brake transitions. Plan your line to put your tires over the most tractable surface. For instance, if there is a slippery white plastic arrow on the surface, plan your line to one side of the arrow without having to make a sudden change.

If slippery surfaces make you nervous, the fix is to get in some riding time on an unpaved road.

If slippery surfaces make you nervous, the fix is to get in some riding practice on unpaved roads. Spend a day riding a gravel farm road, or a national forest road. If you're too cautious to ride gravel on your big road burner, borrow a smaller dual sport machine. But whatever you ride, get in some dirt time to gain familiarity. It's not just a matter of being able to handle a detour now and then; it's a matter of learning more about traction control on all surfaces.

David L. Hough

Keep Speed Within Sight Distance

A lot of motorists get into trouble because they don't adjust speed to what's happening. It may be perfectly sensible to motor down the highway at 60 mph in clear weather, but that's way too fast when the road disappears into a fog bank. One minor collision can quickly turn into a major pileup as drivers continue to slam into the fog-shrouded wreckage at speed. Most motorcyclists would recognize the extreme hazard of riding into a fog bank on a busy freeway, but some riders don't seem to understand that riding into a blind turn is just as hazardous as riding into fog. If you constantly adjust speed to sight distance, you should never be surprised by hazards such as fog, a stalled car, or a decreasing radius curve.

Next time you're out for a ride, make a point of adjusting speed to sight distance. When your view of the road ahead closes up, immediately reduce speed, and don't be timid about using the brakes. Sure, you can just roll off the throttle, but it's a better habit to dab the brakes, too, to prepare yourself for a quick stop. That same technique works for an intersection where a truck blocks your view of side streets, a twisty road where you can't see around the curve, or a hill that blocks your view of what's on the other side.

Keep Bike Speed Within Your Thinking Speed

It's tempting to think that horsepower relates to enjoyment of a ride. A bigger, faster bike should be even more fun, right? Well, there are a lot of high-horsepower machines out there to give you the opportunity to find out. More than a few riders have fooled themselves into thinking that more power makes up for less skill, only to crash more expensive machines at higher speeds.

More horsepower won't make up for less skill.

I bring this up because springtime seems to get a lot of riders drooling over a newer, faster ride, and every year there is a new crop of faster, shinier machines on the showroom floors. A high-horsepower race replica bike may have impressive acceleration and speed, but it also demands intense control that can drain a lot of fun out of riding on public roads.

If you've been driving a car at highway speeds up to 70 mph or so, your thinking speed may be way too slow for a bike that accelerates up to warp speeds with a half twist of the throttle. Symptoms of allowing a bike to get ahead of your thinking include running wide in corners and reacting in panic by suddenly snapping off the gas or jamming on the rear brake.

If you're scaring yourself too frequently, there are several options other than buying more medical insurance or giving up motorcycling. One option is to trade down to a less powerful, more controllable machine. A bike with less peak horsepower but a broader torque curve is easier to control. The truth is, for most of us the limits are determined more by our skill level than by horsepower.

If you're determined to ride a sportbike at 170 mph, you might start thinking about riding the track instead of the public roads. You can start that journey by taking one or more of the track school courses. The big advantage of doing your fast riding on the racetrack is that you don't have to worry about the usual traffic, surface, and roadside hazards.

You will go out and tune up your skills this spring, won't you?

The Slow Ride

I was having a discussion with a German motorcycle instructor who taught fast riding at the famous Nurburgring racing circuit. I was curious whether he thought German riders have as much variation in skill as American riders have. He explained that German riders have to go through much more training and testing to become licensed compared to their American counterparts. But, as in the U.S., some take their riding more seriously, and it shows in their skill level. He went on to suggest that he

Slow speed maneuvers are a tip-off to a rider's overall skill level.

could usually predict a rider's relative skill level by observing the students as they arrived for class: *Let me see a rider maneuvering around the parking lot, and I can tell you how good he is at higher speeds.*

In other words, a rider's slow speed control is an accurate tip-off to his control skills in general. If a rider wobbles around the parking lot, nervously dragging his foot-skids or can't seem to get the bike to make a tight U-turn, it's an indication that he probably doesn't have very good control of the bike at higher speeds either. Good cornering control begins with an understanding of the basics of how a two-wheeler is balanced.

If you haven't watched an observed trial recently, make a point of finding a trials competition this year and watch some demonstra-

The Cossacks stunt team specializes in slow speed maneuvers.

tions of absolute motorcycle control. Or watch a stunt team such as the Seattle Cossacks perform slow-speed maneuvers, often with a rider balanced precariously on his head or several riders stacked up on one machine.

The object of observed trials is to ride a motorcycle through a series of especially difficult sections without losing forward motion, going out of bounds, or having to dab a foot on the ground. A section may lead uphill through a waterfall, make a U-turn on top of a slippery log, or lead down a steep slope composed of 10-foot glacial boulders. Watching a trials competition gives you a fresh idea about proficient riding skills.

Balancing

Although trials riders make balancing a two-wheeler at slow speeds look easy, most of the rest of us find it difficult, especially on heavy machines. To think about balance, let's pretend that gravity is pulling a bike and rider straight down on a single point that we'll call CoG (center of gravity). Since the rider is somewhat flexibly attached to the motorcycle, we should imagine that rider and machine each has its own CoG. And let's imagine that the ring around the tire where it rolls along the ground is just one single point at the bottom of the tire that we'll call the contact patch. Of course, there are two contact patches, one front and one rear.

Now, so long as the CoGs line up directly over the line between the two contact patches, the bike stays balanced, whether it is standing still or rolling along. It doesn't matter whether the rider is in line with the machine, or whether the ground is level, so long as the combined CoGs of bike and rider are balanced over the contact patches.

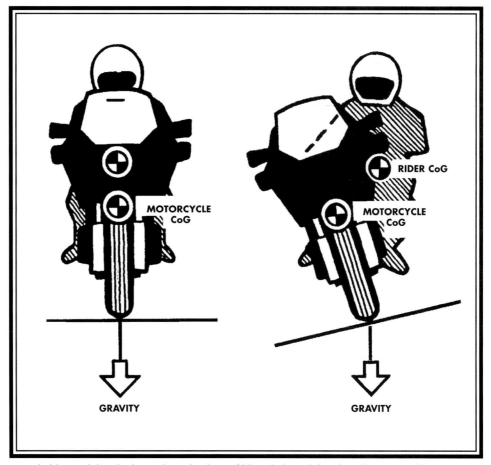

The bike stays balanced so long as the combined CoGs of bike and rider are balanced over the contact patches.

The important question is how do we keep the CoGs balanced over the contact patches? What is it that we do to get the motorcycle rebalanced if it starts to fall over and the pull of gravity is suddenly on one side of the supporting contact patches? Or, to ask the question in another way, how do we get the bike unbalanced so that it leans over into a turn?

As an experiment, try balancing a long stick (a yardstick will work) vertically on your palm. Let go of the top, and try to keep it balanced vertically. You'll discover that you have to control the lean angle by moving the bottom of the stick around. If you don't have a yardstick handy, try an umbrella, a broom, or a couple of vacuum cleaner extensions. When you have mastered balancing it standing still, try keeping it balanced while walking around in a circle.

Hold on! What's all this balancing yardstick business got to do with motorcycles? you may be wondering. Well, it helps explain how we balance a motorcycle or get it leaned over into a corner. Really, put the book down, go get a stick, and do the experiment.

First of all, notice that the most stable part of the stick is somewhere in the middle. Second, notice that to keep the stick from falling over toward the right, you have to move the bottom even farther right. Third, to balance the stick while walking in a circle, you have to lean the stick toward the turn, and you do that by moving the bottom of the stick away from the turn.

The point is that balancing a stick is a lot like balancing a two-wheeler. We control lean angle by moving the front contact patch sideways, not by moving the top of the bike and rider. Steering the front wheel away from the turn makes the top of the bike and rider lean toward the turn.

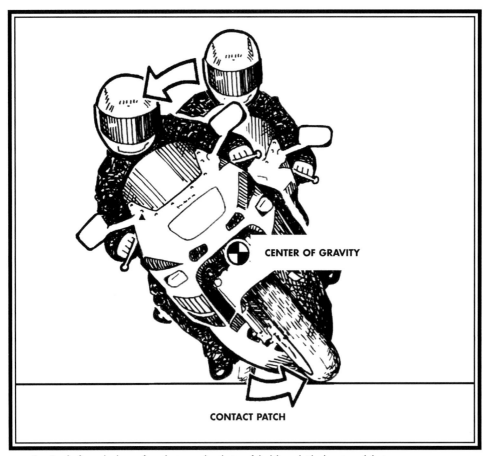

CENTER OF GRAVITY

CONTACT PATCH

Steering the front wheel away from the turn makes the top of the bike and rider lean toward the turn.

As most of us have discovered, it is difficult to balance a big motorcycle while standing still or even rolling along at a very slow speed. Just a breath of wind or a bump in the road can shift things off center, and gravity is eager to pull it all down toward the ground. One reason slow-speed balance is so difficult is that the front contact patch doesn't move sideways very quickly at slow speeds. In order to keep the machine balanced upright, it might be helpful to understand a bit of the physics involved.

Inertia

An object standing still wants to remain where it is. An object in motion wants to keep moving. This is a basic property of matter we call inertia. Kick a brick on the ground or try to catch a thrown brick, and you'll get the idea. A spinning wheel wants to keep spinning. A motorcycle zooming down a straight highway wants to keep zooming straight ahead at the same speed. Technically, inertia isn't a force, but it provides a stability against which other forces can push and pull. Think of this inertial stability of the motorcycle as a sort of rubbery ball joint around which the motorcycle can be leaned.

Gyroscopic Forces

In addition to their other tasks, the wheels of a motorcycle act as gyroscopes. A spinning gyro generates a stabilizing force that gets stronger as the wheel spins faster. So at highway speeds, a motorcycle's wheels and tires provide a great deal of stability, helping the motorcycle remain vertical and pointed straight ahead. At slower speeds, the wheels provide almost no gyroscopic stability. That's one reason it's easier to balance at highway speed than while creeping along at a slow speed.

Gyros have some interesting reactions to the movements of an axle. If you lift a gyro by its axle and pivot the axle toward the left (like turning the front wheel left), the gyro wants to lean over toward the right. That reaction is called gyroscopic precession.

It's tempting to think that gyroscopic precession is what makes the motorcycle lean, but there are a lot of clues that it's not the dominant steering force at any reasonable road speeds. First, remember that a motorcycle wheel is rolling along the ground, not suspended in the air. Second, the actual movement of the front end away from center is slight—perhaps 1/2 degree or 1 degree. Such small angles aren't enough to generate much precession force. Also, it is still possible to balance a two-wheeler at 5 mph, at which point the gyroscopic precession is almost nonexistent.

By comparison, tire traction is much stronger than gyroscopic precession—at least within any speeds attainable by a street motorcycle. Traction can generate side forces equal to the weight on a wheel. If the front wheel is supporting 300 pounds, the front tire can exert a steering force of 300 pounds.

If you think back to how you balanced that yardstick, you'll realize that balancing is a process of steps. Sometimes you are moving the bottom of the stick toward the turn, sometimes away; sometimes pushing forward on the bottom, sometimes pulling back. It's the same way with balancing a two-wheeler, except that we have the advantage of two contact patches.

With the motorcycle rolling along, we control balance mostly by adjusting the relative position of the front tire contact patch. For example, if we start to fall over toward the left, we can shift the relative position of the contact patch toward the left until the bike is again balanced. The way we adjust the relative position of the contact patch is by turning the front wheel slightly away from the direction we want the motorcycle to lean. The wheel tracks off center, shifting its position sideways in relation to the CoGs. The faster the wheel is spinning, the quicker it will track off center, which is the main reason balancing gets easier at road speeds.

We can also help control balance by shifting our body weight around as the trials riders do. Loading one footpeg places more of your weight on one side of the bike. How much effect that will have depends on your weight compared to the bike. The smaller the motorcycle, the more effect you'll get. The heavier the machine, the less influence body steering will have. If you stand on the pegs, hold the bars steady, and lean way over to one side the bike may lean in response to your weight shift but not change direction much. Slam your knee against the tank on a 250 dual sport and it will change direction even if you are trying to hold the handlebars steady.

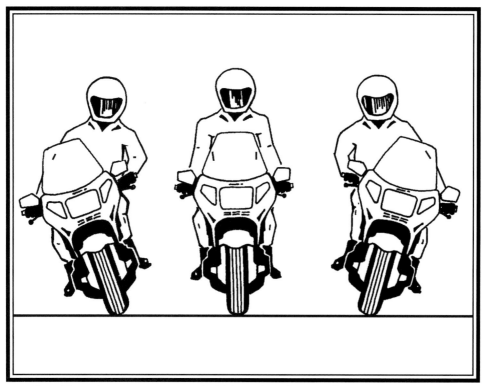

A heavy bike may lean in response to your weight shift but not change direction much.

Next time you're out riding, try it. Get off the saddle and shift your weight over to one footpeg and then the other. If you consciously hold the handlebars steady, you may be amazed to discover that the bike just leans over a bit but doesn't change direction. Of course, with a lightweight bike, just nudging the tank with your knees will probably push the bike onto a new course. Although countersteering the handlebars is the most powerful and accurate steering input, the slower you are riding the more important it is to get your weight off the saddle and onto the pegs, and lean the bike independently of your body.

Front-End Geometry

The front end of a motorcycle has some interesting geometry that contributes to balance. The front tire contact patch trails behind the pivot line (steering axis) of the front end to provide a self-centering effect similar to a front wheel on a shopping cart. But because the steering axis on a motorcycle is leaned back, turning the handlebars left to right causes the steering head to move sideways too. Consider what happens when the front end is steered. With the bike stationary, pivoting the front wheel to the right moves the steering head (and therefore the front half of the motorcycle) to the right.

David L. Hough

The best way to see this for yourself is by sitting on your bike and monitoring the location of the steering head as you turn the bars left then right. Get the bike balanced on both tires, and turn the front wheel toward the left then over to the right. While you're doing this experiment, notice that the bike wants to lean toward the direction you are steering. What's not so obvious is that the steering head drops slightly as the wheel is turned off center. It takes slightly more force to turn the wheel back toward center because you're also lifting the front of the bike.

So, turning the handlebars does help control balance, even when the bike is standing still. That helps explain how trials riders are able to balance the bike at a standstill. Of course they also shift weight on the pegs, and that has a considerable effect on a lightweight trials bike.

Countersteering

While inertia, gyroscopic stability, and front-end geometry all contribute to straight-ahead stability, we can cause the motorcycle to change its lean angle by momentarily steering the front contact patch away from the direction we want to go. It's called countersteering because we momentarily steer the front wheel opposite, or counter, to the direction we want the bike to lean.

We momentarily steer the front wheel opposite to the direction we want the bike to lean.

As the front wheel tracks out on a slight tangent away from center, the motorcycle responds by rolling sideways. It may seem that the bike immediately begins to turn as soon as you countersteer, but the bike must first roll toward the turn before it starts to change direction. Even at highway speed, it takes approximately one second to get the bike rolled over far enough for it to actually begin to change direction. When the bike rolls over far enough for the turn we have in mind, we relax pressure on the grips, allowing the front wheel to re-center, and then swing slightly toward the turn. The bike is balanced in a lean, with gravity pulling against centrifugal force and axles pointed more-or-less toward the center of the turn.

Countersteering is simply adjusting the position of the contact patch by momentarily steering opposite to the direction you want to lean, just like balancing that yardstick. If you rode slowly through a puddle of water and then made a turn, you could go back and look at the tire tracks to see how the front tire out-tracks just before the bike starts to turn. We countersteer whenever we need to adjust the lean angle, whether to stay vertical in a straight line, adjust lean angle while leaned over, or straighten up from a turn.

It's important to recognize that countersteering isn't simply a matter of turning the front wheel in the wrong direction and holding it but rather a process of steps that we repeat over and over as we guide the bike. If you're really interested in the technical details, Hugh H. Hurt, Jr. published a paper, "Motorcycle Handling and Collision Avoidance: Anatomy of a Turn," back in 1973 for the Second International Congress on Automotive Safety. It's an old report but still a concise description of what happens.

Slow Rides and U-Turns

It's more difficult to balance at slower speeds, but I can offer some suggestions for better control. It is usually easier to balance at a slow speed when you are standing on the pegs. It might appear that standing on the pegs raises a rider's CoG. But if you compare balancing a broomstick to balancing a thin book, you'll appreciate that the book requires a lot more effort. The lesson here is that it isn't important to have a low CoG to have good balance at slow speeds. What is important is allowing the rider's weight to be carried loosely from the bike so the rider can quickly lean the bike.

It's also not smart to drag your boots on the ground. Yes, you can push the bike back into balance with your feet, but you can also break an ankle if your foot gets caught under a peg or crashbar. If you feel a need to stick out your foot-skids, that's a hint you aren't countersteering the handlebars enough to control balance, and you're planted too firmly in the saddle.

When making tight slow-speed turns such as U-turns, the technique is to shift your weight to the outside, turn your head to look where you want to go, lean the bike over toward the turn, and ease on enough throttle to pull it around. It's okay to drag the rear brake a little (unless your bike has integrated rear-front brakes), but don't squeeze the clutch and try to coast with the bike leaned over; keep the engine pulling.

Slide your butt over to the outside of the saddle in a tight U-turn.

If you ride a cruiser with forward-mounted footpegs or floorboards, it's almost impossible to balance your weight over your feet. So with cruiser ergonomics, the technique is to slide your butt over to the outside of the saddle in a tight turn.

Reluctant to Turn?

There are some heavyweight bikes around with a limited steering lock that makes them difficult to balance in tight turns. The problem is when the front fork hits the stops, you can't countersteer the bike any farther to prevent it from falling over. All you can do to prevent a fall is to throw your weight to the outside and roll on more throttle. You may instinctively take a dab with your boot in the attempt to prevent a fall, but even expensive plastic bodywork is still cheaper than a broken ankle. So, if you're riding a bike with limited turning angles and expensive bodywork (the BMW K1 comes to mind), it's understandable if you're paranoid about tight slow-speed turns. Don't be bashful about dismounting and pushing the bike around to get out of a tight spot.

But if you're riding a standard machine and can't get it to make a tight U-turn, it's probably your reluctance to force it over to the necessary lean angle. Remember, you control lean angle primarily by pushing on the grips, not by poking your elbows out or hunching your shoulders toward the inside. To turn tighter toward the left, imagine pushing both grips a little harder toward the left. The farther over you lean the bike, the tighter it will turn. The only limiting factor is ground clearance, the primary reason for shifting your weight to the outside. And remember, don't slip the clutch and try to coast around a tight U-turn. Keep your feet on the pegs and the engine pulling all the way around.

One payoff of practicing the slow ride is being able to show off your U-turn skills at a breakfast meeting. But the bigger payoff is being in better control of your motorcycle, whether you're puttering around the parking lot, riding across the slippery grass into the rally site, exploring unpaved roads, or motoring proficiently through the twisties at warp speeds. As the German riding instructor pointed out, your slow speed skills are a giveaway about your general skill level. And we're all watching!

Balance Practice

Your homework for understanding balance is simple: practice the slow ride, both straight ahead and in a figure eight. Take your favorite road burner out to some clean, level pavement, and ride it in a straight line as slowly as you can. Some riders practice their slow ride technique while easing up to red lights or when entering the company parking lot each morning. Try balancing while seated on the saddle, and then try standing on the pegs. While creeping along, shift your weight to the right footpeg, then to the left.

After you've practiced standing on the pegs in a straight line, try circles left and right, and then a figure-eight box. You can mark out a box with chalk or cones if you want, but you can practice the figure eight without any references on the surface. You'll know when you're going wide and when you're turning as tightly as possible.

The trick is to support most of your body weight on the outside footpeg and to keep the engine pulling. At the crossover, smoothly ease your weight onto the other footpeg. The tighter the turn, the farther you must lean the bike to the inside. But if you have trouble with tight turns, set out a 20-foot-wide box. You might surprise yourself when you keep pulling the markers in and find you can turn your bike tighter and tighter once you get the hang of it. My suggestion is to practice a few figure eights at the conclusion of every ride when you have a warm engine. You don't want to attempt the figure eight on a cold engine because it's more likely to stall.

Move It or Lose It

Pulling out onto a busy state highway during the morning rush hour, I was concentrating on accelerating to keep ahead of traffic. It isn't smart to pull in front of someone and then creep along. Quick glances in the mirrors confirmed that I wasn't holding anyone up. But glancing in the mirrors distracted me from what was about to happen ahead.

An oncoming truck hit a piece of steel angle lying in the road. The steel piece instantly flipped and spun into my lane. For an instant, my brain struggled to respond to the crisis. Here was a piece of road shrapnel skittering at me like an incoming missile, heavy enough and strong enough to punch right through me or my bike. I needed to get out of its way as quickly as possible.

Without any conscious decision to swerve, my right hand suddenly pushed hard on the right grip, and held it until the bike responded by leaning right and arcing off toward the shoulder. The swerve was barely in time to avoid a disaster. With a clanging thud, the steel debris bounced off the bike's frame and clattered across the lane. To recover from the swerve and stay on the road, I pushed hard on the left grip until the bike leaned hard left and the howling front tire managed to force the bike back toward my lane. A nudge on the right grip stabilized the bike again. The crisis was over within seconds, but it took a while longer for me to calm down.

A piece of road shrapnel can be heavy enough and strong enough to punch right through the bike.

Usually, if we're looking far enough ahead we can spot potential hazards and make a correction to avoid being in the wrong place at the wrong time. But once in a while, a hazard leaps out at us with no warning, and we need to pull off a last-second evasive maneuver.

The most useful get-out-of-the-way tactic is often a quick stop. Accelerating might help outrun a problem, but speeding up increases forward energy, which makes it even harder to stop or swerve. In a situation like the one described, stopping wasn't a good option, and speeding up wouldn't have helped. The best tactic was to maintain speed and attempt to swerve around the problem.

First, let's review the dynamics of how a two-wheeler is made to swerve. Then let's discuss how to develop the habits that make a quick swerve possible.

Swerving Dynamics

It is important to recognize that two-wheelers take longer to start changing direction than four-wheelers do. When a driver yanks on the steering wheel of a car, the front wheels immediately turn and start pushing the car into a different direction. The tires may complain, but the front of the car starts to turn almost instantaneously.

Although it may seem that a bike starts to change direction immediately, even before it gets leaned over, it's really the top of the bike (and the rider's head) that's starting to roll toward the turn before the bike actually starts to change direction. Depending upon the weight of the motorcycle and how hard the rider pushes on the grip, it may take a half second or longer to get the bike leaned over sufficiently to change direction. The bike doesn't actually start to turn until it leans over far enough that the front wheel can be steered back toward center.

With power steering and power brakes, a car driver can yank quickly enough on the steering wheel or stomp hard enough on the brakes to snap the tires loose without much risk of taking a tumble down the tarmac. If a motorcyclist pushes hard enough to punch through the traction envelope, he or she will be getting up close and personal with the pavement. So, a motorcycle not only requires more actions and more time to get it turned but also demands more of the rider's skill to avoid a fall.

A swerve is really just two quick turns, first one way and then the other. The first turn is to get the bike leaned over and moving away from the problem. The second turn is to get it straightened out again to stay on the road. When we combine a pair of opposite turns in quick sequence, there's a lot of stuff going on in short order, and we need to understand the details.

Traction

Forceful changes of direction can eat up all of the available tire traction, front and rear. There's only so much traction to go around, and during a swerve we can't afford to squander traction needlessly on either accelerating or braking. Even the stickiest tires available don't have enough traction for rapid swerving and hard braking at the same time. Scary as it seems, the best tactic for swerving is to stay off the brakes and hold the throttle steady, conserving all of the available traction for steering. A steady throttle hand is just as important as staying off the brakes because snapping the throttle closed would apply engine braking to the rear wheel, just as if the rider had stepped on the rear brake pedal.

You can brake (or accelerate) either before or after swerving, but the actions need to be separated. In other words, brake, then get off the brakes and swerve. Or swerve, then get the bike straight and upright before you brake. And in case you're wondering, ABS won't help avoid a skid caused by swerving too aggressively.

Countersteering

Motorcycles are balanced and steered by both bodysteering and countersteering, but countersteering is the most powerful input. Push on the right grip to turn right; push on the left grip to turn left. Every two-wheeled motorcyclist does this, whether they understand the dynamics or not. But in spite of years of information about countersteering, I continue to bump into riders who have never heard of it or have never figured it out. They just get on a bike and do it, without understanding what countersteering means.

Is that a problem? Well, yes. You can't make a motorcycle swerve rapidly without pushing forcefully on the grips. For that matter, you've got to know which grip to push on. There have been instances where novice riders have panicked, tried to steer away from a left-turning car, and swerved themselves directly into a collision.

Normally, we apply only modest pressure on the grips, plus a bit of body English, to achieve those smooth cornering lines that maximize traction. But when an emergency swerve is needed, the push on the grip must be forceful. You can shove a lot harder on the grip than you might think before the front tire begins to slide, even on wet pavement. It is also important to keep pushing on the grip until the bike gets leaned over and starts to change direction. The harder you push on the grip, the quicker the machine will lean. The longer you hold the push, the farther the machine will lean and the tighter the radius of turn (up to the limits of traction or ground clearance, of course).

Swerving Sequence

Now, let's think through the swerving sequence, in this case to the right.

1. **Hold a steady throttle, push hard on the right grip, and hold the pressure until the bike leans over far enough to swerve toward the right. As the bike rolls into a lean, the front wheel actually out-tracks to the left until the bike begins to turn.**
2. **Once around the danger, recover from the right swerve and get the bike pointed back toward the lane again. Push hard on the left grip to roll the bike from a right lean into a left lean. The front**

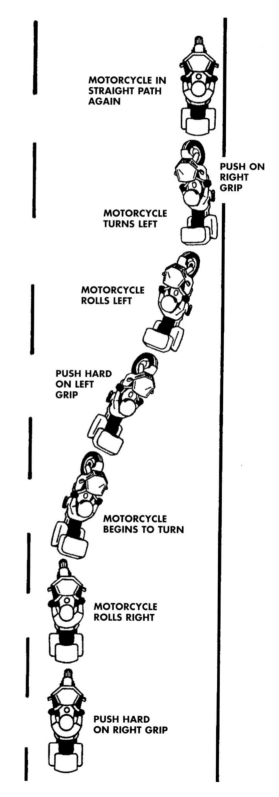

MOTORCYCLE IN STRAIGHT PATH AGAIN

PUSH ON RIGHT GRIP

MOTORCYCLE TURNS LEFT

MOTORCYCLE ROLLS LEFT

PUSH HARD ON LEFT GRIP

MOTORCYCLE BEGINS TO TURN

MOTORCYCLE ROLLS RIGHT

PUSH HARD ON RIGHT GRIP

Emergency swerves aren't much different from a normal S-turn, except a lot quicker.

wheel will out-track even farther to the right as the bike leans, and then tire traction pushes the motorcycle back toward the lane.
3. To recover from the swerve, relax pressure on the left grip and press lightly on the right grip to get the bike stabilized in a straight line again.

If you think about it, emergency swerves aren't much different from a normal S-turn, except that the turns are much closer together and therefore a lot quicker.

Actions Follow Habits

An emergency is just a hazard that arrives more suddenly than you expect. If you know that an oncoming truck is going to launch a missile at you exactly at a big yellow X painted on the pavement, you could just ease out of the way early or get yourself prepared for a major swerve. If you know for sure that the pickup truck at the next intersection is going to make a sudden left turn in front of you just as you cross the pedestrian line, you could do a quick stop before you get there. In real life, we occasionally encounter hazardous situations we can't predict, and we just aren't prepared for any emergency maneuvers. In a microsecond, we are faced with a hazard with no time to get set.

It seems to be some sort of human characteristic that when faced with a sudden need to do something, we react first and think about it afterward. The brain reverts to habits in a crisis. The brain makes a quick decision, the body responds to that sub-conscious decision, and after it's all over we'll think about it consciously. In other words, when push comes to shove, our habits determine what we will actually do.

Of course we also have some instincts left over from our cave dweller days. The trouble is that our survival instincts were developed from thousands of years at walking and running speeds. When we face a crisis at motorcycling speed, we need to overpower our survival instincts and follow the habits that best suit the situation. The solution is to practice a variety of skills to give our brains several options. Swerving should be one of those options.

I submit that learning special emergency maneuvers is not of much value. For me, countersteering is how I control the bike every time I ride. It's not a special evasive maneuver I reserve for emergencies. I suggest that the way to prepare for swerving is to practice countersteering, rather than just thinking, *lean into the turn,* all the time as you ride along.

For the same reasons, it's important to practice good throttle control. If you're in the habit of rolling off the gas every time you lean into a curve, wouldn't you expect to snap the throttle closed during a quick swerve? If you're in the habit of rolling on a little throttle in turns and making seamless throttle-brake-throttle transitions, you're better prepared to hold a steady throttle while swerving.

Quick, Stop!

One of the *MCN* staff writers was riding down out of the hills toward work one morning, as usual a few knots over the limit. It had started to drizzle, but he'd been riding this same urban street every day and knew every curve, bump, and crack. And besides, he was riding a test bike with sticky tires and awesome brakes. The wake-up call came as he rounded a blind turn to discover a giant excavator digging a big hole in the street, with several cars sliding to a halt as the flagman flipped out the one and only warning sign.

The *MCN* guy immediately hit the brakes, but the rain-slick downhill section was getting slippery with mud, and he quickly realized that there was no way he could stop short of smacking into the car ahead of him. He pointed the bike between the cars and the curb to gain a little stopping distance and focused on maximum braking. Those "sticky" tires weren't of much use on mud, but he managed to slither through the mess and bring the bike to a halt inches away from the excavator's crawler tracks.

I frequently suggest that a quick stop is often the most reliable evasive tactic for avoiding crashes, but pulling off a quick stop successfully on slippery surfaces demands considerable skill. Sure, bikes have excellent brakes these days, and some even have ABS, linked, or integrated front/rear systems. But you still need to use that computer between your ears.

Let's think about quick stops in real world conditions. First, we'll consider the bike and its brake systems, then rider capabilities, and finally I'll suggest some practice exercises to help you improve your stopping skills.

You never know when your braking skills will get the big test.

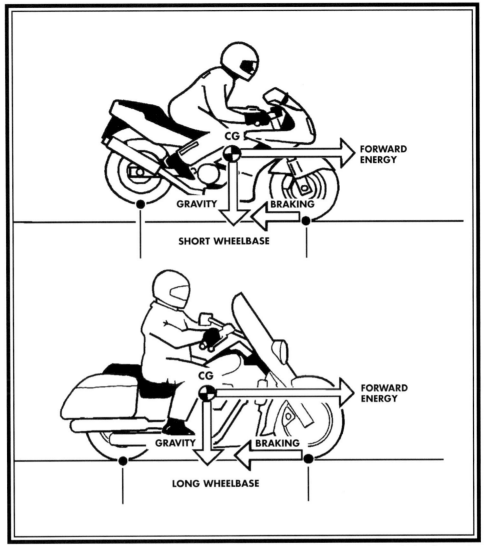

A shorter sportbike requires a more delicate hand on the brake lever than a cruiser to keep the rear wheel on the ground.

Different Bikes, Different Braking

The *MCN* test riders who do a lot of braking agree that every machine is different. It should be obvious that a cruiser with a long wheelbase keeps its rear wheel on the ground better than a shorter, taller sportbike. The surprise is that even two identical cruisers or two "identical" sportbikes don't stop in the same distances, or with the same braking feel. We'd all like to believe that mass-produced machines perform exactly the same, but the reality is that each machine is slightly different. Brake rotors are seldom perfectly true, brake pads aren't exactly the same shape or composition, fork sliders and shocks don't all act the same, and different tires have slightly different traction.

You might think that sportbikes, with their monster-sized race-bred front brakes, would be the kings of the quick stop. But sportbikes, leaning heavily toward a racing heritage, are designed to corner swiftly, not decelerate from 60 to 0 in the shortest distance to avoid an errant car driver. It might surprise you that many cruisers and touring bikes out-stop the sportbikes.

The big limiting factor in braking with any of today's sportbikes is keeping the rear wheel on the ground. The test riders who perform the *MCN* braking tests report that every contemporary sportbike has the same "forward loop" braking limitation. During hard braking, the rear wheel lifts off the ground, and unless the rider eases off the front brake, the bike would literally loop forward over the front wheel. With warm tires on clean pavement, a sportbike will lift the rear wheel before the front tire begins to skid. What that means is that you can't use all the power the brakes are capable of generating. The typical cruiser, with a longer wheelbase, usually slides the front tire before the rear wheel shows much daylight. The longer wheelbase places the CoG farther back from the front contact patch.

Studies such as the Hurt Report have shown that riders involved in accidents made critical errors when braking. The primary sin is applying too much rear brake and not enough front brake. There are indications that riders today are no more skillful at quick stops than they were twenty years ago. So, manufacturers have been busy designing high-tech brake systems that they hope will make up for inadequate rider skill, including antilock, linked, integrated, and power brake systems.

Do Powerful Brakes Produce Quicker Stops?

You might think that power brakes would be great for bikes. Doesn't it make sense that the quicker and harder you apply maximum braking, the sooner you'll stop? Well, no. The stopping dynamics dictate how much braking can be applied. Power brakes can stop the wheel from turning, but that wouldn't necessarily stop the bike. The ABS limits skidding, but it does that by releasing brake pressure, which lengthens the stop.

Motorcycle journalists and other professionals have mixed opinions about high-tech braking systems. One problem is that all the systems are different, and a rider who switches bikes has a tough time allocating the right skills and habits to the right bike. Years ago, motorcycle controls were standardized for this very reason. Now, you have to learn different braking techniques for different machines.

Another issue is performance. Activating the ABS on some bikes actually lengthens the stopping distance, while on others it seems to help stop the bike just as quickly. One machine with a linked braking system may be able to stop quicker than a similar model with independent brakes, but a different machine with a linked braking system may not be affected. When braking while leaned over (trail braking), the linked system on one model may cause the bike to weave, while a different linked system may help the bike settle down.

With computerized braking systems, you lose some control over what's happening. Skilled riders seem to prefer directly controlling which wheel is being braked, when, and how hard. For instance, if you're stopping on a gravel shoulder or trying to make a tight U-turn, you probably don't want to apply any front brake at all, and you probably wouldn't want power brakes that come on suddenly. The gear heads among us are also nervous about complex brake systems, not only because of performance but also because of the maintenance nightmare that could occur a few years down the road.

The BMW EVO power brake system introduced on BMW's 2002 machines has not been accepted with open arms. It's a complex computer-controlled system with power-assist, front-rear integration, and ABS. Police motor officers seem to appreciate ABS on their BMW patrol bikes, but they have generally rejected the fully integrated system in which the rear brake pedal activates both front and rear brakes.

Whether you have ABS, integrated, linked, or power brakes, there is a limit to what the braking system can do for you. For instance, the brake system can't save you from a skid caused by snapping off the throttle in a curve. Quick stops are still dependent upon rider skill and upon brake system maintenance.

David L. Hough

Making It All Work

Sportbikes typically require only a light squeeze on the lever to produce a high braking effect. With powerful front brakes, some riders only use one or two fingers on the lever to help avoid overbraking. Other machines have powerful enough brakes but a low hydraulic ratio, so they will stop quickly—but only if you can provide a King Kong squeeze on the lever. Whatever the brake system, the actual braking effect you get on your particular machine depends to a great extent on the brake pad compound, system condition, trueness of the brake rotors, front tire compound, and suspension compliance.

Brake Condition

Brakes tend to lose their efficiency as the contact surfaces become glazed or worn to strange shapes. Discs wear into concentric grooves from abrasive grit contaminating the brake pads. Automobile brake discs ("rotors") are thick enough to allow regrinding during a brake rebuild. Motorcycle brake rotors are typically much thinner, so they usually aren't reground.

Brake rotors are a big part of the equation. It's relatively easy to ding a rotor while changing a tire or by leaving a disc lock in place while riding away. And even if you don't bend a rotor, it may have a slight high spot right out of the factory or may become warped from heating and cooling. The problem with an uneven rotor is that the brake pads can grab it unpredictably.

Brake pulsing from uneven rotors can be treacherous. At higher speeds, the rotors slam the high spots past the calipers several times each second, which you might feel as a slight vibration. But as the bike slows down, the high spots have more and more time to grab, and you may feel the brakes surging. The danger is when the bike is hauled down to a slower speed during a quick stop and the brake pad suddenly grabs a high spot on the rotor, causing the front tire to instantly start to slide. To prevent a fall down, you must release the lever and then get back on it, which stretches out your stopping distance, possibly right into the side of that earthmover.

Even if the discs and pads have perfect contact and adequate thickness, the friction material tends to become glazed with use. The friction material in the brake pads ages and can lose much of its braking efficiency over a period of years. Brake pads will also soak up hydraulic fluid from leaking brake components or weeping fork seals. A brake pad that is ill-fitting, glazed, brittle, or saturated with fluid might have less than half the friction of the original parts when new.

DISC

BRAKE CALIPER

BRAKE PAD

HIGH SPOT

The problem with an uneven rotor is that the brake pads can grab it unpredictably.

Brake Fluid and Maintenance

Brake systems require periodic maintenance. Pads and rotors need periodic renewing, and the brake fluid and brake lines need replacement on a regular schedule. Rubber brake hoses gradually soften, resulting in a spongy feel at the lever. Systems such as ABS often use special hoses that require more frequent replacement for proper functioning.

Brake fluid also becomes contaminated over time, and the contamination attacks internal parts such as caliper pistons and seals. Alcohol-based brake fluids absorb water from the air. The water sinks to the bottom of the system, corroding the brake components. Rubber bellows in the master cylinders help reduce water absorption, but the only way to avoid costly brake system corrosion is to flush and refill the system every year or two.

Note that each manufacturer chooses rubber compounds to be compatible with a particular brake fluid. When flushing and refilling a hydraulic brake system, it is important to use only the type of fluid specified by the manufacturer.

Tires

Wider, lower-profile tires generally put more rubber on the road. But whatever the tire profile, the big factors in traction are rubber compound, temperature, and pressure. All rubber compounds change their traction behavior as the temperature changes. In general terms, a warm tire has much more traction than a cold tire has. Tires heat up from flexing, so it may take a few miles of a twisty road to get the tires up to normal traction. I'm not talking so much the air or pavement temperature but the temperature of rubber in the tire. A soft racing compound can have much greater traction than a long-distance touring tire but only after it's heated up to racing temperatures. Racing rubber also cures, and once the tires cool down, they lose much of their sticky quality. And that affects braking as well as cornering.

It's also important to maintain tire pressure. Pressure that's too high results in lower traction. Inadequate pressure results in excessive temperatures and premature tire failure. With tube-type tires, underinflation can allow the tire to slip on the rim during a quick stop, tearing the valve stem or inner tube.

Suspension

The suspension also contributes to your ability to make a quick stop without losing control. When you are braking hard, telescopic sliders tend to hang up from the axle being pushed back toward the engine. If the front fork sliders have excessive stiction, the front tire may not maintain contact with the surface of the road as the wheel rolls over a bump or dip. If you hit a bump while braking hard and the suspension hangs up, the tire will rebound off the surface. At that instant, the brakes will instantly lock up the wheel while the sliders will be free to rebound. Then as the locked wheel slams back to the pavement, the sliders bind again, and the cycle repeats itself: BAMchirpBAMchirpBAM.

If it isn't obvious, the brakes can't stop the bike if the tires can't maintain a grip on the road. Maybe your fork tubes need a simple alignment or the fluid topped up. If your brakes or suspension are doing some funny things, it would be smart to do a little maintenance before you encounter a left-turning car (or an earthmover) around a blind turn.

Squeezing the Lever

How you squeeze the lever is perhaps the most significant part of the braking equation. Regardless of the system on the bike you are riding, with few exceptions, you get the quickest stop by using the computer between your ears to apply maximum braking on both wheels just short of skidding the tires, lifting the rear end, or activating the ABS.

What you're doing to accomplish that is feeling how hard you are squeezing the lever or pushing on the pedal, and comparing that to your seat-of-the-pants feel of inertia ("g-force") pulling your body forward, the bike's attitude, and the sound of the tires. If the bike seems stable and the tires aren't howling, you can squeeze a little harder, and expect to feel the g-force increase slightly. If the rear end starts to fly or the front tire starts to wiggle, you can ease up on the lever pressure and expect the g-force to lessen. That's why it is so important to maintain your awareness of what the bike is telling you.

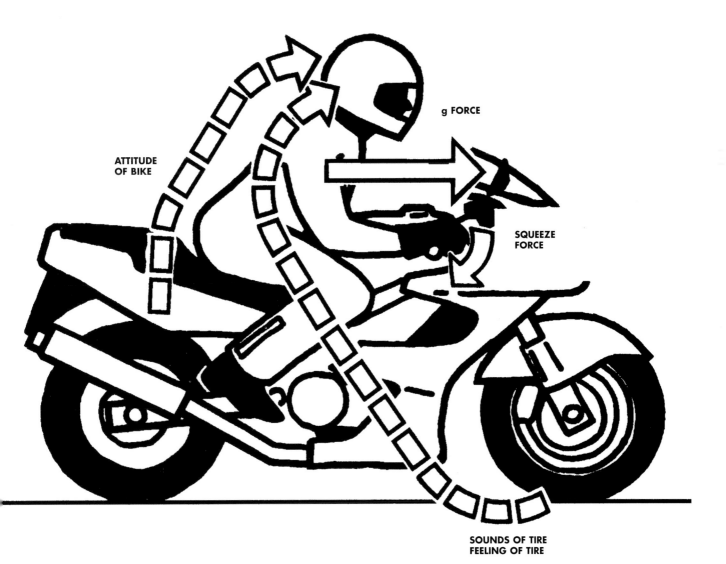

g FORCE

ATTITUDE
OF BIKE

SQUEEZE
FORCE

SOUNDS OF TIRE
FEELING OF TIRE

If the rear end starts to fly or the front tire starts to wiggle, you can ease up on the lever pressure and expect the g-force to lessen.

Don't Panic

We sometimes call quick stops "panic stops" because we're faced with scary and unpredictable consequences with little time to react. But successful quick stops really demand that the rider avoid panicking and focus on braking. If you suddenly discover an earthmover in your path ahead, the normal reaction is to stare at the heavy steel and let your brain waste time running through scenarios of what the impact is going to feel like and how you're going to explain this to your significant other. That sort of panic won't help you stop the bike. To make a successful quick stop, you need to push all that bad stuff to the back of your mind, point the bike in the best direction, and focus on maximum-effort braking. The slower you're traveling on impact, the less the pain and expense are going to be, so the best thing to do is concentrate on braking and ignore everything else.

Be aware that in a panic situation, muscles tend to overreact. You might think you are squeezing the brake lever steadily, but with the adrenaline suddenly pumping into your muscles, you can be applying a King Kong squeeze without realizing it. In your panic, you might also grasp the handlebars with a death grip, which makes controlling the bike harder. Being familiar with quick stops is the key to avoiding panic and the death grip.

Practice

Of course, you can read all about it, understand exactly what to expect, and believe you are prepared to do a perfect quick stop but still not be able to pull it off when the emergency happens. The only way to gain better braking proficiency is to get your bike out and practice quick stops. Find yourself some pavement you can borrow for a few hours and get in some braking time. If you have a new subdivision going in, there may be a nice new paved street with no one using it yet. Or maybe you can find an abandoned section of highway or a vacant parking lot or industrial street early on a Sunday morning. You definitely don't want to be practicing quick stops in traffic or with children or pets running around.

It is helpful to mark off your braking chute and the point at which you will initiate the braking so your practice is consistent. Remember to allow plenty of run-off room. Some riders just pick up a scrap of sheet rock to chalk some marks on the pavement. I prefer brightly-colored tennis balls cut in half. They are easy to see, pack easily into a tank bag, won't cause a tire to slide, and don't leave any evidence. Quick stops from speeds of only 40 mph are scary enough. If you gradually work up from 20 mph to 60 mph, you'll need a minimum of 120 feet on both sides of the braking point.

Since I'm not going to be there to help you if you goof up, I strongly urge you to strap on your best crash padding, including abrasion-resistant pants and jacket, leather boots, full-fingered gloves, and a helmet (preferably full-coverage). It would also be smart to do some brake maintenance before you start your braking practice. Bleed the brakes, top off your brake reservoirs, adjust the levers, pump your tires up to correct pressure, and snug up the various pinch bolts.

Braking Drill
1. **Make a series of quick weaves to warm up the tires, or put in fifteen to twenty minutes of a twisty road getting to your practice area. Serious riders actually stop and feel the tires with their bare hands, pushing a fingernail into the rubber to see how it's softening as it warms up.**
2. **Practice a few "easy" stops from 20 mph right down to 0, using both brakes. Keep practicing well within the traction envelope until you begin to get a feel for how your bike stops.**

3. Continue practicing easy stops with both brakes, but gradually increase pressure on the rear brake to find where the rear tire begins to skid.
4. Now get serious about stopping in the shortest distance, increasing front brake pressure to the maximum, short of either skidding the front tire or lifting the rear wheel.

I want to point out that test riders who do a lot of braking might not be fazed by a 60-0 stop, but for the rest of us, a quick stop from 60 mph is seriously risky. If you aren't experienced at hard braking, it's a lot smarter to do your initial stops at a modest speed and gradually work up the dial as you gain confidence and skill. A speed of 20 mph is not too slow for your first run.

Straight-Line Braking Techniques

To practice braking in a straight line, get the bike up to speed, shift up as appropriate, and keep the bike vertical and headed straight down the chute. Cover both the clutch and brake levers. Keep your head and eyes up, focusing on the spot at which you intend to stop the bike, not at the cones. Grip the sides of the tank with your knees to prevent sliding forward.

At the braking point, squeeze the clutch, roll off the throttle, and apply both brakes. Try not to grab the front brake instantly but squeeze the lever progressively harder over the first half second as the weight transfers onto the front wheel. That initial squeeze

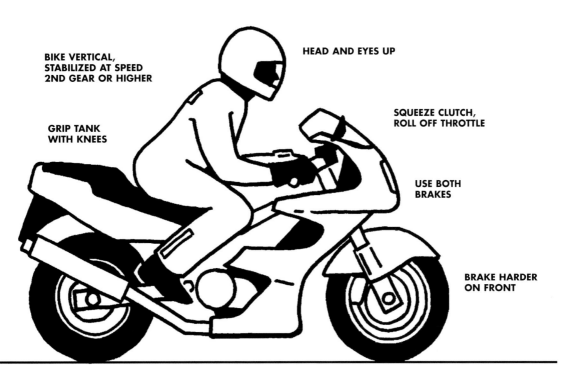

BIKE VERTICAL, STABILIZED AT SPEED 2ND GEAR OR HIGHER

HEAD AND EYES UP

GRIP TANK WITH KNEES

SQUEEZE CLUTCH, ROLL OFF THROTTLE

USE BOTH BRAKES

BRAKE HARDER ON FRONT

IF REAR TIRE SKIDS, STAY ON BRAKE TO COMPLETE STOP

COME TO COMPLETE STOP LEFT FOOT TO GROUND RIGHT FOOT ON BRAKE PEDAL

Before you take off to return to the start again, think about what you did right and wrong.

needs to be smooth and progressive to avoid sliding the tire before weight transfer. You'll need to ease up on the rear brake as weight transfers to the front.

Toward the end of the stop, shift down into first gear, and come to a complete stop with your right foot on the brake and your left foot on the ground. Before you take off to return to the start again, think about what you did right and wrong.

Expect steering to require more effort under hard braking. If steering suddenly gets easier while braking, that's a danger sign the front tire is about to wash out.

If you slide the rear tire and the rear end drifts sideways, it's important not to release the rear brake. Steer into the skid and stay on the rear brake until the bike stops to avoid a high-side flip. If you continue sliding the rear tire when you aren't trying to, use less pedal pressure on subsequent passes. With a lightweight sportbike on clean, dry pavement, any rear braking may be counterproductive. When carrying a passenger, or on slick surfaces, you'll be able to use more rear brake.

Quick Stops in Curves

Quick stops in curves are much more difficult because the tires are already consuming much of the available traction when you're leaned over. There are two different techniques for quick stops in curves. You can either get the bike vertical and attempt a maximum-effort, straight-line stop, or you can apply the brakes while continuing around the curve, trading cornering traction for braking traction. In tests, the straight-line-stop technique produced shorter stopping distances, assuming conservative cornering speeds. The straight-line technique also works well with high-tech braking systems.

As cornering speeds increase, you quickly run out of room to make a straight-line stop without running off the pavement. So, if you enjoy cornering more aggressively, it's important to practice maximum-effort braking while leaned over. Remember, in a corner, the tires are using most of the available traction to force the bike into the curve. You have a limited amount of traction, and you can only use traction for braking that isn't being used for cornering.

The technique for braking while leaned over is to apply the brakes gently at first, and increase brake pressure as the bike lifts up. As the bike gets more vertical, the cornering forces decrease, and you can use most of the available traction for braking.

Whether your favorite road burner has independent, integrated, linked, antilock, or power brakes, the tech-

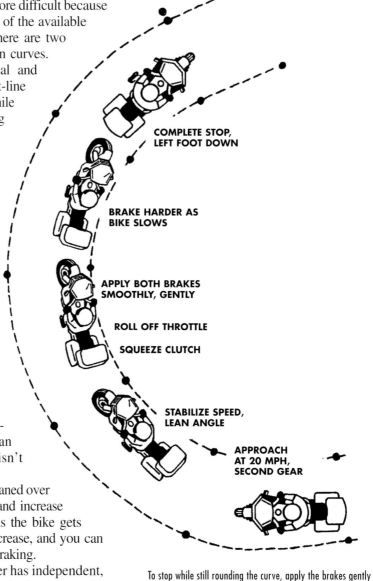

COMPLETE STOP, LEFT FOOT DOWN

BRAKE HARDER AS BIKE SLOWS

APPLY BOTH BRAKES SMOOTHLY, GENTLY

ROLL OFF THROTTLE

SQUEEZE CLUTCH

STABILIZE SPEED, LEAN ANGLE

APPROACH AT 20 MPH, SECOND GEAR

To stop while still rounding the curve, apply the brakes gently at first, and increase brake pressure as the bike lifts up.

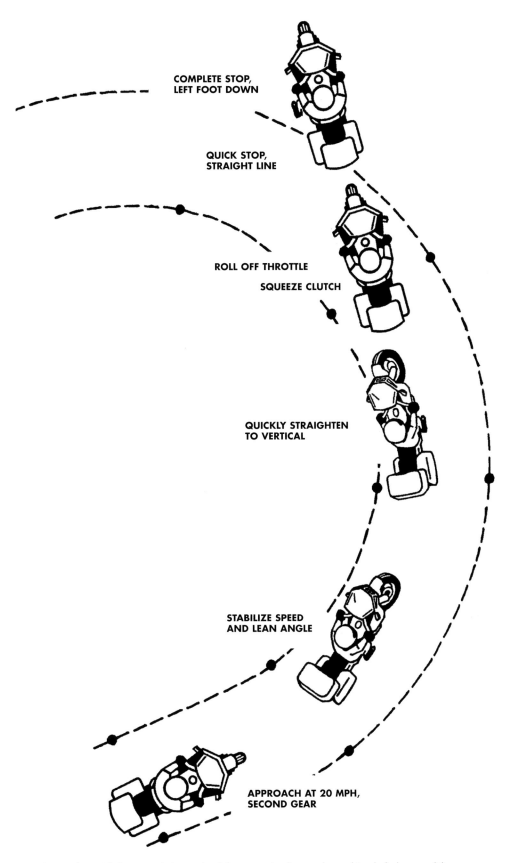

COMPLETE STOP, LEFT FOOT DOWN

QUICK STOP, STRAIGHT LINE

ROLL OFF THROTTLE

SQUEEZE CLUTCH

QUICKLY STRAIGHTEN TO VERTICAL

STABILIZE SPEED AND LEAN ANGLE

APPROACH AT 20 MPH, SECOND GEAR

In tests, the straight-line-stop technique produced shorter stopping distances than applying the brakes around the curve.

nique for a quick stop is the same: apply maximum braking on both wheels, just short of skidding the tires or lifting the rear wheel. And once quick stops are familiar to you, most of the panic will go away, too. That *MCN* staffer I mentioned back at the beginning confides that if he had not had a lot of experience practicing maximum-effort quick stops, he would have been picking his teeth out of that excavator.

Homework

While it is important to have an intellectual understanding of the principles of steering and swerving, sooner or later the rubber needs to meet the road. Yes, you can practice emergency swerves on a training course, but I suggest that the way to prepare yourself for swerves is to practice aggressive cornering, preferably on a twisty road.

The ideal twisty road for gaining swerving skills is out in the desert or any place away from traffic, and one that has an unobstructed view through every corner. If you have such a road available, then get out and ride it again and again. The problem is that there are few public roads with unobstructed views or scarce traffic. In Oregon, police motorcyclists are taking to go-cart tracks for cornering practice.

The "PM" Cornering Range

Years ago, some other instructors and I designed a "parking lot" practice exercise (the "PM" cornering range) that would provide a continuous circuit of difficult corners, stops, and turns from a stop. The concept behind this exercise is that a continuous circuit of exercises is more like real life than a sequence of individual exercises interrupted by wait time. You simply ride it against a stopwatch. You are required to put a foot down three times, including the quick stop at the end, and you're penalized one second for running over any line. Elapsed time is a good indication of rider skill. Variations of this range have been tried at different locations, and the feedback from riders is typically positive and often enthusiastic.

The corners are designed not only to fit the maximum skill practice on the minimum area but also to keep speeds low and therefore limit potential injury. The layout allows an instructor standing near the start line to observe a rider's performance throughout the entire range and announce the elapsed time to the rider at the end.

The circuit includes three locations at which the rider must come to a complete stop. Two are stops followed immediately by right-angle turns. The final stop is a maximum-effort quick stop in a straight line. There are two decreasing radius turns (one left and one right), plus S-turns of different radii.

You can draw up your own rules for riding performance. The suggestion is to time the rider with a stopwatch, with elapsed time from when the front wheel crosses the start line to where the bike comes to a complete stop with the rear wheel clear of the final stop line. A penalty of one second is suggested for each occurrence of tires crossing outside any lane boundary, failure to come to a complete stop, or failure to put the left foot down at a stop.

If you want to create your own cornering range, you'll need to find a relatively large area. This type of range is complex enough that it needs to be painted down rather than marked with temporary cones. The range can be chalked down for temporary use, though. The most difficult part is getting permission to use someone's pavement. College parking lots are ideal because they are usually available on weekends. A motorcycle dealer may be open to the idea of painting down a motorcycle practice area in his parking lot. Or perhaps you can convince your local rider training site to add it to its training range. It is more likely that a training program

David L. Hough

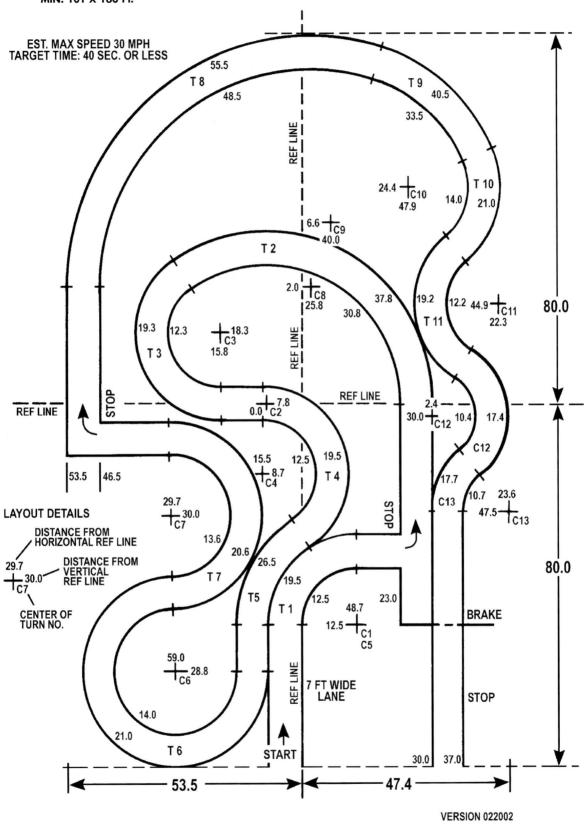

"PM" CORNERING RANGE
MIN. 101 X 160 FT.

EST. MAX SPEED 30 MPH
TARGET TIME: 40 SEC. OR LESS

LAYOUT DETAILS

DISTANCE FROM
HORIZONTAL REF LINE

DISTANCE FROM
VERTICAL
REF LINE

CENTER OF
TURN NO.

VERSION 022002

or a motorcycle club would do it. But be aware that while various staff members at the MSF like our idea for a cornering range, and some state rider training managers have used it, no one in authority has ever given it an approval.

Start the layout by chalking down two reference lines that cross at a right angle. Then locate the centers of the turns. The centers of the turns are located by measuring from one vertical and one horizontal reference line. The inside and outside of the turns are measured from the indicated radii from the centers. The basic lane is 7 feet wide throughout the course. Dimensions are given in feet and tenths, which can be approximated when measuring with a tape with feet and inch measurements. A 100-foot steel surveyors tape makes measurements easier.

Layout is easier with a pin held exactly at the turn centers. A heavy steel plate with a bolt in the center makes a good tool for holding the end of a measuring tape. It is suggested that the layout be done in chalk and then painted after the turns have been smoothed together.

The course can be laid out in approximately two hours and painted with a 3-inch roller in approximately one hour. Painted lines should be a light color, not dark. For temporary use, the lines can be marked with chalk or duct tape.

The range requires a minimum length of 160 feet and a width of approximately 100 feet, but all of the turns should have additional run-out space beyond the lines for a safety zone. Start the layout by dividing the range approximately in half in both directions, with the reference lines crossing at a right angle. Before laying out any turns, measure from the reference lines to the maximum dimensions to ensure that the range will fit. If necessary, move one or both reference lines.

Measure from the reference lines to locate all the turn centers. The turn centers are coded C and the turns coded T. In other words, turn 2 is labeled T2, and the center for T2 is C2. It's helpful to identify these centers with the number of the turn chalked next to the exact center. When measuring, try to keep the measuring tape parallel to the reference lines.

With the turn centers located, you can lay out the turns in any sequence. Position the pin holder over any turn center, secure the loop end of the measuring tape around the pin, and chalk the inside and outside of the turn at the radii shown. There are several short straights. Lay out all the turns first, then connect the straights.

Note that the transitions from one turn to the next occur along a line running through both turn centers. These transition points are indicated by tick marks on the layout and are for reference only. The transition points should not be painted on the circuit.

It is not desirable to use any cones on the turns, but cones may be added at important points such as the start and stops. A cone positioned at the inside of the right-angle turns will make it obvious if the rider crosses the line.

Bear in mind that it is not necessary to have this course laid out exactly as shown, only that the lane is approximately 7 feet wide and the turns all connect. After all, roads in real life change in width, radius, and direction. The range can be modified as necessary to fit the available area or surface conditions. For instance, turns 8 and 9 could be moved left or right, with short straight sections added as necessary to connect. Pay particular attention to the surface at turns 9 and 10, where riders will be decelerating from fastest speed on the exercise into a progressively tighter turn. These turns should be located over tractable pavement to help avoid slideouts.

Ultimately, it's important to take your cornering skills to the road. Yes, I realize that a conservative touring rider may look down his nose at squidly riders who blast through twisty canyon roads at dizzying lean angles. But those quicker riders have experienced the grip pressure and lean angles needed for quick swerves. They don't have to pull any emergency maneuvers out of their hats, even if they could.

Riding in the

Real World

CHAPTER 6
RIDING IN THE REAL WORLD

Sight Distance

Knee-Dragger Nellie is on the way out to her favorite canyon road. It's been a frustrating week, and she really needs to get away from the office to get an adrenaline fix by blitzing a curvy road on a fast motorcycle. But first she has to work her way through urban traffic to get out of town. And frankly, all those other drivers seem to be conspiring to get in her way. There was some nervous housewife in a minivan pacing an old geezer in a motor home side by side. She was finally able to swerve between them when the minivan driver pulled a few feet ahead. But now she's trapped in the right lane behind a transit bus. She's getting really anxious to get past the creepers and get out to the canyons.

Approaching an intersection, the bus driver signals to pull into a bus zone, and Nellie pulls up close behind, anticipating a quick pass as soon as the bus gets out of

her way. But in the instant before Nellie can get around the bus, a delivery truck, aimed directly at Nellie, pulls out of a parking space. There is no time to swerve or brake. They are both locked into a collision by the physics. BAM! The truck slams into the bike.

Mercifully, Nellie gets thrown clear with only a broken left leg, two broken ribs, some skin missing from her right arm, and a concussion. Sprawled on the pavement, it takes Nellie a few seconds for the world to stop spinning. She gradually remembers what happened, and then it dawns on her that it might be a long, long time before she gets to ride again. Nellie is pumping adrenaline, all right—but not the way she had expected.

Lessons to Be Learned

While Nellie is being hauled off to the emergency room in an ambulance, let's think through what happened and see if we can learn a few lessons from her disaster. When another vehicle knocks down a motorcycle, we tend to sympathize with the hapless rider and blame the driver. Yes, Nellie had the legal right-of-way, and the other driver should have yielded. The problem was that the truck driver had no idea there was a motorcycle hiding behind the bus. From his perspective, there was a space behind the bus, just big enough for him to make a quick pullout if he didn't waste any time.

Before we go on, let's note that regardless of the legal right-of-way, it was Nellie who got seriously nailed, not the truck driver. If you want to avoid getting crunched, you need to be much more aware of the situation around you than drivers of larger vehicles do. Let's also note that Nellie wasn't focused on avoiding a collision—she was thinking about that canyon ride and concentrating on squirming her way through traffic. Think back through her ride and you can see that Nellie put herself in several bad situations in which the view was blocked by other vehicles such as the van, motor home, and bus. By riding through traffic tailgating the bus with her view blocked, Nellie was slipping her own head in the noose.

What Is Sight Distance?

There is an important concept at work here: sight distance—the relative amount of road space ahead we can see at any given moment. Sometimes we can see several miles ahead; other times the view is limited by foliage, roadside obstructions, the crown of a hill, or a large vehicle. Bear in mind that the closer we are to a visual obstruction, the larger the visual shadow, or the area you can't see. To confirm how this works, hold your arm out straight, and squint at your upraised palm with one eye. Now, pull your hand closer and closer toward your eye and see how it blocks out more and more of a visual shadow.

If Nellie had been thinking about traffic instead of the canyons to come, she would have stayed out from behind any large, view-blocking vehicles, or at least positioned herself to give other drivers a better chance of seeing her. For instance, moving into the left-wheel track often provides a better view of what's happening ahead, such as a vehicle about to pull out of a side street, a jaywalking pedestrian, or a driver backing into a parking spot.

Dropping back an extra second or two from behind a big vehicle shrinks that visual shadow and allows you to see more of the traffic ahead. Dropping back also gives oncoming drivers more of a chance to see you. Even on a one-way street, dropping back two or three seconds gives you a much better picture of what's happening.

Moving into the left-wheel track often provides a better view of what's happening ahead.

Dropping back an extra second or two behind a big vehicle will open up the view even more.

You should always plan a complete stop before moving beyond a visual obstruction.

David L. Hough

Prepare to Stop

When you can't do much to improve the view, the only reliable tactic for avoiding a collision is to be prepared to stop short of the point at which your sight distance is severely limited. When you can't see around an obstruction, consider making a complete stop to take a look. In a situation such as a hedge or building right up to the corner of the intersection, you should be planning a complete stop at the corner, just as if you had a stop sign. And don't be amazed to discover a stop sign hidden in the bushes.

Positioning for Corners

Even if Knee-Dragger Nellie had made it out to the canyons, the same concept would apply there. Whether it's a left-turning cabbie in the city or a slow-moving silage wagon on that twisty back road, you should always be able to bring your bike to a complete stop within your available sight distance.

Approaching this turn from the outside gives you a better view of what's about to happen.

Every sunny weekend, on all the favorite curvy motorcycle roads around the country, a few motorcyclists splatter themselves into the roadside. If the police happen upon the accident and make out a report, the official reason is usually "excessive speed for conditions."

I remember a recent incident in which I was following a rider I'll call Big Dawg Dan, who was cruising at what I perceived to be the edge of the speed/traction envelope. When I observed a blind corner ahead that appeared to be tighter than the others, I backed off. The turn looked really tight, and the road apex was at the top of a rise. I braked harder, thinking, *Holy schnitzel! I can't believe Big Dawg can keep it on the road, diving into such a tight turn at warp speed!* When I rounded the turn, Dan had already disappeared. I was dumbfounded that he had been able to make that tight turn and then accelerate fast enough to be gone around the next corner.

Then I saw a flash of color in the bushes as I rode by and realized that Big Dawg hadn't made the turn— he had launched himself into the bushes as the bike lifted up on the suspension and the tires lost traction. Luckily, he managed to miss the big trees and stumps, and was able to limp home with only sprains and bruises after several other riders helped grunt his bike back up onto the road.

That story illustrates how different riders judge cornering speeds differently on the same road. You need to remember that you're in charge of your bike, not the other guys. One big trick to riding fast is to get on the brakes *right now* when the sight distance closes up or the corner looks like it might have some surprises. You can't depend on other riders to keep speed within the physics of the situation. If you allow yourself to get suckered into following others, you could be following them into a ditch.

One big issue on twisty roads is getting good information about the shape of the road ahead. Approaching turns on a twisty back road, you can improve the view by moving over to the outside of the turn. That is, approaching a left-hander, move over to the right edge of the lane. Approaching a right-hander, start your lean-in from a location closer to the centerline.

It may not seem like much, but being able to see the road ahead one or two seconds sooner gives you that much more time to set up for what's about to happen. The sooner you can make a prediction about the curve, the earlier you can get set up.

Let's also note that even if you have the talent and traction to stay on the road at impressive speeds, there are often hazards lurking around blind corners. You might be suddenly faced with a boulder rolled into the road, a truck halfway over the centerline, or an AWOL steer. I'm not going to suggest how fast you should ride—that's between you and the boys in blue. But I will suggest that if you prefer to do your riding on a bike rather than in an ambulance, it's important to adjust your speed to how much road you can see ahead as well as to your real-life stopping abilities.

Stopping Distance

For a given speed and traction situation, your bike requires a certain amount of distance to stop. In the city, most motorcycle accidents seem to occur on straight, level streets, so our quick stops most likely involve straight-line braking. But out in the country, accidents happen more frequently in curves.

Think about that for a second. Are there more hazards located in curves than in the straights? No, it's not that more hazards lurk near curves but rather that we can't see them soon enough when the view ahead is limited by the shape of the road. Since we are most likely to be surprised in curves, we'll need to brake hard in curves from time to time. Remember that you can do a maximum-effort quick stop in a curve either by lifting the bike up and doing a straight-line stop or by braking progressively harder as you continue around the curve.

While a straight-line quick stop slows the bike more quickly with less risk of a slideout, that option goes away as your road speed increases. Higher speed means much longer braking distance. Let's say that on a particular curve, you could just barely bring your bike to a complete stop in a more-or-less straight line from a speed

Imagine what your stopping lines in this corner might look like for speeds of 40, 60, and 80 mph.

of 50 mph without running off the pavement. But if you were to attempt to brake in a straight line from a speed of 60 mph on the same curve, you'd still be braking hard as the bike runs off the pavement. And from a speed of 70 mph, you'd be flying off the road with the bike still making 20 or 30 mph.

What's the lesson here? Well, faster speeds mean you probably won't be able to make straight-line stops in curves. You'll have to brake while leaned over, so you'll be stopping well around the curve. For instance, think about what your stopping lines might look like for speeds of 40, 60, and 80 mph if you suddenly discovered the road ahead blocked by a hay truck backing up to a barn.

What's the importance of this? The faster you ride, the more important it is for you to be skilled at maximum braking while leaned over. Even if you follow my advice to enter curves from the outside and slow down to match your sight distance, the time will come when you will need to make a quick stop after you've leaned the bike over.

The obvious problem with braking while leaned over is that the tires are already close to their limits pushing the bike around the curve. When braking while leaned over, you need to be very smooth at applying both brakes, and skillful enough to modulate brake-lever pressure. You progressively brake harder as the bike straightens up and consumes less traction for cornering.

Front wheel braking prior to leaning the bike over should be part of your cornering habits. Even barely applying a light squeeze on the front brake lever to help slow the bike helps you build the habit. You should also be familiar with trail braking (front wheel braking while leaning over). When the turn has a fast-sweeping entry rather than a straight leading into a tight corner, the road curves more gradually, allowing the rider to maintain greater speed. But the road eventually curves tighter, requiring the rider to treat the last half of the curve as the actual corner. There is no purpose in slowing down too soon in the gradual entry part of the curve, but you need to get speed down prior to the tight part of the curve. So the trick is to squeeze on a little front brake to decelerate while you're leaned over.

If bike skeletons were left lying around the curves, we might have a better understanding of the hazards.

What's Wrong with a Steady Pace?

There are a lot of riders who are proud of their ability to cruise through the countryside at a brisk but steady pace. Sure, it's entertaining to find a pace that allows you to maintain almost the same speed through the corners as down the straights. Leaning over hard into turns without slowing the bike does take a bit of talent and provides a thrilling ride. But as I've pointed out, your sight distance shrinks and expands dramatically as you motor along. If you intend to be able to stop within your sight distance at any point, you'll need to make speed adjustments as the view shrinks or expands.

A few optimistic riders snicker that it can't be as bad as I've suggested since they don't see broken bike skeletons littering the roadside. No, there aren't a lot of crushed bike skeletons littering the roadsides to caution you about the hazards. That's not because there aren't many crashes; it's because the bent bikes get hauled off to the repair shops and wrecking yards. If you want verification of the problem, go visit a motorcycle wrecking yard.

Putting It Together

Imagine riding an urban street where sight distance changes from moment to moment. When riding a long, straight boulevard, it may appear that you have unlimited sight distance, but remember that vehicles can appear suddenly from side streets, alleys, and entrances to big parking lots. So, your sight distance must also include the possibility of intruders who haven't appeared yet.

In city traffic, you need to be aware of vehicles that might be in the process of pulling out into your path at intersections. Can you see whether there are any vehicles approaching or is your view blocked? If you can't see what's happening, that's the indicator you need to scrub off some speed and get prepared for a quick stop. Automatically squeezing on a bit of front brake when your view is blocked is an important habit that gives you an edge if you do need to make a sudden stop. Slowing down just 10 mph at typical urban speeds chops your stopping distance in half.

Out on those twisty country roads, the temptation is to turn up the wick and have a little fun, but temper your enthusiasm according to the sight distance. When you are approaching a sweeping turn with no obstructions, where you can see the surface and the situation all the way through the corner, it's not critical to slow down, because your sight distance isn't limited. But as you approach a corner with a limited view, it's important to slow down to a speed at which you could pull off a quick stop within the amount of roadway you can see at any point in the turn. If you choose to ride faster than that, you're gambling your life that a hazard won't pop out in front of you.

Yes, we know it's seductively easy to ride just a little faster, and a little faster, and, if nothing bad happens, ride a little faster. And if you're riding with others, it's awfully difficult to control the urge to jack up your speed to avoid being seen as a wimp. But if you intend to keep on riding for a few more years, remember the experiences of Knee-Dragger Nellie and Big Dawg Dan, and make a better effort to keep your speed within your sight distance.

Expert Eyeballs

Here's Rapid Ralph, zipping through Boston rush hour traffic on his way to work. Ralph watches for errant drivers and covers the front brake in case he needs to make a quick stop. But he is also paranoid about surface hazards such as loose gravel, edge traps, and steel construction plates, so he tries to maintain his awareness of the pavement. The trouble is that traffic is so dense he can't see the surface very well.

It's no surprise when the car ahead bounces over some steel construction plates, but it's a big shock when Ralph realizes his front tire is headed directly for a slot between two plates. He tries to swerve around it, but it's too late to do anything. His front wheel drops into the opening and clangs down onto the brake discs. Instantly, the front wheel wedges into the hole, the forks are bent back under the engine, and Ralph is pitched forward over the bars. He's bouncing down the street on his back before he comprehends what has happened.

Okay, let's rewind the tape now and figure out what precipitated Ralph's painful and expensive tumble. Sure, the construction crew left a motorcycle hazard exposed, but that's a fact of life in cities such as San Francisco, Boston, New York, and Chicago. Could Ralph have been able to swerve around the slot if he had been more skillful? Sorry, he tried to apply his swerving skill, but there just wasn't time. Does this mean Ralph was doomed to an accident? Nope. This wasn't a matter of inadequate control skills. The problem started because Ralph wasn't looking far enough ahead to see what was happening in time to do something about it.

Let's not downplay control skills. As you ride through city traffic, your survival may depend upon your ability to put your tires exactly in the space between a pave-

Most of the information about what's happening around us comes through our sense of vision.

ment groove and an open manhole, or to bring your bike quickly to a stop to avoid a double-parked delivery truck. But consider that control skills such as countersteering and braking are only half of the equation. Before you can swerve or brake, you need to decide what to do. And before you can decide what to do, you have to figure out what's happening. Most of the information about what's happening around us comes through our sense of vision.

Eyes Up

You may see more than a few riders glancing down at the pavement just ahead of their front wheels. They get a great view of what's about to roll under their tires, but it's a useless habit because whatever is about to roll under their front tires at that moment is out of their control. Remember, it takes a second or two just to initiate a swerve or get on the brakes, even if you are prepared. At a street speed of only 30 mph, you're covering 44 feet every second. So, whatever occurs in the 44 feet of pavement just ahead of your front tire is already history. You need to see any hazards—such as that slot between the steel plates—at least two or three seconds ahead. Had Ralph been looking farther ahead instead of down at the pavement in front of his bike, he would have had more time to react.

Safety experts often use the term *seconds ahead* to describe distance: five seconds ahead is whatever distance you will be covering in five seconds at your same speed. Measuring distance in seconds is more accurate than trying to compute feet or car lengths because it relates to the time we have to react. If you have five seconds to react to a hazard, that's enough time to change your line or adjust your speed.

Rider training instructors often suggest that a rider should be looking twelve seconds ahead, or the distance he or she will be covering over the next twelve seconds. That doesn't mean you should be focused only on what's happening at a point twelve seconds ahead. Instead, you should focus on everything that's going on within that twelve-second zone.

At 40 mph, twelve seconds computes to roughly 700 feet.

At 60 mph, you'll cover more than 1,000 feet in twelve seconds.

To help you understand what twelve seconds looks like, here are some visual examples. Riding an urban street at 40 mph, twelve seconds computes to roughly 700 feet. Riding the highway at 60 mph, you'll cover more than 1,000 feet in twelve seconds. The point is that twelve seconds represents about as far ahead as you can see details. If you're not in the habit of looking twelve seconds ahead, you should work on that important technique.

Dense Traffic

If you've been riding around in aggressive urban traffic, you know that twelve seconds is way too much territory to observe. The traffic situation changes so rapidly that you must make frequent split-second decisions. It may seem that there is little point in thinking more than three or four seconds ahead. Like Ralph, you often find yourself boxed in between cars, so you seldom get a clear view of the road surface. And if you try to drop back to increase following distance, an aggressive driver quickly occupies the space ahead of you.

But that doesn't mean you can't be aware of what's happening ahead. You just need to be more clever about looking for clues when you're riding in big city traffic. For instance, when you spot those orange work zone warning signs, you should try to open up some space and increase your awareness of the surface in that area. You may need to look through the windows of other vehicles, peer under trucks, or dodge over to one side of the lane to catch quick glimpses of the pavement. Or when you're stopped by a traffic signal, leave a car length between you and the vehicle ahead to avoid being surprised by hazards hidden under it. And while you're stopped, use the opportunity to look over and around the vehicles ahead to spot surface hazards in the intersection and beyond.

You can also glean some clues from what other drivers are doing. If you see taillights coming on ahead for no apparent reason, you might suspect a surface hazard. If the other drivers are all swerving over to the left side of the lane, you can predict a problem on the right side, even if you can't see it yet. Most drivers instinctively avoid surface hazards, so riding in the cars' wheel tracks makes sense.

If you commute over the same route every day, keep track of the areas where construction has been going on. If you're just a visitor, you won't have that advantage. If you're just making a transit through town, try to schedule your ride to avoid the morning and evening commutes.

Bike Follows Nose

The tendency of people to point their vehicles wherever they are looking is called target fixation. For whatever physical or psychological reasons, the act of turning your head seems to help aim the bike in that direction. Think of this as the bike following wherever your nose is pointing. Try it and see if it works for you.

Keep Your Eyes Level

Most riders find that it helps to keep their eyes level with the horizon when cornering. If you keep your head square on your shoulders as you lean over, your view of the curve will be at an angle to the horizon and will give you a sense of disorientation.

Try an experiment right now: First, look around the room with your eyes level. Then lean over in your chair with your torso and head at about a 45-degree angle, and scan the room. Do you get an uneasy feeling that the walls have changed shape, or the furniture should be sliding downhill? Try walking in a circle or climbing stairs with your head tilted at an angle to see how it affects your muscle coordination.

Human vision pulls some psychological tricks when we view life at an angle. What most people discover is that they get much better spatial orientation with their eyes level, even when riding a bike that's leaned over at an angle. If you fit the pattern, you'll find it easier to keep track of the curvature and camber of the road if you keep your head level with the horizon.

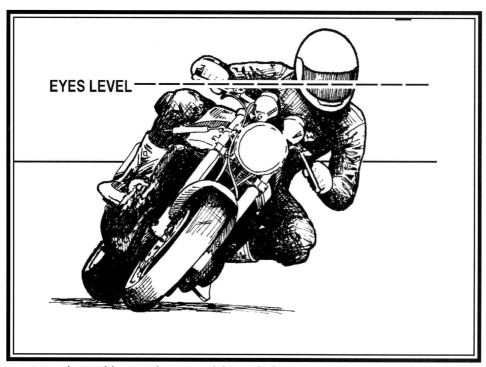

EYES LEVEL

Most people get much better special orientation with their eyes level.

What Are You Looking for?

Assuming you can get in the habit of looking far ahead, pointing your chin in the direction you want to go, and keeping your eyes level, we can bring up the question of what should you be looking for?

The classic city collision is with a car making a quick left turn across the path of a bike. So, you should be looking primarily for other vehicles on collision courses, either merging into or about to turn in front of you. But you must also be watching for other scenarios, including jaywalking pedestrians, bicyclists riding against traffic, and car doors opening into the traffic lane. Remember that in many cities, transit buses have a yield sign on the back and have the right-of-way, even if they pull out of loading zones into the path of oncoming traffic. If you know this is the situation where you

YIELD
RCW 46.61.220
for Buses

In many cities, transit buses have the right-of-way, even if they pull out into your path.

are, watch for any clues that a bus is about to pull out in front of you, and be pre-pared to take evasive action. Better yet, stay out of the right lane, where buses are likely to merge.

Just as important, we must watch for potential chain reactions. For example, a driver approaching a bus loading zone may be surprised by a bus pulling out and react by swerving into the adjacent lane or across the centerline. So, we need to watch for other drivers reacting to a hazard as well as the hazard.

There are some distinct clues that should put the urban motorcyclist road warrior on the defensive. Most of the following situations involve a driver being preoccupied with thoughts other than driving:

★ **A driver on a cell phone, lighting a cigarette, reading the paper, or putting on makeup**
★ **A vehicle with bulky loads inside or on the roof**
★ **A vehicle carrying several passengers, especially teenagers or young children**
★ **A vehicle moving at a higher or slower speed than surrounding traffic or one that is constantly changing lanes**
★ **A vehicle with out-of-state license plates, a rental car, or a car towing a rental trailer**
★ **Large trucks or motor homes on streets where they are not normally present**
★ **A car or truck with body damage, broken glass, or inoperative equipment**

A car's broken mirror doesn't just indicate that the driver can't see out of that mirror but is also a hint that the driver may be just as careless about driving as he or she is about vehicle maintenance.

Where to Look

Remember that other vehicles can make left turns from four different directions. In traffic, it's important not only to spot vehicles that might turn in front of you but also to get the quickest visual clues about what the vehicle is doing before it moves into your path. If you wait until after the other vehicle moves to take evasive action, you won't have much time to react.

For cars approaching an intersection from the opposite direction, monitor the level of the hood. The hood dipping slightly is an indication the driver is braking, a hint that

If the hood dips, it's a clue the driver is braking to make a turn. If the hood rises, it's a clue the driver has stepped on the gas.

the car may soon be turning across your path. The hood rising is a good hint that the driver has stepped on the gas. If you look closely, you may also see the front wheel turned in your direction.

It doesn't really make any difference whether you establish eye contact with the driver or not; you need to know if the vehicle is starting to move. The driver may be looking past you, or may see you but not predict how quickly you are approaching. For vehicles on side streets or in left turn lanes, monitor the vehicle's front wheel. The top portion of a wheel moves forward at twice the speed of the vehicle.

If you can see only the front bumper of a car hidden behind other vehicles or buildings, you can assume the driver can't see you and will enter the street. It is also smart to proceed more cautiously if your view of side streets or alleys is blocked by a bus or truck.

Even if you can't see a car starting to poke its nose out of a side street, you should predict that possibility and prepare for evasive action. If you find yourself approaching a blind intersection on the right, move to the left side of the lane to provide greater separation and a better view.

The top of the tire moves twice as fast as the car.

Approaching a blind intersection on the right, move left to get a better view.

Curves

On curving roads, it's common for an overly aggressive rider to drift wide halfway through a tight turn. While accident reports often indicate excessive speed as the cause, a competent rider on the same bike likely could have made the same curve at the same speed. One cause for such an accident, though, is pointing the bike toward an early apex as the result of focusing on the inside edge of the pavement or white fog line. A second cause is failing to grasp the character of the curve (the camber of the surface, the tightness of the curve, or the road changing elevation or camber in midcorner).

In sharp right-handers, the view is often limited.

Remember, pointing your nose toward where you want to go helps guide your bike in the right direction, and keeping your eyes level with the horizon helps you figure out the character of the curve. So, when approaching a curve, point your nose toward the outside of the curve—the centerline in a right-hander—until you initiate the lean. Then tilt your head level as you lean the bike, and swivel your nose around toward your intended apex.

It may not be obvious, but you get your best clues about the curvature of a road by monitoring the outside edge of the pavement as it unwinds into view. In a left-hander, we get a good view of the outside edge—the right side of our lane. But in sharp right-handers, our view around the curve is often limited by trees, rocks, or a hill.

When you aren't quite sure how tight the a curve is, it's more difficult to plan the best line. Since the opposite side of the road comes into view first, that's where many riders tend to focus as they try to calculate which way the pavement turns next. You also get clues about road camber changes from the opposite edge of the pavement. If the road seems to be getting wider, that's a clue the camber is tilting toward you. If the road seems to be getting narrower, or the other edge disappears, that's a clue the camber is tilting away from you. If it isn't obvious, you want the camber to be tilting in the same direction as the curve. If you suspect an off-camber situation, it's time to get on the brakes.

Here's a nasty off-camber left turn on Deals Gap's "dragon."

But remember, the bike tends to go where you point your nose, and you don't want to be carving off the road just because you glanced over there. One technique is to use your peripheral vision to track the curvature of a road, even while you are pointing your nose toward your proper apex. Some riders call this "getting the big picture." Most of us are receiving a lot of visual information from our peripheral vision but ignoring it. Using your peripheral vision is a valuable technique.

Seeing Is Believing

We should all be aware of common vision quirks as well as any specific vision problems we might have. One important quirk is speed-related tunnel vision. As speed increases, the eyes focus farther and farther out in front, and the brain blurs out the dizzying view toward the sides. That's why it is important to mentally keep track of surrounding traffic while motoring down the superslab.

Our brains also have a deceptive habit of filling in missing information and ignoring new information that doesn't fit the old memory. That's good for reading a mystery novel but not so good for motorcycling. For example, let's say I glance behind and see no other traffic, so my brain remembers the road as vacant. A few seconds later my eyes pick up a car right behind me, but my brain momentarily refuses to accept the new information: *No, there can't be anyone there because I remember that the road is vacant.* That's one of the main reasons for looking behind more than once during a maneuver and turning your head to look rather than depending only on the view in the mirrors.

Vision Problems

The human eye is an amazingly complex gadget. I'm not going to try to explain how it works, but motorcyclists should be aware that all eyes have small blind spots. Normally, the blind spot of the right eye is to the left of center, and the blind spot of the left eye is to the right of center. So theoretically, both eyes together see the whole picture. But if you have a problem with vision in one eye, you could have a blind spot right where you need to see that left-turning car or that hole in the pavement.

Even if you have healthy normal eyes, your vision is likely to be slightly nearsighted (myopic) or farsighted (hyperopic), or portions of the visual field may be distorted or blurred (astigmatic). These problems can usually be solved with corrective lenses, either eyeglasses or contact lenses.

The bad news is that vision tends to fade with the years. It is normal for the lens in the eye to harden by about age forty, reducing the ability to focus at close distances. Even if you have good distance vision, can you focus clearly on the instruments and then quickly refocus back to what's happening ahead? Night vision also fades with age. Older eyes typically have more trouble with the glare of oncoming headlights. The additional bad news is that smoking, diabetes, high blood pressure, hypertension, and some diets all have a negative effect on vision.

Considering how important vision is to motorcycling, it's worthwhile to have your eyes examined periodically by an eye specialist. Sure, you can squint more or buy cheap eyeglasses off a rack at the drugstore, but it's important to have a specialist look for eye problems such as glaucoma (blurred vision), cataracts (clouded vision), or macular degeneration (distorted images or blind spots in central vision). Ophthalmologists and optometrists are eye specialists.

I have problems with my own vision. I've always been nearsighted, but now I need different eyeglasses for driving, motorcycling, and writing at the computer. I'm getting more floaters in my eyes and even a few episodes of sparklers in my peripheral vision. I wonder how many more years of riding and writing I can squeeze out of this old body. That's a question all riders must eventually answer for themselves. If you're having trouble with nighttime vision, maybe it's time to give up riding at night.

In the meantime, take advantage of all that information your eyes are giving you. Get your eyes up and level, look far ahead, point your nose to where you want to go, and position the bike for the best view.

Being Seen in All the Right Places

We'd all like to believe that we can manage our risks of motorcycling by being smart, attentive to what's happening, and skilled enough to avoid problems. If the road twists and turns into a killer corner, we can handle it because we're looking far enough ahead, braking when sight distance closes up, and following a delayed apex line. Loose gravel, shiny construction plates, edge traps, V traps, sunken drains, wet leaves, or slick plastic lines: Hey, no problem! We've studied the surface hazards, and we know what to do. We see that road shark making a three-lane merge onto the freeway and we're already moving out of the way. In other words, we're prepared to handle anything that comes along, right?

Well the bad news is that there are a few situations where we just can't get out of the way. For instance, let's say you find yourself on a narrow bridge with a car approaching from the opposite direction, the driver yakking on a cell phone and wandering over the centerline. If the car strays over the centerline, you're toast because there just isn't any escape route. Even the veterans who have learned to dodge out of the way of most errant drivers sometimes get boxed into situations from which there is no escape. Like it or not, we often depend on other drivers to see us and give us our road space.

Seeing vs. Believing

The famous Hurt Report offered some sage conclusions about motorcycle accidents and being seen; what the safety experts call conspicuity (being conspicuous to others). In those accidents in which being seen was critical to avoiding a collision, only 5 percent of the motorcyclists who crashed were conspicuous. In 46 percent of those involved in collisions, the bike/rider was difficult to see.

The logic from the Hurt Report goes something like this:
1. Most motorcycle accidents are caused by human factors rather than environmental or vehicle factors.
2. Multivehicle motorcycle accidents are most often caused by the other driver

**failing to see the motorcycle and violating the right-of-way of the motorcyclist.
3. Therefore, increasing motorcycle conspicuity will decrease the risks of collisions.**

That seems pretty open and shut. Other drivers tend not to see us, and then they are surprised when they run us over, right? So, conspicuity tactics such as wearing high-visibility gear and turning on the headlight should help them see us, and then they'll avoid us. Some riders go a few steps further. If having the headlight on helps, then why not switch it on high beam, pop in a 100-watt bulb, or wire in a modulator that flashes the headlight?

Well, many of us suspect that conspicuity isn't that simple. How is it that a driver can pull out in front of a yellow motorcycle with its headlight blazing on high and the rider wearing a glowing orange "safety" vest and leaning on a pair of air horns? Well, think about those newspaper accounts of drivers who motored across the railroad tracks right in front of a freight train, apparently unable to see the flashing lights or hear the blasts of the locomotive's horn.

So, is it really a matter of conspicuity or is something else going on? Was the driver actually unable to see the motorcycle, or did the driver see the bike but his or her brain ruled out another vehicle because he or she wasn't expecting a motorcycle? Or, did the driver see the bike but didn't believe a motorcyclist had the same rights as a car driver? Did the errant driver make a quick left turn in front of the motorcyclist because he or she really didn't see the bike or because that driver hates motorcycles and wanted to teach the rider a lesson? Or did a driver who would have respected the rider's road space see the motorcycle but fail to judge its approach speed?

There haven't been enough research projects to give us solid answers. There is some evidence that the human brain disregards objects it doesn't expect to see, even if the objects are conspicuous. And there have been studies that hint that drivers yakking on a cell phone fail to perceive what's happening around them in traffic.

For the moment, let's be optimistic and assume that the majority of drivers out there will give us our road space if only they can see us. If you really want to increase your conspicuity, what's the best way to go about it?

The Hurt Report suggests:
★ **keeping your motorcycle headlight on at all times;**
★ **having a high-visibility color on the motorcycle;**
★ **that both passenger and rider wear high-visibility clothing.**

Let's face it: motorcycles are narrower than automobiles and easier to miss in poor light conditions. Riding gear in brighter colors with reflective patches can make it easier for other motorists to see you. Most motorcycle accidents occur on sunny days, but of course that's when most motorcyclists are out riding. If you find yourself riding in rainy or foggy conditions, be aware that it might be awfully difficult for other motorists to see you. In those circumstances, it certainly pays to be as conspicuous as possible.

Motorcycling gear manufacturers are paying more attention to conspicuity these days. Riding gear often includes reflective panels in key areas such as across the shoulders or on the back of the pants legs. Aerostich even offers a riding suit made of a new hi-viz fabric that's lime yellow in the daytime and a blazing, reflective white in headlights at night.

There are also vests with reflective panels, reflective belts, and reflective helmet bands, all designed to make you more conspicuous at night. Reflective tape on the back of your jacket or saddlebags might just catch the attention of a driver who

In poor visibility conditions, it certainly does help to make yourself more conspicuous.

The rider on the left is wearing a red suit with reflective patches. The rider on the right is wearing the Aerostich Hi-Viz Lime Yellow jacket that reflects brilliant white at night.

The white leathers are more conspicuous than the darker suit, but the bright vest with reflective stripes would make either suit more visible.

couldn't pick your taillight out of the maze of other lights on a dark, rainy night. Motorcycles typically have limited electrical power, so adding extra lights to the bike can quickly exceed available charging capacity. Retroreflective panels don't consume any bike electrical power, but rather light up from the illumination of other vehicles' lights. The big advantage of reflective panels such as Scotchlite is that they light you up using the other car's electrical power. If you don't want to have reflective patches sewn to your riding suit, there are mesh vests with reflective stripes.

Extra Lights

If your motor has enough charging capacity to keep extra lights glowing, you might think about modifying your lighting to increase conspicuity. For example, consider adding amber running lights to the front of your bike. Perhaps you can add dual-filament sockets to your turn signals. Running lights might make the difference between an oncoming driver seeing your motorcycle and misinterpreting your bike's headlight as a streetlight reflection.

While it might seem like a good idea to have amber running lights on the back of your bike too, equipment laws generally require taillights other than turn signals to be red. If you're thinking about installing dual-filament sockets in your rear turn signals to provide extra taillights, think that through again. Your local law enforcement might ignore amber taillights, but the legal eagles in other states may be watching more carefully. Rather than add dual-filament sockets to a turn signal, why not add a second pod with a red lens on each side?

Three-Bike Test

Years ago, a pessimistic *Road Rider* journalist didn't think much of the conspicuity suggestions offered by the Hurt Report. So he did a little informal test of the high-visibility suggestions during his daily commutes to work. On different weeks, he rode with different levels of conspicuousness and tallied the number of drivers who violated his right-of-way. One week he rode a "stealth" bike: a narrow dark-colored machine with no accessories and the headlight turned off. To decrease his conspicuity he wore dark riding gear. The next week he rode a "conspicuity" bike: a white machine with a big fairing and the headlight and taillight blazing. When riding the conspicuity bike, he wore a bright-colored riding suit and flashy helmet. The third week he tried the "motor cop" appearance: the black stealth bike outfitted with white saddlebags and a clear windshield, but with the headlight turned off. His motor cop costume included a short-sleeved khaki shirt, tall leather boots, a half helmet with a shiny visor, and sunglasses. Okay, he also attached his club name badge to the left breast pocket. His conclusions: there were far fewer infractions when he was riding with the motor cop setup. The conspicuity package didn't do any better than the stealth package.

All right, we know that wasn't a scientific study. But think about it. Why would drivers pay no more attention to the conspicuity setup than the stealth outfit? And why would drivers apparently notice the "cop bike" even though it didn't follow the conspicuity suggestions from the Hurt Report?

My personal conclusion is that drivers have little difficulty seeing bikes but treat them with different concern. Perhaps the motor cop bike registered because it hinted at a threat to them—the threat of a ticket. In other words, drivers are able to pick a "threatening" bike out of the traffic stream even if it isn't conspicuous in terms of bright colors and flashing lights.

I'm not suggesting you run out and buy khaki shirts, blue sunglasses, and half helmets, or that you paint stars on your tank and bags or wear those toy sheriff badges you bought in Tombstone. There are laws about such things, and Officer Friendly may not be charmed by your roadside logic. Besides, I think there's something else going on here other than being conspicuous. I suggest that it's also a matter of others judging our approach speed and proximity.

Judging Speed

It is important that other drivers correctly judge your approach speed. If it appears to another driver that you are thousands of feet away and creeping along at 20 mph, there is plenty of time to make a leisurely left turn in front of you. But if you are actually a hundred feet away and approaching at 60 mph when the driver makes his or her turn, it is going to be a shock for both of you. Could it be that drivers didn't pull out in front of the cop bike because the white saddlebags made the bike look bigger, closer, and approaching at a higher speed?

Obviously there are two parts to the equation: (1) What your distance and speed really are, and (2) what the other driver thinks is happening. Try a couple of experiments right now to observe how the eyes and brain determine distance and speed.

First, with both eyes open, hold one thumb out in front of you as far as you can reach, and then focus on it as you slowly pull your thumb back toward your nose. If your eyes and brain are working normally, you should see a single thumb coming at you. Now focus on your outstretched thumb, but place it a few inches in front of this book, held at arm's length with your other hand. Slowly pull your thumb back toward your nose. Focus on the thumb as you pull it toward you, and you'll see two fuzzy images in the background. Focus on the book, and you'll see two semitransparent thumbs. If you continue to focus on the book while pulling your thumb back toward your nose, you'll see what looks like two transparent thumbs appearing to get farther apart.

Now, here's the question: Based entirely on vision, how do you know your thumb is getting closer to your eye and not just inflating in size? Well, seeing is primarily in the brain. The main optic nerves run from the back of the eye directly into the brain. The eyes just send signals. The brain does some quick calculations, pulls up some memory about thumbs (or cars or airplanes or motorcycles), runs through some logic, and comes up with what it thinks is happening.

David L. Hough

Can you judge the approach speed of a motorcycle entirely by its headlight?

Based on the changing angles reported by the eyes, and the memory that objects such as thumbs (or motorcycles) don't change size very rapidly, the brain calculates that the thumb is getting closer, not larger. Two signals from two eyes a few inches apart also help confirm that the angle between the edges is changing. The point is that the speed of the changing angles helps the brain calculate how quickly the thumb is approaching.

The same thing happens with an approaching motorcycle. Take the scenario of a driver waiting on a side street, watching an approaching motorcycle for a second or two. His or her eyes report the changes in angle, and his or her brain calculates the distance and approach speed of the motorcycle. If the bike is small or narrow, the brain tends to calculate it as far away. And if the angles measured by the eyes don't change rapidly, the brain assumes the bike isn't approaching quickly.

Now, here's a potential problem for motorcyclists: a narrow motorcycle doesn't give a driver much in the way of changing angles. An approaching automobile is wide enough to give the brain some visual angles to compute. It's difficult to calculate the approach speed of a narrow motorcycle or a single 7-inch headlight, even if it's on high beam. It may be that a driver gets a more accurate idea of approach speed from a fairing than from the headlight.

This visual perception could explain why running with the headlight on high beam doesn't seem to help visibility any more than running on low beam. It's not a matter of brightness but the apparent size of the bike. A headlight on high beam might even distract a motorist from observing other, more important speed clues such as the edges of the fairing. If that theory is correct, then it would make more sense to have two small lights at the ends of the handlebars rather than a single large headlight at the center.

We might also surmise that today's large touring bikes have a conspicuity advantage over cruisers and sport tourers. A bike that's physically wider makes it appear closer and faster, encouraging other drivers to wait for it to pass rather than pull out in front of it. And the front lights on bikes such as the 1800 Gold Wing make it look even wider than it is. Not only are the dual headlights much wider than a single headlight, but the running lights on the mirror housings add reference points that make it appear to be closer and approaching faster than it actually is.

That doesn't mean you need to trade your narrow sportbike for a monster tourer just to increase your conspicuity. But it does mean that if you're riding a narrow bike, you need to be much more aware of how other motorists perceive your distance and approach speed.

Colors

It might seem that bright colors such as white, red, or yellow would be much more conspicuous than dark colors such as black, blue, or green. But the background is just as important as the color of the bike's paint. A white bike against a dark background is much more obvious than a black bike against the same background. But background is constantly changing when you're on the road. Consider what these same bikes would look like out in the desert under a bright sun.

Colors also influence the brain when it's judging distance. Consider a red ball painted on a blue background and a blue ball painted on a red background. The red ball appears to be a sphere suspended well in front of a blue sky. The blue ball appears to be a small area of sky seen through a hole in a red wall. It's difficult to judge the distance of a red object. That's something to remember when you're adding reflective patches to the back of your bike and riding gear.

One reason fire trucks and school crossing signs are changing from red and regular yellow to hi-viz lime yellow is that the lime yellow is more conspicuous, and it's much easier to judge the distance of something in the green spectrum. Given what we know today about colors, it was a big mistake to make taillights red rather than green, but don't expect that ever to be reversed.

The dual headlights and running lights on the GL1800 mirror housings make the bike look even closer and faster than it really is. The top of the tire moves twice as fast as the car.

David L. Hough

Relative Speed

Whatever the speed of traffic, a driver waiting to merge makes a mental calculation of whether there is sufficient time to pull in front of any approaching vehicle based on the relative time it takes other vehicles to pass. On a highway where most traffic is moving at 60 mph, a driver makes automatic assumptions on the space needed to pull in front of other drivers approaching at 60 mph. But if a vehicle is approaching at 75 mph, it's going to eat up the distance a lot quicker than the driver had anticipated, even if he or she correctly judges its distance. And if the vehicle is a small or narrow bike, it's likely the driver will misjudge both its distance and approach speed. The lesson here is that if you're riding a narrow, naked bike in traffic, you should ride at conservative speeds and be prepared for quick stops to avoid collisions.

Above: Consider what these two bikes would look like on a bright desert road.

I'm not going to suggest never exceeding the speed limit, but I do suggest that when you twist up the throttle to warp speed on public roads, you need to accept some increased responsibility for what happens. You should be prepared to scrub off a lot of speed quickly when you approach other vehicles that could get in your way, so the motorists can judge your approach speed and distance more realistically, and you have a shorter stopping distance in case those motorists guess wrong.

If you choose to twist up the throttle to warp speeds on public roads, you need to accept some increased responsibility for what happens.

Cornering

CORNERING

DEMANDS MORE
TRACTION

DEMANDS LESS
TRACTION

CA

CONTINUE TO
ACCELERATE
OUT OF TURN

MORE
THROTTLE

Cornering   CORNERING

CHAPTER 7
CORNERING

The "Trendy Delayed Apex Line"

More than once over the years, I've suggested that a delayed apex cornering line is often the most appropriate line for riding public roads, especially through corners with a limited view ahead. Lately, I've been hearing a few snide remarks from track school instructors and motorcycle scribes scoffing at the cornering suggestions in the *MCN* column "Proficient Motorcycling." Some attempt to dismiss me with snide comments such as, *We don't teach the "trendy delayed apex line."* Frankly, I'm pleased to hear that my suggestions are trendy. Let's revisit the subject, and I'll offer some additional insight.

Now, don't flip the pages just because you ride a cruiser or touring bike and don't think this applies to you. If you're interested in managing the risks, stay with me here. Your cornering lines have a lot to do with maintaining traction and avoiding collisions, regardless of the style of bike you're riding. First, I'll define *delayed apex line* and consider why I think it's smarter for public roads. Then I'll offer some suggestions for applying this information to your street riding.

Delayed apexing is just mentally sliding your apex a little farther around the corner than where you think the road apex occurs.

What's a Delayed Apex?

The apex is the tightest point of a curve, the location where a motorcyclist would come closest to the inside edge. A delayed (or late) apex is mentally sliding your intended apex a little farther around the corner from where you think the tightest part of the curve occurs. The road has the same shape regardless of your cornering line, so a delayed apex is just a different way of thinking about your cornering line.

Remember that for a two-wheeler, the straightest line generally results in the least lean angle and therefore the least slideout forces on the tires. The straighter your line, the less likely you are to slide out, and the more traction you'll have in reserve for potential emergencies. A two-wheeler can carve a much straighter line through most corners than an automobile. Now, don't get the idea that I'm suggesting a rider pass a car on the inside in a corner; I'm just comparing cornering lines here.

Racetrack vs. Public Roads

Of course, the ideas about fast cornering lines generally start on the racetrack, with the focus on absolute maximum speed rather than on mundane matters such as avoiding potholes or rock slides or wandering moose. The main reason I preach delayed apexing for riding public roads is that they have a much different environment from the racetrack.

The racetrack is more predictable because the racer usually has a good view through the corner, the pavement is wide, the surface is clean, and everyone is going in the same

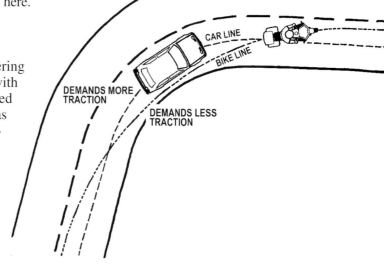

The bike line uses less traction than the car line.

David L. Hough

direction. On public roads we often can't see what's happening around a corner, or we can't get a good enough view of the surface to pick the most tractable line, or we don't know where a particular corner is heading.

The delayed apex line may not be the fastest line through a turn on the racetrack. But if we're talking public roads, then the "trendy" delayed apex line has some advantages over racing lines. The racing lines you generally see on a track are typically midturn apexes, or sometimes early apexes. That's fine for the racetrack with its wide surfaces and good views, but an early apex on a narrow public road often leads to an excursion across the centerline.

If you study the different lines from an bird's-eye view above the road you'll realize that the delayed apex line has its tightest, slowest part of the turn right after the point where you lean the bike. So, the delayed apex requires you to slow down more at the lean-in point. Slower speed means you can use more of the available traction for turning without increasing the risks of a slideout.

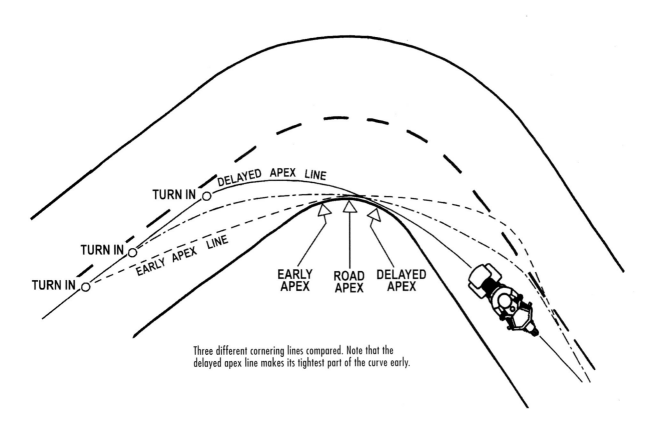

Three different cornering lines compared. Note that the delayed apex line makes its tightest part of the curve early.

You'll also notice that the delayed apex line straightens out more after the apex. That helps maintain more traction in reserve, giving you more options for changing your plan during the last half of the turn. For instance, if you're suspicious about that surface change ahead, you have more options for changing speed or line.

The temptation is to maintain speed when entering a corner and point the bike toward an inside line. But that requires you to make the sharpest part of your curve (and therefore the maximum lean angle) about two-thirds of the way around. The big problem with an early apex is that you may not realize you're pointed too wide until you're well into the turn. Then, when you suddenly find yourself going too fast, crossing the centerline, or running out of traction, you don't have a lot of options for corrective action.

A delayed apex line gives you more options for changing your plan during the last half of the turn.

Your cornering line also relates to your throttle and brake technique. If you lean into a turn while decelerating on a trailing throttle or dabbing at either brake (trail braking), you're consuming traction for braking that might be better spent on resisting slideouts. The smarter tactic for street riding is to slow while in a straight line, then get off the brakes and gradually roll on the gas as you carve through the turn. Rolling on the throttle helps stabilize the bike, and it happens to work very well with a delayed apex line that straightens out as you increase speed.

Trail braking is usually an attempt to help stabilize the bike. Racers may use front trail braking to help the bike turn more quickly. Trail braking is not the ideal tactic for normal curves, but there are situations in which you'll want to be braking while leaning. For instance, if the turn entry is a gradual sweeper, or downhill, you may want to trail brake all the way to the apex.

You might think it would be better to brake only on the rear, but remember that when heading downhill, there is more weight on the front, and therefore more traction on the front. If you're already on a trailing throttle, you're applying engine braking on the rear. So, trail braking on the front only helps balance braking between the two wheels.

Racetrack techniques are not wrong, but the public road is a different environment that requires different priorities. Out on the state highways, you're not going to have corner workers with warning flags or medics standing by to rescue you if you guess wrong.

Real World Observations

I've had a lot of opportunities to observe many different riders cornering. I won't name any names or publish any embarrassing photos, but too many riders don't really apex, or they apex too early or way too late. Many riders seem just to follow one car-wheel track all the way around a curve, not apexing at all. Some riders eventually cruise over toward the inside of the curve, but they move over so late that the advantages of the motorcycle line are lost.

Is it bad just to just follow one of the car-wheel tracks through a corner? Isn't it important to avoid crossing the grease strip that sometimes collects between the two

David L. Hough

Entering a downhill curve, you may need to trail brake all the way around.

wheel tracks? Well, cruising along in one of the car wheel tracks isn't "bad," but it does increase your risks out on those narrow highways in the country. And the grease strip is much less of a problem out in the country.

The car line consumes more traction and requires a sharper lean angle than the bike line for the same curve. Spilled oil or slick tar snakes aren't limited to the center of the lane. If your rear wheel steps out on a tar snake, you can quickly find yourself slipping sideways.

Also, following the left-wheel track puts the bike close to spots where oncoming drivers tend to wander over the line. Imagine yourself getting ticked by one of those big chrome mirrors of a motor home at a closing speed of 100 mph. And following the right-wheel track severely limits your view around blind right-hand corners. Approaching a right-hand curve, start your lean-in from the left side of the lane to provide a much better view of what's happening ahead.

Okay, add it all up. The delayed apex line maximizes traction, helps guide you away from potential collisions, and gives you a better view around blind turns. If you like those priorities, consider adopting the trendy delayed apex line yourself.

Tricks for Delayed Apexing

Let's consider some practical tactics for incorporating delayed apexes into your riding skills. First, get your eyes up and your brain thinking as far ahead as you can see. Even if you have quick reflexes, you'll need about one full second to make the bike do anything. At 55 mph, you're eating up about 80 feet per second. You need to be looking several seconds ahead, getting your approach to the next corner lined up when you still have time to make adjustments.

Remember that it's important to actually turn your head and not just swivel your eyes around. If you keep your chin pointed toward where you want to go and your eyes level with the horizon, you'll probably find it much easier to put the bike right where you want it to go. If you find that you get momentarily disoriented as you swivel your head around, then try moving your eyes first, and then following with your chin.

Once you've got the bike pointed toward your apex, you should already be looking toward the next corner and setting up for your next apex.

Visualizing your intended apex will help get the bike there.

David L. Hough

As you approach the turn-in point, quickly decide where you think the road apex might be, then mentally slide your intended apex a little farther around the corner. Imagine a nice sweeping line that curves gracefully from your turn-in point past that delayed apex. You don't have to focus on the exact location of your delayed apex because it's just a general area. Once you've got the bike pointed toward your apex, you should already be looking toward the next corner and setting up for your next apex.

As you point toward your next delayed apex, you should already be looking for the following one, which may be hidden behind a hill. Just imagine where it is, and that will help you point the bike in that general direction.

The most hazardous corners are those that tighten up more in the last half (decreasing radius turns). You know, that corner that keeps turning and turning as your brain wonders, *Where the heck is this road going?* Decreasing radius turns are especially dangerous for a rider in the habits of following the left-wheel track or apexing too early.

The best clue about where the pavement goes is your awareness of the opposite edge of the road. If the opposite edge of the pavement appears to be getting closer to the inside edge (converging), then the corner is probably still tightening up. If the opposite edge appears to be getting farther away (diverging), that's a good clue the curve is straightening out. Of course, the road unfolds in perspective, so the edges of the pavement always appear to converge, even on a straight section. It takes a bit of practice to judge whether the opposite edge is converging or diverging.

The opposite edge also gives you clues about camber (road slant). If you can see the opposite edge continuing around the turn, that's a good clue that the road is cambered to your advantage. If the opposite edge disappears, that's a hint the pavement slants the wrong way (off-camber), which in a left turn is especially hazardous.

If the opposite edge of the pavement appears to be getting closer to the inside edge (converging), then the corner is either tightening up or off-camber.

If you can see the opposite edge continuing around the turn, that's a good clue that the road is cambered to your advantage.

If the opposite edge disappears, that's a hint the pavement slants the wrong way (off-camber)

Cornering Performance

The best clue about your cornering performance is what happened in the last half of that last turn and the one before that. If you regularly find yourself snapping the throttle closed or dabbing at the rear brake while rounding a curve, it's a message that your cornering tactics need a little updating. The usual culprits are not looking far enough ahead, not slowing enough prior to turn-in, apexing too early, and not easing on the throttle all the way around.

If you practice the techniques and lines I've suggested, you'll probably discover that there are fewer panics. Controlled cornering isn't a matter of just wringing the throttle and trying to hang on. Rather, it's a result of the correct techniques at the right speeds and right times.

Before I get off this subject, let's note that a delayed apex line is just one pattern in your bag of riding skills, not the only one you'll ever need for all situations and every bike. For instance, a sweeping turn on a freeway doesn't require apexing. For all practical purposes, a sweeping curve is a straight line. Nor can you find a useful apex on a road that goes around in a circle, such as a freeway off-ramp, or a corkscrew parking garage.

If you are riding a cruiser with limited leanover clearance, you may prefer more of a V-shaped line in which you brake toward the point of the V, make a tight, slow-speed turn, and accelerate away from it. With the V-line technique, you slow way down, which allows you to turn the bike through a tighter radius over a shorter period of time; hence you're able to make a "quick" turn. A V-line really has two apexes: one early and one late. On the flip side, if you are riding a sport tourer, have a wide-open view of the corner, and there's no traffic, you can take a racing line with a midturn apex.

But for most of us riding those unfamiliar secondary roads with a lot of twists and blind turns, the delayed apex line is often the best ticket.

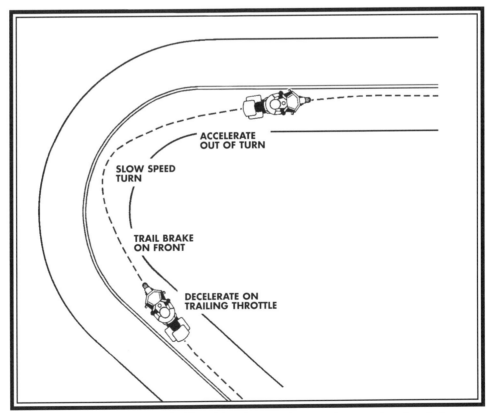

ACCELERATE
OUT OF TURN

SLOW SPEED
TURN

TRAIL BRAKE
ON FRONT

DECELERATE ON
TRAILING THROTTLE

The V-line is an acceptable technique for bikes with limited cornering clearance, cruiser ergonomics, or heavy loads.

Mastering the Throttle

More than a few riders have taken soil samples trying to negotiate strange turns. Downhill left-handers seem to cause the most problems. How and when you roll on—or off—the throttle has a lot to do with whether you make it around a corner or end up lifting your chin out of the dirt.

Back in the days when I was teaching motorcycle classes, the time came to get re-certified to teach the new curricula, which included the now familiar "slow, look, lean, and roll" cornering sequence. I really rebelled against the idea of teaching novice riders to roll on the throttle as they leaned over into corners. Surely, rolling on the gas while leaned over would cause people to run wide or slide out.

Up to that point, I'd believed only in decelerating toward the apex on a trailing throttle, making a quick turn, and accelerating away from the apex. That V-line technique allows a quicker, shorter turn at a slower speed. And it's still an acceptable technique for bikes with limited cornering clearance, cruiser ergonomics, or heavy loads.

The chief instructors eventually wore down my resistance to the concept of getting on the gas earlier in the turn. They talked about things such as stabilizing the suspension, managing traction, and making smoother lines. And while I was trying to make up my mind, they suggested that I'd teach the party line or else. While we were learning how to coach the new exercises, I gradually thought it through. Rolling on the throttle as you lean the bike does have some theoretical advantages. But if I was going to teach it, I needed to see whether the theories actually worked in real life or were just more officious techno-wackiness from the control freaks. Over the next week, I tried rolling on the throttle in corners and discovered that it does what the chiefs had promised.

So, ever since I got dragged, kicking and mumbling, into better throttle control, I've been preaching it myself. The technique is to decelerate in a straight line, then smoothly roll on a little throttle as you lean the bike over. You continue to ease on the gas all the way through the corner, accelerating toward the exit.

Rolling on the gas as the bike is leaned over accomplishes several things: First, it smoothes out the wobbles at midturn; second, it keeps the bike up on the sus-

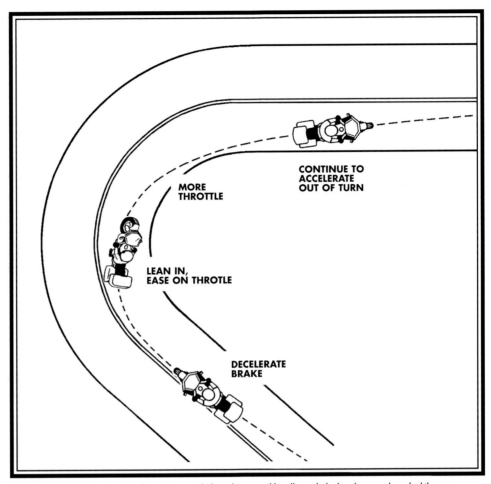

CONTINUE TO ACCELERATE OUT OF TURN

MORE THROTTLE

LEAN IN, EASE ON THROTLE

DECELERATE BRAKE

The ideal technique is to decelerate in a straight line, then smoothly roll on a little throttle as you lean the bike over.

pension and the weight better shared between the wheels; and third, it helps conserve traction. Put it all together, and it helps achieve a smoother, more predictable cornering line.

Smoothing Out the Wobbles

One of the disadvantages of the V-line is that you have to transition from decelerating to accelerating while you're getting the bike leaned. If you are decelerating toward the apex on a trailing throttle, you need to get back on the gas as soon as the bike is turned, and that transition from deceleration to acceleration while leaned over tends to make the bike wobble.

Remember that the tire contact rings shrink slightly in diameter as the bike leans over. The maximum diameter of a tire is at the center of the tread, as when the bike is straight up. Out toward the sidewall, the contact ring is smaller in diameter, which means the wheel needs to turn faster to maintain the same bike speed. That's one of the reasons rolling on the throttle while leaning produces a smoother turn.

But also be aware that rear wheel thrust and braking have different effects at different lean angles. When the bike is leaned over, the tire contact rings are off center from the bike. So, accelerating or braking will pull or push the bike more on the low side. And, of course, decelerating on a trailing throttle is applying engine braking to the rear wheel. The drag on the front wheel is also off center with the bike leaned over. So, trail braking on the front while leaned will have an effect on steering.

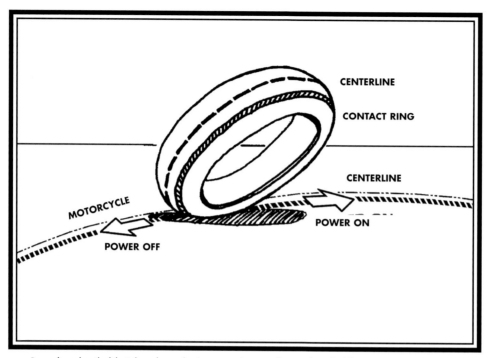

Remember, when the bike is leaned over, the tire contact rings are off center from the bike.

The point is that if you try to hold a steady throttle while leaning into a curve, the bike tends to wobble as the engine tries to synchronize with wheel speed. Rolling on the throttle slightly while leaning over keeps the engine pulling and the wheels turning at a more constant speed. It also maintains a steady push on the offset contact patches, which helps reduce wobbles.

One advantage of today's wide oval tires is that there is less difference in diameter between the straight-up contact ring and the leaned-over ring. Speed is more constant as the bike leans over. But the disadvantage of wider, lower-profile tires is that the push or pull leverage of the contact patches is farther from the bike centerline than with narrower tires. That's one reason hanging off in corners on a contemporary sportbike can have a greater effect than on an older bike with narrower tires.

Up on the Suspension

With most motorcycles, rolling on some throttle lifts the bike up on the suspension. It's most obvious at the front end, but the rear end typically rises, too. On chain drive bikes, the geometry of the swing arm pivot and transmission sprocket determines whether the rear end will lift or dive. But almost all motorcycles jack up both ends during acceleration. One exception is parallelogram rear ends (such as the BMW Paralever system) that resist either jacking or squatting.

Keeping the bike up on its suspension another inch or two not only increases leanover clearance, but it also gives the suspension a better chance to absorb bumps. For example, let's say your bike has 6 inches of suspension travel, and you've got it set up for 2 inches of sag. That leaves 4 inches of compression to absorb a bump, right? Well, at a 30 degree lean, that 4 inches of travel absorbs only a 3.3-inch bump, and at 45 degrees, maybe 2.8 inches. The farther over the bike leans, the less effective the same suspension travel.

Of course, as the bike leans over, a sharp bump will try to push the wheel straight up, not in line with the suspension. So, the farther over the bike is leaned, the greater the effect of bumps pushing the contact patches sideways.

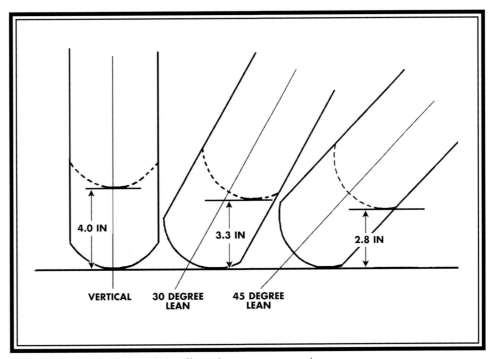

The farther over the bike leans, the less effective the same suspension travel

Front/Rear Weight Shift

Rolling on or off the throttle also shifts weight between front and rear wheels. Consider a straight-line wheelie, when the rider rolls on enough power to lift the front wheel off the surface. All of the weight of bike and rider has been shifted back onto the rear wheel. The wheelie is caused mostly by wheel traction pushing forward, and the mass of bike and rider resisting. But once the front wheel is up, the weight can be balanced entirely on the rear wheel.

Braking also causes weight shift from rear to front. Really hard braking can lift the rear wheel off the pavement—known in some circles as a stoppie. The big message for cornering is that rolling on the throttle transfers weight rearward, and rolling off the throttle transfers weight forward.

Traction Control

Leaned over in a corner, your big concern is traction. You'd prefer that the tires maintain their grip on the pavement to avoid a slideout. Now, remember that weight on a tire is a big factor in available traction. Since both tires have about the same traction, it might seem that a 50/50 weight distribution between the front and rear would be ideal. Some bikes are notable for almost perfect front/rear weight balance; others are biased toward more weight on the rear wheel.

The weight distribution is often determined by the configuration of the engine and drive train. For instance, a shaft drive typically places more weight on the rear wheel. Obviously, carrying a passenger places considerably more weight rearward. A chain drive and engine positioned across the frame typically results in weight bias toward the front wheel. The point is that the front/rear weight balance determines the traction relationship.

It's easy to forget that the engine provides braking as well as forward thrust. We realize the bike is slowing as we roll off the throttle, but we may not appreciate that decelerating on a trailing throttle applies engine (compression) braking through the rear wheel only. A lot of riders of lightweight sportbikes have been surprised by the rear end stepping out in a corner. And that's more likely in a downhill corner with the rider applying trail braking on the front, because applying front brake shifts weight forward.

Okay, rolling on a bit of throttle while leaned over helps keep the bike up on the suspension and maintains constant thrust on the tire, but wouldn't rolling on the throttle punch through the traction envelope? Remember that weight transfer. Unlike braking, rolling on the throttle shifts weight rearward, increasing available rear wheel traction.

Smoother, More Predictable Lines

If you think through all the theory, you can understand why throttle control in corners contributes to smoother, more predictable cornering lines. Rolling on a bit of throttle as the bike is leaned over helps stabilize the suspension, lifts the bike up to increase leanover clearance, distributes weight between the rear and front to maximize traction, and smoothes out the midturn wobbles. Hey, that's what we said back at the beginning, right?

Let's put it all together now and see how you can improve your cornering. Start the turn from the outside—the left side of your lane approaching a right-hander, or the right side of your lane approaching a left-hander. Roll off the gas, brake, and shift down as necessary to slow the bike to the desired corner-entry speed, and then get off the brakes. Keep your head and eyes up, looking as far through the corner as you can. Swivel your chin around to point exactly at your intended line, and keep your eyes level with the horizon. If you intend to hang off, get your weight shifted and your low, or inside, toe tucked in before you turn in, not while you're leaning the bike.

At the turn-in point, push the bike over with one smooth push on the low grip, and simultaneously ease on the throttle. Your goal is to be able to keep easing on a little more throttle all the way through the turn. As you lean the bike, keep your eyes level with the horizon. Point the bike—and your nose—at a delayed apex. At the apex, roll on more throttle, lift the bike up, and start planning for the next turn.

One steering input per curve is the ideal. Yes, you can make small adjustments to your line while turning, but every steering input eats up traction, which can become a precious commodity if you suddenly encounter a dribble of oil midway around the corner, or if the turn tightens up more than you had anticipated. Ideally, push the bike over toward your intended line with one precise push, and then stabilize it with the throttle.

Sweepers

The slow, look, lean, and roll technique works well for level corners and those with more-or-less constant radius. But it's not ideal for a sweeping turn with a gradual entry because there isn't an obvious point where you should be off the brakes and on the throttle. For such turns, you'll need to decelerate while also leaning toward the entry to the sharpest part of the curve. And at the turn exit, you'll need to be accelerating while turning.

The line for a sweeping curve is more like the V-line we discussed earlier. And rather than just rolling off the throttle and using compression braking to slow down, it can be helpful to trail brake on the front. Remember, there will be more front tire traction when decelerating. There is no single technique for trail braking that works for all curves, other than being smooth. Sudden transitions from deceleration to acceleration cause sudden demands on available traction.

What About Hills?

Riding down a steep hill, you'll probably round corners on a trailing throttle and add some trail braking. Trail braking on the front is much more predictable when pointed downhill because more weight is transferred to the front tire, and therefore there is more traction. If you are concerned about overbraking during downhill turns, brake while in a straight line, favoring the front brake, and then ease off the brakes for tight turns.

Going up a steep hill, there is a significant weight transfer to the rear wheel, and that reduces front wheel traction. During a steep uphill corner there is limited front wheel traction to turn the bike. And that's even more of a problem when you are carrying a heavy load or a passenger. To help carry the bike up and around the turn, don't slow down as much as you would for a level or downhill turn. A slightly higher speed maintains more kinetic energy to coast uphill around the turn, and you can roll on more throttle as the bike straightens out.

Camber

In right-handers, the crown of the road usually tilts the surface in the direction you want to go, but in a left-hander the surface is likely to be cambered the wrong way. That not only reduces leanover clearance but also reduces available traction on both wheels. So, when diving down a steep hill with a left-hander at the bottom, plan on braking harder to get speed down before you lean in. It's especially important to reduce speed while in a straight line when the surface has reduced traction.

It's especially important to reduce speed while in a straight line when the surface has reduced traction.

Throttle-Brake Transitions

Sudden control inputs such as snapping off the gas or slamming on the brakes can upset a bike. When you're riding aggressively, it's important to smoothly transition from throttle to brakes or brakes to throttle, and a smooth transition is especially important when the bike is leaned over in a turn. By "transition" I don't mean snapping the throttle off and then squeezing the brake, I mean easing off the throttle at the *same time* as you ease on the brake. I'll suggest a practice exercise to help you gain some smoothness.

Next time you find yourself on a straight section of vacant road, practice transitioning from throttle to brake to throttle as smoothly as possible. At a speed of 40 to 50 mph, ease the throttle closed as you squeeze on the front brake, then ease off the front brake as you roll back on the throttle.

I don't mean you should snap off the gas and then grab the brake lever. You should ease the throttle closed as you squeeze progressively harder on the brake, then ease off the brake as you roll back on the gas. Yes, this is difficult, but practicing this exercise will prepare you for smoother corner entries as well as limit those nasty wobbles if you have to change speed at midcorner.

So, What's Your Technique?

Next time you're out for a ride, think through how you are using the throttle during curves. If you consistently find yourself running wide halfway around a tight turn, that's usually a result of leaning toward the inside too soon. Concentrate on getting the bike way out toward the edge of your lane and slowed down before leaning it over, and then ease on the gas as you point it toward a nice curving line that kisses a delayed apex. In other words, go into a corner slower and exit faster than you're used to.

If you keep getting the urge to snap off the throttle halfway around, that usually means you didn't achieve a slow enough entry speed before leaning the bike. Concentrate on slowing down more before you lean until you can ease on the throttle all the way around. And, whether you're getting on the gas or rolling off, smoother is better.

Coming Unglued

My personal motorcycling hero from the good old days is Mike "The Bike" Hailwood. Mike is no longer with us, but in his prime back in the 1970s he could ride a motorcycle around the tricky Isle of Man circuit faster than anyone else. He knew the 37-mile course like the back of his hand and rode every race consistently, smoothly, and absolutely in control without ever hanging a knee off the bike. It was like Mike was glued onto the saddle.

Is hanging off a real advantage, or just a show-off gimmick?

Well, sports fans, times have changed. Today when you see road racers in action, they all hang off the bike toward the inside of turns. They hang off so far they actually slide their knees on the pavement, which is why they have plastic sliders (pucks) outside their leathers. You may have wondered whether hanging off is something the street rider should even consider:

What's so important about hanging off?
Is hanging off a real advantage or just a show-off gimmick?
Hanging off may be an advantage on the track, but is it a skill
I should use on the road?

In a nutshell, hanging off in turns can help stabilize the bike, reduce steering effort, and increase leanover clearance. If that's all you need to know about hanging off, skip the rest of this and go riding. But if you're curious about why it works, or if you'd like a little coaching on how to do it, get your head on tight and stay with us.

Front-end geometry and tire profiles contribute to the way motorcycles balance themselves. Sometimes we get strange feedback from the bike or find ourselves struggling for control. If you haven't yet studied the first *Proficient Motorcycling* book, or if you didn't really take the time to wade through the details, the rest of this might not make sense to you. If you find this confusing, we suggest you do a little homework and reread the Motorcycle Dynamics chapter in the first book.

One major difference between Mike Hailwood's style and that of today's road racers is that motorcycles have been refined. Let's consider tires, for instance. Back in the 1970s, motorcycle tires generally had round cross sections. Today's motorcycle tires are typically much fatter and wider, with oval-shaped profiles and more tractable rubber. Tire profiles, compounds, and belt patterns contribute greatly to what happens as a bike is leaned over into turns.

Today's rubber compounds offer better traction and better wear. The wider, flatter footprint puts more rubber on the road and bridges across surface problems such as grooves or cracks. The oval profile results in more consistent engine revolutions per minute (rpm) as the bike leans over. The tread pattern is carefully designed to allow water to squirt out from under the tire even with the bike leaned over. Steel cords in the tire carcass can be spaced to provide better braking stability and a more predictable loss of traction at maximum lean angles.

Tire Profile vs. Drag

One characteristic of a wider-profile tire is that as the bike leans over, the contact ring shifts farther toward the sidewall than with a narrow tire. What's important about that? Well, it affects steering. The axle pushes the front wheel down the road, but rolling friction drags the tire backward, down at the contact ring. As the bike leans over, the contact ring moves farther and farther from the centerline of the bike, and the drag on the tire has more leverage to pull the wheel toward the turn. In other words, a wide tire's drag steers the wheel more toward the turn as the bike is leaned over.

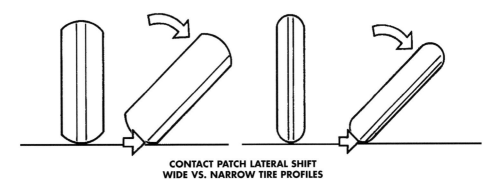

CONTACT PATCH LATERAL SHIFT
WIDE VS. NARROW TIRE PROFILES

A wider-profile tire shifts the contact patch farther to the side as the bike leans over.

Now, remember that a two-wheeler balances by countersteering. To lean the bike right, you momentarily steer the front wheel left, which forces the motorcycle to lean (roll) toward the right. Even if the rider isn't pushing on the grips, front-end geometry is usually designed so that the bike countersteers itself upright into a straight line. For instance, in a right turn, if the front tire steers itself more toward the right, the effect is that the motorcycle wants to roll itself upright, back into a straight line again.

If the motorcycle wants to straighten up from a turn, then the rider must maintain a slight pressure on the low grip to keep the bike leaned into the curve. Relaxing pressure on the low grip at the curve exit allows the front wheel to steer itself a little wider, rolling the bike back vertical again. And of course, rolling on the throttle helps push the bike upright, too.

A few motorcycles are engineered so well that they have almost neutral steering when leaned over, whether fast or slow. But most motorcycles don't meet that ideal, and even the great handling machines respond differently

If the front tire steers itself more toward the turn, the effect is that the motorcycle countersteers itself upright.

under different conditions. You may have noticed that sometimes your bike seems to hold a lean with only slight pressure on the low grip, and sometimes you've got to push hard on the low grip or even pull on the low grip to maintain the same line. What's going on?

Part of the answer is road camber. Consider a bike leaned over to the same angle in three different curves: one with positive camber, one with the pavement level, and one off-camber. Notice that the lean angle of the wheels is the same in all three turns, but the positions of the contact rings are quite different.

The difference in bike behavior is a result of the contact ring changing position. In the positive-camber turn, the contact ring is close to the bike centerline, side drag from the tire is minimal, and steering should feel neutral. If the pavement under the tires is level, there is a moderate amount of offset drag as the bike is leaned over, and a stronger push on the low grip will be necessary to maintain the same curving line. On the off-camber surface, the tire drags much more toward the inside of the curve, requiring a much stronger push on the low grip to keep the bike leaned over.

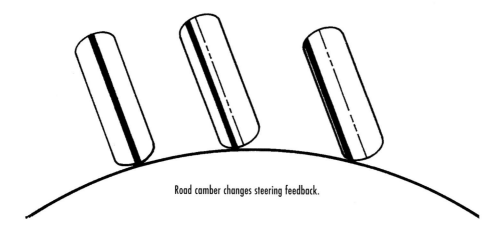

Road camber changes steering feedback.

Changing Road Camber

If you think about how roads snake up and down hills and around corners, it should be obvious that road camber is constantly changing. Even on a straight road, the surface may stagger from a left slant to a right slant and back again. Most of those twisty two-lane roads we like to ride have a crowned center to allow rainwater to run off, so where you position the bike in the lane makes a difference in the camber under your tires at any particular moment. If you follow my suggested delayed apex line, your tires will cross different cambers at different parts of the curve.

Back in the good old days, road camber didn't have as much effect because those old round-profile motorcycle tires didn't cause as much of a sideways shift in the position of the contact ring as the bike leaned over. There can't be much side drag on a tire that's only 3 inches wide. Dunlop even designed a trigonic front tire that had a triangular cross section more like a V than an O. The idea was to maintain the location of the contact ring close to the bike centerline right up to 40- or 45-degree lean angles. And with the harder rubber compounds available in those days, riders had to be pretty nervy to lean the bike over that far. Those few riders who were adequately nervy discovered that when the tire suddenly made contact on the flattish side of its tread, the bike developed some scary weaves and wobbles. If you're interested in photos of old British racing bikes, including Nortons that raced on trigonic tires, try the "Phantom Oiler" Web site at www.vintagenet.com/phantom.

But let's get back to contemporary bikes. Consider a sportbike leaned over into a curve, with the rider seated exactly on the centerline. The bike has its CoG, the rider has his or her CoG, and at any point in time the two have a combined CoG. With the rider sitting balanced in the saddle, the combined bike/rider CoG is close to the centerline. Gravity pulls the bike into a lean toward a curve, balanced against centrifugal force pulling outward. The rider controls balance and direction by slight adjustments in the position of the contact ring.

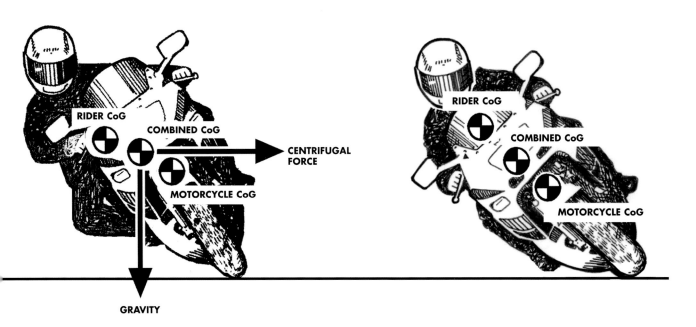

Hanging off shifts the position of the combined CoG, which allows the bike to corner at less of a lean angle for the same speed. With the rider's weight shifted toward the inside of the curve, the motorcycle itself won't have to be leaned as far as if the rider was balanced on the centerline of the bike for the same cornering speed.

Shifting rider weight to the inside of the saddle (hanging off) moves the bike/rider combined CoG to a slightly different position that allows the bike to follow the same curve at the same speed at less of a lean angle. It's obvious that the bike has more leanover clearance with the rider hanging off toward the inside. What's not so obvious, but just as important, is that moving the position of the contact ring changes steering feedback.

Let's say a rider sitting upright and centered has to maintain a strong push on the low grip to keep the bike leaned over. That means the front wheel wants to countersteer the bike upright. Or, to put it another way, the contact ring is too far from the centerline to allow the bike to stabilize at the desired lean angle. Hanging off moves the contact rings back toward center, reducing the self-countersteering effect. Hanging off doesn't change the traction equation, which means you don't increase the risks of a slideout by leaning your body to a different angle than the motorcycle.

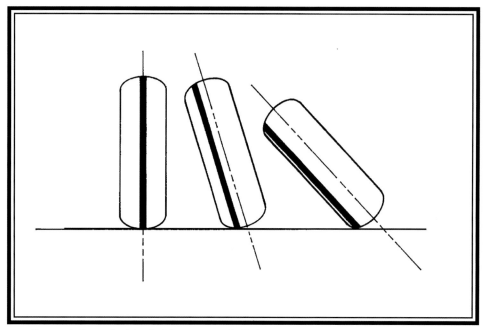

Changing the lean angle of the wheel changes steering feedback.

Getting Yourself Unglued

The first step in learning to hang off is to get unglued from the saddle. Many of us are paranoid about moving around in the saddle because we've noticed that wiggling around on a bike does strange things to the handling. The first place to start is to try some exercises with your bike. As with any practice exercises, you'd be smart to wear your crash padding and find some unused parking lot away from traffic.

Get the bike in a straight line at 25 or 30 mph and gradually lift your butt off the saddle by standing more on the footpegs. At first, balance your weight equally on both pegs. When that gets familiar, try loading your weight more on one peg and then on the other peg. To do that, you'll have to lean the bike away from the peg you're standing on. Remember, you control lean angle and direction by countersteering—to lean the bike left, push the grips more toward the left.

Once you're comfortable with standing on the pegs and shifting your weight around, try sliding your butt to one side of the saddle and riding along sitting on the edge of the saddle. Then shift your butt to the other side. Try sliding over farther and farther while holding the bike in a straight line. The trick to keep from falling off is to hook your outside knee against the tank. Shift your weight so smoothly that you don't wiggle the bike.

Now, practice making small steering corrections while hanging off both left and right. See if you can relax that death grip on the handlebars and make small steering inputs without pushing your body around or wiggling the bike.

Ergonomics

Of course, your ability to move around in the saddle depends on the ergonomics of your bike. For best control, you should be able to move your body around in the saddle independently of the handlebar grips. That means that most of your body weight should be balanced over the footpegs in your normal riding position, and your arms should be slightly bent reaching for the handlebar grips. If you have to brace yourself against the handlebars to move around or hold yourself on the bike, you will be making steering inputs whether you intend to or not.

There are a lot of bikes around with ergonomics that severely limit a rider's ability to move around or hang off while riding. For instance a cruiser with forward-mounted footpegs or floorboards will make it very difficult to lift your weight off the saddle. Some handlebars are so low or curve back so far that it's impossible to stand on the pegs and still reach the grips. Or the angle of the grips may be so awkward that you can't move out of your assigned seat without twisting your arms.

Touring and sport touring bikes tend to have footpegs, handlebars, and saddle arranged in a good relationship for control. But some touring machines have deep bucket saddles that pretty well lock the rider's butt into a single position. A comfy saddle may be great for the long haul in a straight line but limits your ability to control the bike in situations such as crosswinds or off-camber turns. You'll have to decide for yourself whether style or comfort is more important than better control.

On the Road

Assuming your bike has tolerable ergonomics that allow you to move around, it's time to go for a ride and try sliding your weight around in the saddle. First, try to feel what the bike is telling you as you negotiate a few turns. Is steering light and responsive while the bike is leaned over, or does it demand more and more push on the low grip as you increase cornering speeds and lean angles? Does the bike have a lot of leanover clearance, or does it make sparks if you try to corner too swiftly?

If your machine scrapes or bends things when you lean over too far or requires a lot of steering effort to hold your intended line, hanging off may be a helpful tactic. You may discover that hanging off a few inches makes a big difference, reducing steering effort and allowing you to follow a smoother line with less muscle input. And regardless of the good or bad manners of your machine, hanging off may be a smart idea for a severely off-camber surface or a steady crosswind.

Timing

If hanging off gives you easier steering and greater control, be conscious of when you shift your weight. Shifting your weight at the same instant you lean the bike tends to make the bike wobble because you're tugging on the grips to move around as well as countersteer. You want to get your body stabilized in the correct position for the turn before you get there. Approaching a left-hander, slide your weight to the left two or three seconds before the turn-in. Hook your right knee over the tank, get your left toe tucked in, and point your chin toward the turn as you lean the bike.

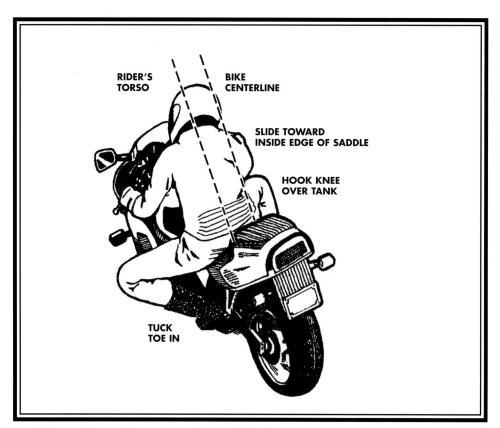

RIDER'S TORSO

BIKE CENTERLINE

SLIDE TOWARD INSIDE EDGE OF SADDLE

HOOK KNEE OVER TANK

TUCK TOE IN

Slide your weight toward the curve two or three seconds before the turn in.

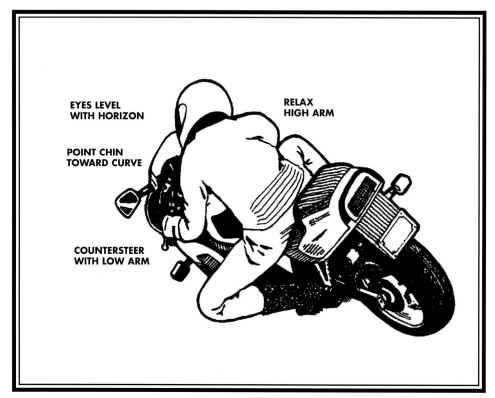

EYES LEVEL WITH HORIZON

RELAX HIGH ARM

POINT CHIN TOWARD CURVE

COUNTERSTEER WITH LOW ARM

You may find it helpful to steer with the "low" arm and relax your "high" arm.

David L. Hough

You may also discover that it's helpful to countersteer with your low arm and let your other arm relax. That helps avoid fighting one arm with the other. So, in a left turn, you'll be countersteering with your left hand, and your right elbow will be relaxed.

Two or three seconds before the turn exit, shift your weight back toward center, so that the bike is stable as you lift the bike up and accelerate. In an S-turn, shift your weight a couple of seconds before you lean the bike from one side to the other.

The point is, don't throw away better control of your bike just because your habits have you glued to the saddle. I suppose even Mike the Bike would be hanging off his machine these days if he were still around and riding a contemporary sportbike.

Countersteering vs. Bodysteering

Over the years, I have frequently suggested that countersteering is the primary way to cause a motorcycle to turn. It's called countersteering because you momentarily turn the front wheel opposite (counter) to the way you want to lean. Some riders call it push steering because you normally push on the left grip to turn left or push on the right grip to turn right.

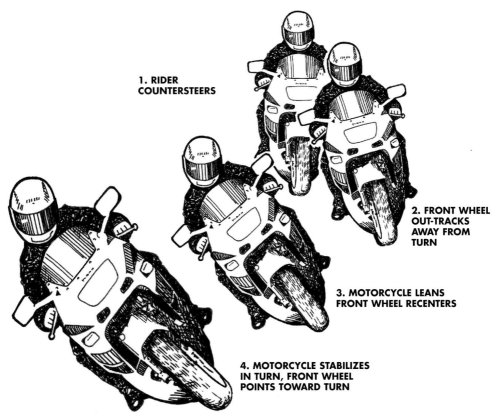

1. RIDER COUNTERSTEERS

2. FRONT WHEEL OUT-TRACKS AWAY FROM TURN

3. MOTORCYCLE LEANS FRONT WHEEL RECENTERS

4. MOTORCYCLE STABILIZES IN TURN, FRONT WHEEL POINTS TOWARD TURN

Countersteering is just the first step in the leaning process

The Leaning Process

Before we move on, let's make some observations about countersteering. Note that countersteering is just the first step in the leaning process—the momentary steering input needed to cause the motorcycle to start to lean. The front wheel contact patch shifts its position sideways, causing the bike to roll (lean) toward the turn. Once the bike is leaned toward the curve, the front end is allowed to re-center and then steer slightly toward the curve.

Let's think about how we move the front wheel contact patch sideways. Steering the front wheel slightly away from center causes it to roll off on a different track from the central mass of the bike. At road speeds, even a slight countersteering input results in the front contact patch quickly moving away from center.

That first countersteering action to get the bike leaned is followed by a second action to stabilize the bike at the desired lean angle. So, first you countersteer away from the curve to lean the bike, and then you steer the front wheel back toward center. Leaned into the curve, it may not be obvious from the saddle, but the front wheel and rear wheel don't follow the same lines. In a curve, the front wheel tracks outside the arc of the rear wheel. This is called out-tracking.

Bodysteering

You can also affect lean angle by shifting your weight on the bike, which is known as bodysteering. Bodysteering is applying pressure on the bike through your butt, knees, hands, and feet to cause the bike to steer itself into a new direction. Shift your weight to the left to turn left; shift your weight to the right to turn right.

Some riders believe they control mostly by countersteering. Others feel they control the bike primarily by bodysteering. Keith Code, track school guru and author of the book *A Twist of the Wrist* says, "Countersteering is the only way you can direct a motorcycle to steer accurately." But other equally famous track school instructors are adamant that they control the bike by bodysteering and that countersteering is of less importance. What's going on here? Do different race bikes perform differently? On our street bikes, should we lean the bike by countersteering with the handlebars—or by bodysteering with our butt, knees, and feet? Or is there some relationship between the two tactics?

Roger Racer is an experienced road rider, mechanic, and MSF-certified instructor. He also campaigns a race bike on the West Coast and occasionally teaches for one of the better-known track schools. I assumed that Roger, with his riding, racing, and teaching experience, would be able to offer some sage advice about how he combines countersteering and bodysteering. His answer surprised me. He explained that he used to countersteer, but one day on the racetrack he pushed so hard on the grips that he slid the front tire out and crashed. So, he stopped using countersteering and now feels that he only uses bodysteering.

I've had a few other serious conversations about how track schools deal with countersteering and bodysteering. Flyer Fred is an airline pilot and veteran motorcyclist who has gone to numerous track schools. Fred happened to stop by soon after attending a school where he had ridden on the back of a bike piloted by a famous bodysteering guru. During the classroom sessions, the instructor emphasized bodysteering, not countersteering, which Fred uses. Later in the course, each student was given the opportunity to ride as a passenger behind the instructor and Fred accepted. Watching over the guru's shoulder during turns, Fred could see him countersteering. Sure he leaned his body, but he also turned the handlebars.

Self-Countersteering

One hang-up with understanding countersteering is that the bike countersteers itself. It's important to recognize that the bike countersteers itself, because otherwise we might think our own pushes and shoves on the grips or footpegs are the only steering inputs.

Let's also note that countersteering isn't always a push on the low grip. Changing road camber, crosswinds, and speed all change the front end's dynamics. For instance, if you're leaned over into a left turn but not pushing on either grip, does that mean there is no countersteering going on?

If you're pulling on the low grip, does that mean you aren't countersteering?

Imagine yourself leaned into a right turn with the bike stabilized. If the bike wants to straighten up, you need to maintain a slight push on the low grip. But if the bike wants to keep falling over, you have to pull on the low grip to maintain your line. If you're pulling on the low grip, does that mean you aren't countersteering?

Perhaps the answers would be more clear if we defined *countersteering* in terms of what happens down where the rubber meets the road rather than up at the handlebar grips. Now, it should be obvious that the tire contact surface is a ring around the tire, not a single patch, but to simplify our observations, let's pretend that at any moment in time the only contact is the contact patch at the bottom of the tire. Let's define *countersteering* as steering the contact patch opposite to the way you want the bike to lean.

For example, let's say you're leaned over in a right-hander and the bike wants to keep falling over and turning tighter. It wants to lean *down*. You want it to lean *up* a little more. So, you maintain your line by pulling on the right grip, steering the contact patch slightly more toward the right. Are you countersteering? Sure, because you want the bike to lean more upright—toward the left, so you're steering the contact patch the other way—toward the right.

The point is, don't get hung up on countersteering having anything to do with left or right of center, or always feeling the same in all circumstances. Better-handling bikes such as the BMW R1150R or Ducati ST4s have almost neutral steering even when leaned over into a sharp turn. A well-balanced bike can maintain its own steady line in a curve with little or no additional input at the grips. And since steering consumes traction and changes stability, neutral steering is the ideal.

A bike that resists turning demands more traction. It requires a stronger push on the grips to keep it leaned over. And a bike that wants to fall over in turns is more confusing because you first push the grips toward the turn to initiate the lean, then push the grips away from the turn to keep the bike from falling over too far.

Leaned over into a turn but pulling on the low grip, the rider may perceive that steering toward the curve is what is causing the bike to turn, but the pull on the low grip is actually to counteract the bike's overenthusiastic cornering geometry. The rider may not appreciate that the pull on the low grip is countersteering to prevent the bike from falling over. The point is, even with a bike that has less-than-ideal geometry, the pressure on the grips is opposite (counter) to the desired lean angle and line. If the bike wants to fall down, he or she will need to countersteer it up.

This reaffirms that countersteering isn't just a matter of pushing on one grip but steering the front tire contact patch counter to the direction you want the bike to go, whether that takes a push or a pull on the grip and whether the bike is vertical or leaned over. All two-wheelers respond to countersteering, whether as a result of front-end geometry, rider input, or both.

Perception vs. Reality

There are some experiments you can do to help understand the relationship between countersteering and bodysteering. Next time you get your bike out for a ride you can try this for real, but for the moment let's think it through from your armchair. Sit in your chair the same way you sit on your bike, and reach for a pair of imaginary handlebars.

Pretend you are approaching a sweeping turn to the left and will be leaning the bike into the curve using only countersteering. Sit centered in the saddle and push on the left grip. The bike would respond by leaning left, so pretend to lean those handlebars over toward the left, leaning your shoulders along with the bike. When it has leaned far enough, relax your push on the grip, imagine the bars re-centering and the bike carving around the turn at a stabilized angle.

Now, same sweeping turn, but you're going to use bodysteering. Approaching the curve, shift your butt to the left, point your nose in line with an imaginary left mirror, tuck your left foot in, and press against the tank with your right knee. Careful, don't fall out of your chair! Just lean everything toward the left, including your shoulders, arms, and hands. Imagine the bike leaning left and carving around the turn.

Okay, now do the same sweeping turn, but this time focus on holding the grips absolutely straight. Shift your butt, push on your right peg, press against the tank with your right knee, and lean your torso toward the left mirror, concentrating on not moving the handlebar grips. When you try this experiment on a real bike, you'll probably discover that the bike is reluctant to lean if you aren't pushing the grips toward the turn.

Riders who believe they bodysteer are likely pushing the grips toward the turn without being aware of that input. Of course, with the handlebar grips positioned behind the steering axis, pushing both grips toward the turn is countersteering the front wheel away from the turn.

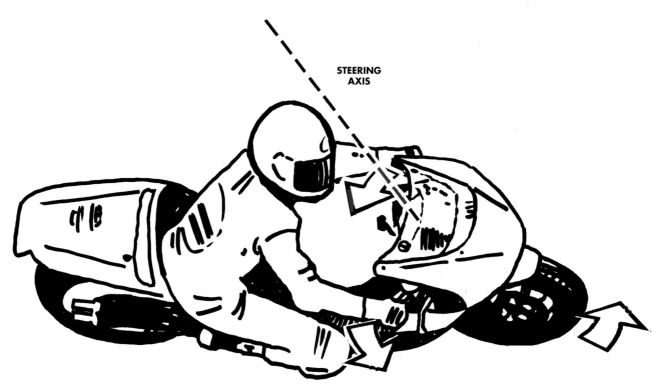

STEERING AXIS

Pushing both grips toward the turn is countersteering.

David L. Hough

The point is that if you just lean everything toward the turn while holding onto the handlebars, you are probably countersteering, whether you realize it or not. I suspect that riders who deny that they countersteer either don't realize they are doing it or don't define it as I have here.

I've also received reports from riders who felt they didn't have the muscle power to countersteer, but they could easily corner by bodysteering. That's not so much an affirmation of bodysteering, but a hint that some riders are unintentionally strong-arming the upper grip while trying to push on the lower grip in their attempts to countersteer. With one arm fighting the other, it seems as if they don't have enough strength to countersteer.

Bodysteering may be a useful psychological crutch for those riders who have difficulty with the idea of countersteering. By focusing on leaning everything toward the curve, the rider pushes both grips toward the turn and believes that the bike leaning is a result of the shift in body weight, not countersteering input through the grips.

Front-End Pivoting

When the bike leans into either a left- or right-hand curve, does the front end actually turn? Yes, it does. The actual movement is so slight that many riders do not perceive that the front end (front wheel, forks, etc.) actually does pivot away from center. At slow speeds it's more obvious. In a fast sweeper, it may seem that the front wheel points straight ahead and doesn't pivot at all as the bike leans. Even as you lean the bike into a tight turn, it may appear that you don't turn the front wheel off center, but the front end really is pivoting first to one side and then to the other, if ever so slightly. At highway speeds, just a slight change in the path of the front wheel results in considerable out-tracking of the front wheel, and that results in obvious changes in lean angle.

Race crews who have attached measuring devices to the front end of bikes report pivoting (front end turning left-right) up to 10 degrees going through a fast S-turn. On the street, you'll probably never exceed 4 or 5 degrees, but the point is that the front end does pivot. I bring that up because if the front end does pivot and steer toward one side, it should be obvious that the front wheel contact patch out-tracks away from the curve.

Pushing Forward or Down?

When you are pushing on the grips, should you push sideways, down, or forward? You can do a little experiment right now to draw your own conclusions. Hold one hand out as if gripping that imaginary handlebar again. Use your other hand to point a finger down toward the floor at an angle similar to the slant (rake) of the steering head on your motorcycle. Now, rotate your imaginary handlebars around that pivot axis. The grip pivots forward and up, or backward and down, correct? If this isn't obvious with imaginary handlebars, go out to the garage and try it on a real bike.

So, why does it feel on a moving bike that the grip moves down rather than forward when you push on it? Well, remember that the actual pivoting of the front end is only a degree or two, but the out-tracking of the front contact patch results in an obvious change in lean angle.

Grasp both imaginary grips again and try this: Pretend you're motoring along at 55 mph. Push on the right grip just a quarter of an inch, and imagine the bike leaning over a foot toward the right. What you're doing is rotating the grip slightly forward. What you perceive is the bike leaning over. It's not much of a stretch to believe that you are pushing the bike over by pushing *down* on the grip.

Don't worry about the actual direction of the push. It's acceptable to think in terms of pushing the grips toward the direction you want the bike to lean. Approaching a left curve, push the grips toward the left, and the bike will lean left.

It's okay to think that you are pushing the bike over by pushing down on the grip.

If you find it hard to control the bike by countersteering, think about what you're doing with your high arm. If you realize that you're "stiff arming" the high grip (say the right grip in a left turn) the suggestion is to steer with one hand and relax the high elbow. In other words, in a right turn, focus on steering with the right hand, while intentionally relaxing your left elbow. In a left turn, steer with your left hand, and relax your right elbow.

And if you're riding a cruiser with "feet forward" ergonomics, you're probably leaning back and pulling on the grips. Leaned back, you aren't really braced to push forward on either grip. So, imagine pulling both grips toward the turn. In other words, approaching a left turn, pull both grips toward the left. Or if you want to steer with one hand, use your right hand to pull the right grip toward the left (and relax your left elbow) to lean left. It's still countersteering, just a different way of thinking about it.

What About Bodysteering?

Yes, you can cause a bike to change direction just by bodysteering, hands off the grips. Now, we all know someone who can sit in the saddle hands off and steer a bike for miles and miles. Some can even take a bike through an S-turn hands off. Such examples might appear to be proof that countersteering isn't required. But remember that a bike countersteers itself, and small changes in balance causes a bike to steer slightly off center.

More importantly, bodysteering by itself doesn't provide very forceful or accurate steering. There may be someone out there who can make a tight U-turn or figure eight with hands off the grips, but most of us find that trick incredibly difficult and not very useful for day-to-day riding.

The effect you will have leaning your body depends on the weight relationship between you and the bike. A heavy rider on a lightweight bike is able to shove the bike into a different line just by throwing weight to one side or the other. A lightweight rider on a heavy bike may not have much success changing direction just by bodysteering. The bike may just wobble to one side and then straighten up again.

The real point of bodysteering is to fine-tune steering feedback. If steering isn't neutral, you can adjust feedback by shifting your weight in the saddle. For instance, if your bike requires a strong push on the low grip to hold a turn, you might make steering more neutral by hanging off slightly toward the turn.

David L. Hough

I also might suggest that with the proliferation of surface hazards on most roads, riding hands off potentially increases the risks. For instance, if the front wheel happens to encounter a groove in the pavement, the bike may go into a sudden side-to-side oscillation (speed wobble) trying to correct itself. Accurate control of the bike under both normal and emergency situations requires countersteering via the grips.

The bottom line is that bodysteering has an effect, but countersteering is the most powerful input. My suggestion is to use countersteering as the primary technique for accurate, forceful steering control and bodysteering as fine-tuning the steering feedback. Next time you're out for a ride, try the experiments I've described and see if you agree.

Feeling the Bike

When you first learn to ride, you've got your hands full figuring out how to balance, shift gears, and avoid surface hazards. That's why the advice offered to novice riders in training courses reflects a somewhat simplistic view of motorcycling life. As you gain experience, alternate tactics reveal themselves. For instance, a new rider may be advised to ride with the headlight on high beam to be more visible to other drivers. After a few years of riding—and perhaps a few close calls—most of us outgrow such simplistic advice and move up to more comprehensive tactics such as adjusting our position to maximize the view, predicting what errant drivers are going to do, and getting out of the way.

Controlling the motorcycle has a similar growth process. We start out learning how to get a bike rolling without stalling the engine and how to make turns from a stop without running outside the painted lines or dropping the bike. After a few years, we figure out how to make cornering lines that demand less traction, roll on the throttle while leaned over, and avoid rear-end skids during quick stops.

One big step in becoming a proficient motorcyclist is learning to recognize what your bike is telling you. Feedback through the handlebar grips provides a measure of what your tires are doing. Feedback through the seat of your pants can tell you how the suspension is working. Strange noises or vibrations can be a signal that a mechanical problem is developing.

Most riders just rest their hands on the grips, but don't perceive whether the grip is pushing back on their hand. When you learn to feel what's happening, sud-

denly you get new input on what the bike is doing. With practice, you'll begin to detect feedback through the seat, footpegs, and handlebar grips. For instance, you may suddenly realize that your bike requires constant pressure on the low grip to maintain your cornering line. Or perhaps you realize that with the bike in a straight line, it always wants to ease to the left.

The point is to learn to feel what the bike is telling you. There are no right answers here because every corner and every bike is different, and even the same bike may give different feedback at higher or lower speeds. The selection of tires, direction of turn, camber of the road, and even the horizontal position of your swing arm all cause the bike to behave in a certain way. The only right answer is to correctly figure out what the bike is telling you at that moment so you can better control it.

How do you support your weight on the bike?

Steering

If you haven't really paid attention to your palm pressure on the grips, you may be surprised at how much subtle feedback you can get once you focus on what your hands are doing. While cornering, do you favor one hand for steering or do you push on one grip while pulling on the other? As the bike leans over, can you feel the subtle change in grip pressure as you stabilize the bike in the corner?

Does the bike balance itself exactly in a lean, or do you have to hold pressure on the grips to hold your line?

What are you doing with the handlebar grips while turning a corner? Do you lean over onto the low grip and relax your other arm? Do you push both grips toward the turn? Or do you pull both grips toward the turn?

How do you support your weight on the bike? Is almost all of your weight supported on the saddle, or do you support your weight partially on the footpegs and handlebars? Do you sit upright in the saddle; do you lean forward, supporting your torso on the handlebars; or do you lean back, pulling on the grips? Do you just rest your feet on the footpegs or floorboards, or do you push down to change balance? Do you put more weight on one foot than the other? Do you let your knees hang out in the breeze, or do you press your knees against the tank?

Riding Experiments

Your assignment is to take your bike out for a spin and try to feel what it's telling you. If you're not comfortable trying experiments while you're riding your bike down the road or sliding your butt around in the saddle that's okay—wait a few more years until you're ready. For those who are ready, it's time to analyze what your bike is telling you. First, try some straight-line experiments, then find a twisty road and see if you can figure out what your bike is telling you about corners. Here are some experiments to try and questions to ask yourself about your riding:

1. **Riding down a straight, level road does the bike steer exactly straight ahead, or does it keep trying to curve left or right?**
2. **Is steering rock steady, or does the bike weave slightly? Does the rear end steer the bike left or right when you accelerate and decelerate?**
3. **Approaching a left-hander, sit on the absolute centerline of the bike, rest both feet equally on the left and right footpegs, rest both hands equally on the left and right grips, and lean the bike into the turn. As it settles into a stable arc, feel the feedback from the grips. Is steering so stable that you can guide the bike with your hands barely touching the grips, or do you need to hold pressure on the grips to maintain your line?**
   If steering isn't neutral, do you need to pull on the low grip to keep the bike from falling over farther? Or do you need to press on the low grip to hold your line?
4. **Try the same experiments in a right-hander. Does the bike give you the same feedback in right turns as in left turns? Or does this particular machine corner differently in left and right turns? For instance, do you need to hold pressure on the low grip in a right-hander but pull on the low grip in a left-hander?**
5. **Approaching a left curve, intentionally shift your butt toward the left side of the saddle (hang off left). Get the bike stabilized in the turn and see how hanging off changes the feedback. With the bike leaned over in a left curve, does steering get lighter, or do you have to push even harder to hold your line? Try hanging off to the right when approaching a right-hander and see if steering feedback is any different.**
6. **Now, approaching a left curve, intentionally shift your weight to the right side (the high side) and push down on the right footpeg to place more weight on the peg and less on the saddle. Does that make steering easier or harder?**
7. **If you have access to a different bike, swap to the other one, and try the same experiments on the different bike, in both left-hand and right-hand curves.**

If you discover that your bike needs a strong push on the low grip to maintain a cornering line, you may also observe that hanging off toward the inside makes steering more neutral. Being aware of steering feedback is more than a curiosity. As you figure out what the machine is telling you in various situations, you can try some fine-tuning to adjust what's happening.

If you're concerned about absolute traction, remember that the more pressure you apply on the grips, the more traction is being consumed for balancing and steering. If your bike has some strange quirks, think about what you could do to improve handling.

Suspension

Suspension performance has a lot to do with traction control. In a nutshell, if your bike's suspension can't keep the rubber on the road, you can't maintain control. If you haven't been listening to your suspension lately, it's time.

Take your bike for a spin, find a rough road for a test track, and try to feel what the suspension is doing. Does the suspension soak up dips and bumps easily, or does the bike buck and bounce? When you hit a dip, does the suspension hold the bike reasonably level, or does it bang down to the stops? Do bumps or dips cause the front end to bounce up and down? On a rough road, do you hear strange gurgling, clanking, rattling, or squeaking sounds from the front end or rear shocks? Do the front forks compress smoothly, or do the sliders move in a sequence of jerks and stops? When the suspension extends, does it clang up against the top, or does the damping work quietly all the way to the limits? If your suspension isn't doing its job, you should try to tune it up.

While novice riders might not understand why it is necessary to set up the suspension on a brand-new bike, veterans know that different riders and different riding styles each require a different suspension setup. Small adjustments can result in big changes in handling. If you've been avoiding the suspension setup clinics for fear they are too technical, it's time for a reality check. If you're serious about your riding, you need to be serious about suspension maintenance and setup. Track schools typically include suspension setup. If you get the opportunity to attend a suspension setup seminar, take it.

If you're serious about your riding, you'll be serious about suspension setup.

Ideally, your suspension preload should be set to hold the bike up in the top two-thirds of suspension travel with your weight on the saddle. The forks and shocks should compress smoothly with no strange noises and absorb both bumps and dips without pitching the bike up and down.

That steering feedback I talked about earlier is also related to suspension setup. For instance, a bike that is reluctant to turn might be improved by dropping the triple clamps on the fork tubes a few millimeters or increasing rear shock preload. If you have discovered that your favorite bike requires you to keep pulling on the low grip during a corner to prevent the bike from falling over too far, you might help neutralize steering by raising the triple clamps on the fork tubes or changing to a front tire with a slightly wider profile.

If your suspension is worn out or in need of servicing, it's time to take care of that. Original equipment shock absorbers are built on a budget. Most original equipment shock absorbers are sufficiently worn by 20,000 or 30,000 miles so that they no longer perform adequately. By listening to your suspension, you should be able to figure out how to make it work better for you.

Brakes

Brake performance changes so gradually that you may not realize it has degraded. But if your brakes aren't working properly, you can't expect to do quick stops, let alone make smooth throttle-brake transitions.

You should be able to squeeze firmly without the lever contacting the grip.

First, before you even start the engine, feel your brakes for air bubbles. Squeeze the lever very hard and feel for sponginess. The lever should feel firm—not rubbery—when the brake is fully applied. You should be able to squeeze firmly without the lever contacting the grip.

The rear brake should also feel firm. If either brake feels spongy, it's time to bleed the system before you're ready to do any road tests. If any caliper won't release instantly, it's a hint the calipers need a rebuild and the brake lines need to be flushed. Squat down with a flashlight and check your brake pads for wear. You should be able to see a wear-indicator slot in the middle of each pad. If the friction material is worn down to the bottom of the slot, it's time to replace the pads.

With your brakes checked and serviced, try some normal stops using both brakes. When applying the brakes lightly, listen and feel for any irregular braking. Even brand-new brake disks may be warped or have high spots. When braking, does the front end wiggle from side to side? That's an indication that one or both discs are warped or have high spots. Screeching brakes are a symptom of glazed brake pads, imbedded debris, missing parts, or a corroded caliper piston.

Chassis

At highway speeds, it's important for the wheels to track true. Weaves, wobbles, or vagueness in steering are symptoms of problems, from misadjusted or notched bearings to broken parts.

If the rear wheel is not in line with the front wheel, you can expect strange steering. With chain-drive bikes, check wheel and sprocket alignment carefully. The marks stamped on the chain adjusters are seldom accurate, so don't be bashful about getting down on the ground and sighting between front and rear tires. And for bikes with the engine/swing-arm rubber mounted in the frame, it is important to align the rear wheel with the front wheel. With shaft drive machines, it may be possible to adjust the swing-arm pivots to better center the wheel or to improve balance.

Steering head bearings are often overlooked because they are hidden from sight. But ball or roller bearings that are adjusted too loosely will pound tiny dimples (notches) into the races from repeated road shocks. And because the steering head bearings rotate only a few degrees, the dimples form in the same radial locations. The notching makes accurate steering difficult because the bearings don't turn smoothly.

To feel for loose or notched steering head bearings, support the front wheel off the ground. Grasp the front wheel facing back at the bike and try to jerk the front forks back and forth in the steering head. A clunking sound from the bearings or looseness in the bearings means it's time for adjustment and possibly replacement.

Notched steering head bearings result in vague steering.

With the front wheel off the surface, it takes only a moment to check the wheel bearings. Spin the wheel and listen for any clicking, rattling, or grinding. Then face the wheel from the side, grasp the top and bottom of the tire, and yank alternately on the top and bottom to check that the bearings do not have any free play.

After you've checked the front end, jack up the rear wheel and check the swing arm and wheel bearings. If your wheel, steering head, or swing-arm bearings are not exactly right, it will be difficult to diagnose steering feedback or suspension setup.

Frame

Motorcycle frames sometimes fail. If the motorcycle weaves from side to side or wobbles when leaned over, examine the frame for cracks or loose connector bolts. Cracks are more likely to occur adjacent to welds. A crack in a steel part typically shows traces of a cinnamon-colored powder: rust. Cracks in aluminum may show traces of black colored powder: aluminum oxide. While you're looking over the frame, check every major nut and bolt, especially fork pinch bolts, axle nuts, and shock fasteners. Bolted frame joints that have become loose exhibit that vague steering feedback.

Be aware that mass-produced frames are not all alike. It's also possible to bend a frame during a seemingly minor accident. If your bike develops odd tire wear patterns or unbalanced handling, the solution may become apparent with a detailed measurement of the bike's frame geometry. There are companies, such as G.M.D. Computrack, who specialize in measuring and straightening motorcycle frames.

It's a good idea to check your machinery before a ride, but it's also important to feel what's happening as you ride along. If you get the same feedback over many miles, you may just becoming aware of how a particular bike handles, or getting a hint from the bike that some minor adjustments are needed. But if you feel a sudden change in handling, that's a warning message from the bike to you that you need to stop and find the problem before it turns into a disaster.

Getting Your Head

in the Ride

CHAPTER 8

GETTING YOUR HEAD
IN THE RIDE

Riding Systems

Different Strokes for Different Folks

Commuter Kenny

Commuter Kenny fires up his bike and zooms off toward work. Kenny was up into the wee hours last night partying with some friends, and he is running a little late this morning. But he's familiar with this road, and he knows he can make up some time if he pushes a little. He accelerates hard around the familiar right-hander and pushes hard on the left grip to lean the bike aggressively into a tight left-hander beneath the towering fir trees.

Just as the motorcycle leans hard left, there is a sudden incomprehensible banging, screeching, grinding noise, and the rear end starts sliding off toward the shoulder. Kenny instinctively snaps the throttle closed and steers hard right to try to control the slideout. But the rear tire hooks up with the pavement again, snapping the bike into a high side flip and catapulting Kenny off the saddle. Unfortunately, his flight is cut short by the base of a monstrous and immovable tree.

Kenny survives, but in the year it takes for his fractured leg to heal, he loses all interest in motorcycling. Kenny's accident resulted from a trivial error made during his hasty departure—he left his sidestand down. When he leaned the bike into the left-hander, the sidestand prevented the bike from leaning over far enough to make the turn.

If we wished to be charitable, we could say that a design flaw in the motorcycle caused Commuter Kenny's final motorcycle accident. He's not the only rider who has crashed because of an extended sidestand. That's why most motorcycle manufacturers now incorporate safety devices such as starter lockouts or spring-loaded retraction to help us avoid riding away with the stand extended. But there are a lot of other things that can go wrong while motorcycling, and manufacturers can't design for each case of rider carelessness or inattention.

Let's be less than charitable and suggest that Kenny's attitude was probably a leading contributor to the crash. You see, Kenny is one of those people who prefers to take life as it happens rather than plan it out ahead of time. As a motorcyclist, he wasn't interested in studying the boring details about collisions or edge traps or traction management. He wasn't the least interested in reading safety stuff or submitting to rider training. He just hopped on the bike and did whatever felt right at the moment.

Captain G

Captain Geoff (a.k.a. Captain G) is at the other end of the spectrum from Kenny. As an airline pilot, the captain learned to follow strict drills and checklists for every phase of flight to make sure he forgot nothing.

On a couple of occasions, the captain and his wife have flown in to borrow my old BMW airhead for motorcycle trips around the Northwest. That machine had a small panel with light switches and circuit breakers scrounged from surplus airplane parts. Recognizing the old airplane switches, Captain G got a kick out of following a cockpit-style starting drill on the Beemer, calling out the memory items as if they were part of a checklist:

Ignition key: Inserted.
Ignition: On.
Gloves: On.
Fuel tap: On.
Choke: Set.
Sidestand: Up.
Gearbox: In Neutral.
Neutral light: Green.
Kill switch: To Run.
Starting number one.
Headlight: On.
Taillight: On.

Captain G followed this starting drill as a bit of humor, but, funny or not, the advantage of a drill (a set of memorized steps) is that everything gets done in a logical sequence, and nothing gets forgotten. Captain G is less likely to forget something important, such as leaving the sidestand down. He seems to have just as much fun as Commuter Kenny ever did, and what's more, the captain is still riding motorcycles twenty years after Kenny hung it up.

The major problem with a bump-and-feel rider, such as Kenny, is that a lot of motorcycling hazards aren't obvious. Let's say you are making a fast transit across Montana, and you pull off I-90 for lunch. You haven't encountered cattle guards before, so it doesn't register that the cattle guard on the exit ramp drastically reduces traction right where you need to brake for the stop sign. You brake, and suddenly you're sliding down the asphalt on your face. You may not understand what caused the crash until you take a close look at the hazard, in this case half shiny steel and half air.

A motorcyclist has a lot of things to think about while motoring down the road. The situation continuously changes, demanding changes in speed, position, lean

If you haven't encountered cattle guards before, it may not register that the shiny steel drastically reduces traction right where you need to brake for the stop sign.

angle, or direction. Veteran motorcyclists seem to develop riding skills of a higher order, including an apparent sixth sense of being able to predict what is going to happen before there are any obvious clues. The veterans also seem to have instinctive responses to the changing conditions.

There is no magic in this, but rather a well-honed set of skills and habits. For example, consider the situation of a motorcyclist who gets stuck in the wrong lane approaching the planned exit from a freeway. A bump-and-feel rider such as Kenny is likely to do whatever is necessary to make the exit, even if that means an impulsive dive across two lanes of aggressive traffic. A veteran such as Captain G is more likely to forget that exit and change plans, concentrating on an alternate route to the same destination. The habit of not doing anything impulsive in traffic helps avoid close calls with vehicles that suddenly come out of nowhere.

If you could chart all the detailed events leading up to a typical accident, it would become apparent that at some point in the sequence the rider made an error that subsequently allowed the situation to deteriorate beyond his control. The mistake may be not understanding a certain surface hazard, forgetting to check the mirror, or not noticing a truck about to pull out of an alley.

Riding Strategies

Another way to help focus on important details is to use what the experts call a strategy. The MSF uses several accident avoidance strategies, including the well-known SIPDE: search, identify, predict, decide, and execute. Another strategy is the Smith System used in truck driver training.

The Smith System:
1. Aim high in steering.
2. Get the big picture.
3. Keep your eyes moving.
4. Leave yourself an out.
5. Make sure they see you.

If it isn't obvious, the primary way to avoid accidents is to remember all the details so you don't make a mistake. Those of us who are more like Commuter Kenny, getting through life by bump and feel, might feel uncomfortable with the concept of trying to use riding systems. Others become better riders by comparing their riding habits to a logical plan. If you want to become more proficient, you need to be more like Captain G and less like Commuter Kenny.

Commentary Driving

One way to maintain your awareness of the details is to describe what's happening to yourself out loud. The British call this commentary driving. It might go something like this:

Green light, watch for cross-traffic, first gear, accelerate, shift up, shift up. Bus ahead, expect to pull out, check mirror, possible lane change left. Bicyclist ahead. Move over. Oncoming car could turn left into parking lot, cover brake, shift down, check mirror for tailgaters. Look out, streetcar track ahead, swing wide and cross at angle, pedestrian stepping into street, squeeze brake lightly. Check mirror, cab moving up fast, change lanes to get out of the way. Ease over to left to avoid sunken drain grate, signal light changing, shift down, shift down, stop. Check mirror.

It may sound silly to be talking to yourself, but it can be a useful check on your observation and planning. You've got to be concentrating and thinking ahead to describe what's happening. You probably wouldn't talk yourself through several hours of riding, but you might discover that a few minutes of commentary driving once in a while helps you improve your awareness. And if you find yourself fatigued or in aggressive traffic, talking yourself down the road can be a definite advantage.

The British System

Motorcycle police officers in Great Britain use a strategy that they call The System of Motorcycle Control. I'll refer to it as the British System here. At first blush, the British System seems a bit quaint and repetitive, maybe just the ticket for an aging Birmingham gentleman motoring through Lyme Regis on a 348 cc Royal Enfield Bullet. But this system has been used at the Metropolitan Police Driver Training School at Hendon, a school with a reputation for turning out some of the best motorcycle riders in the world. And the same system is used by the Institute of Advanced Motorists, whose members must all pass a ninety-minute driving or riding test in traffic while being scrutinized by an officer on a separate bike.

The system is a drill, or set of steps, that is accomplished in sequence when approaching any hazard:

1. Select course
2. Look behind, signal, adjust speed
3. Change gear
4. Look behind again and signal again
5. Use your horn
6. Look behind again
7. Maneuver and accelerate

The System of Motorcycle Control (the British System) is the basis for what is called roadcraft, the science of becoming an accomplished motorcyclist. The implication is that motorcycling is a craft worthy of mastering, not simply a fun thing you attempt by bump and feel.

Riding a motorcycle in England, Scotland, or the Isle of Man demands considerably more attention than it does in most parts of North America. Traffic is dense

The Ten Commandments of Motorcycling

1. Perfect your roadcraft. Good roadcraft means being less stressed as well as avoiding awkward or dangerous situations. Be courteous and acknowledge courtesy to you. Never be provoked.
2. Ride deliberately. Think clearly and ride decisively. Overtake quickly but safely so the road is left clear for other traffic.
3. Develop bike sense. Know your own limitations. Know your bike and treat it sympathetically. Ride smoothly so as to reduce wear and tear.
4. Use your horn, signals, and lights sensibly. Aggressive use of the horn is as bad as never using it at all. Give good, clear signals. Use your headlight in poor daylight conditions.
5. Concentrate. Total concentration is the key to good riding. It improves control and ensures that nothing is missed or misunderstood.
6. Think first and then act. A good biker never rides automatically. Every hazard is different and needs to be thought through in plenty of time to negotiate properly.
7. When in doubt about passing, hold back. Keep your distance until it is safe to overtake, and don't cut in too quickly.
8. Corner safely. Safe cornering means being fully aware of the forces at work on your bike, and applying correct cornering principles.
9. Use speed intelligently. Never go faster than you need to. The speed limit is not the same as safe speed.
10. Know and obey the highway laws.

If the British System works in such an intense environment as London traffic, we ought to be able to glean some insight from it for riding in the U.S.

and aggressive in Great Britain. The national speed limit is 70 mph on main highways, and it is common to ride well over the "double nickel" even on the narrow B roads, where the trees, hedgerows, and stone walls are right at the edge of the pavement. If the British System works in such an intense environment, we ought to be able to glean some insight from it for riding on this side of the "pond."

The British System is a set of deliberate actions that can be used when approaching any situation, including both normal maneuvers and hazards. At first, practicing a sequence of decisions and actions while riding may seem overly complex. But once the process has been practiced a few times, the decisions and actions become a simple habit.

Note that the British ride on the left side of the road. To help explain the British System in North American terms, I will convert the British descriptions of maneuvers from the left side of the road to the right side. To see how a rider uses the system, let's apply it to perhaps the most dangerous maneuver on a North American road: a left turn.

1. Select course. You've considered the risks of a left turn across traffic but have decided you can do it with reasonable safety. Obviously, a left turn is a lot safer where there is a left turn lane or when traffic is less dense. Your course includes your position within your lane, moving toward the left-wheel track to make your intentions more obvious or to avoid the grease strip in the center.
2. Look behind, signal, adjust speed. Look behind you to see if the traffic will allow you to slow and make a turn. If a truck is bearing down on you, you don't want to be in the way. If traffic allows a turn, signal your intentions, not merely because it's the law but because it's to your advantage to help other drivers understand what you intend to do. Unless there is a separate left turn lane, adjust your speed to complete the turn through a break in opposing traffic without stopping. It would be unwise to come to a stop in an unprotected traffic lane to wait for a break in traffic.
3. Change gear. Change gears to match your speed (in this case, shifting down as you decelerate) so that the engine is capable of accelerating at any time during the maneuver.

David L. Hough

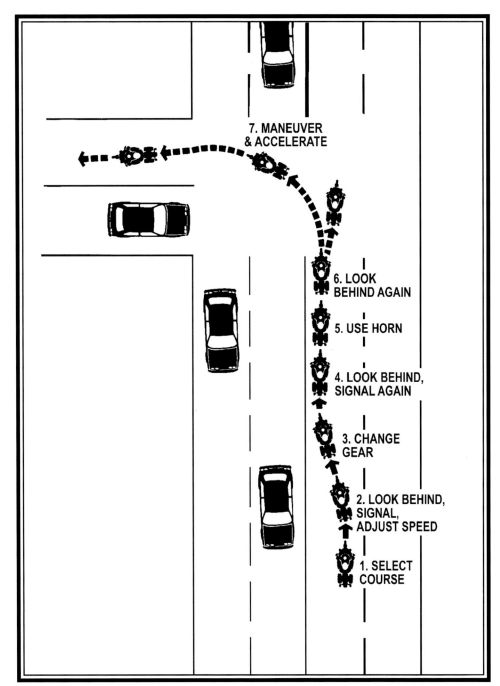

The British System may seem overly complex, but it's one way of remembering all the important steps.

4. Look behind and signal again. While you are slowing and shifting down, look behind you again to check whether the traffic is also slowing. Consider signals, such as a hand signal or flashing your brake light, in addition to your turn lights to reinforce your intentions.

5. Use your horn. If it would help to make others aware of your approach, especially pedestrians, sound your horn politely.

6. Look behind again. Just before you begin your maneuver, look behind one last time to check that the traffic has reacted to your signals and slowed, and that no one is on a collision course. This is your last chance to decide whether to complete the maneuver or abort it.

7. Maneuver and accelerate. Assuming the path is clear, keep the bike under steady power through the turn to maximize traction. As the turn is completed, smoothly accelerate back to an appropriate speed for traffic and surface conditions.

This same system applies to other maneuvers, including riding straight through an intersection, stopping for a traffic signal, negotiating intersections, and passing other vehicles. Depending upon the maneuver, some of the steps may be ignored or emphasized.

The View Ahead

Looking

Notice that the British System doesn't include specific steps to search the road ahead. It's assumed that you are already looking way ahead to select a space between oncoming cars, watching for traffic, and allowing adequate space behind other vehicles. As you ride through a busy neighborhood, look for clues about what's happening. Look through car windows, over fences, down alleys, under trucks, and behind hedges. Sometimes small clues are your only warning of problems.

Quick looks behind you are important, especially when slowing down in traffic, because the focus tends to be on what's ahead rather than on what's happening behind us. If the drivers behind you don't seem to be reacting to your signals, you could decide on a new course and start the process over again.

But What Can You See in Your Mirrors?

Maybe you can't see as much in your mirrors as you think you can. Does your motorcycle have blind spots? It can be educational to check the field of view in your mirrors. The best way to do this is to enlist the help of another rider and do the check while parked. Sit astride the machine as you would if you were riding and have your buddy try to move to a position where you can't see him. If you can't see as well in your mirrors as you thought you could, consider repositioning your mirrors or changing to different mirrors. Using bar end mirrors is one answer to your rear view being blocked by your arms or shoulders. Even with well-positioned mirrors, you might miss something behind or alongside you. Momentarily turning your head and looking over your shoulder (a head check) might save you from a fatal error.

Concentration

A large part of road craft is being able to assess the ever-changing riding situation and making quick decisions without confusion or hesitation. We've got to process a huge amount of information, especially in urban areas, and the faster traffic is moving the quicker we must make the right decisions.

One important consideration is that few of us can sustain the concentration needed for controlled high-speed riding on public roads. When a rider exceeds about 75 percent of the skill limit, fear consumes attention and promotes errors. So, one of the keys to maintaining concentration is to control speed to stay well within that perceived 75 percent limit.

Homework

Try following the British System while riding. See if you can remember the drill while still maintaining awareness of all the other things going on around you. Practicing the drill myself, I realized I often forgot that final look rearward, a critical step I've been working to correct. If Commuter Kenny had been more intentional about his riding, he might still be riding today. How about you? What critical steps are you forgetting?

Positioning

Novice riders often ride down the center of a lane, perhaps to stay as far away from other vehicles as possible or maybe because they are still learning how to control the bike. Most of us soon graduate to following the wheel tracks of other vehicles to avoid surface hazards and debris. With additional experience, we learn about cornering lines, apexing, and positioning to improve the view.

But some experienced motorcyclists have what appears to be a sloppy habit of wandering all over the lane, even drifting over the centerline or across the fog line onto the shoulder. Is this a matter of unskilled riders who really can't stay within the lines, or are there good reasons for moving around in a lane?

One of the unique features of a two-wheeler is that its narrow track allows more choices and much more accurate road positioning than wider vehicles have. We can move our machines around as needed to improve our view, establish our presence, separate from traffic hazards, maximize traction, and negotiate surface problems.

Predicting

When the view is limited, you can't just wait for hazards to emerge. You need to predict the potential for accidents and take action early to position the bike for an escape path. For instance, riding a narrow side street, you must predict hazards such as a car approaching over the crest of a hill or pulling out of a side street even if you don't see any vehicles yet. In the photo below there is a narrow side street on the right, hidden from view by the parked cars. It's possible a car could be about to pull out into the bike's path. Or a car coming over the hill could be about to make a quick left turn.

Observing hazards such as hidden side streets helps avoid accidents.

Improving the View

Approaching intersections, it's essential to see what's going on so you can be prepared to move out of the way of errant motorists. But on narrow streets, buildings, signs, or vegetation often limit your view of other vehicles and pedestrians. Because of the angles involved, the view of an intersection opens up quickly just as you get close to it. You can improve the view and decrease the risks of a collision by adjusting your lane position.

The farther away you are from other vehicles when you see them, the more time you have to react to potential collisions. More to the point: the greater your separation from them, the farther they have to go to hit you. Positioning can give you both a better view and greater separation. For example, consider a car on a side street to the right, hidden behind a building. Moving over to the left side of the lane not only allows an earlier view but the path of travel is farther away from a potential collision.

Out in the country, entering curves from the outside allows you to see more of the road ahead. That is, approaching a right-hand curve, you get a better view from near the centerline. But what can you do to improve the view when you're following a line of cars or a truck? By temporarily swinging over to the extreme edges of the lane, the motorcyclist can often see beyond the traffic and get a better idea of what's happening. Some veterans even dart momentarily over the centerline or over the fog line to catch a quick glimpse around a curve.

You should also be aware of vehicles entering or leaving the freeway and take steps to separate yourself. Sure, you have the right-of-way, and those other drivers are supposed to yield. But why not just change lanes to get out of the way? A little politeness goes a long way toward encouraging other drivers to give motorcyclists a little respect.

If you can see the opposite edge continuing around the turn, that's a good clue that the road is cambered to your advantage.

Blind Spots

It's important to understand the locations of blind spots of other vehicles and avoid riding in those locations. With vehicle drivers sitting in the left front, cars and trucks typically have a large blind spot at the right rear quarter and a narrower blind spot at the left rear quarter. Long-haul commercial trucks (18-wheelers) are so big that a small vehicle such as a motorcycle is easy to lose in the driver's mirrors. The entire right side of a truck can be considered a blind spot that truckers call the no zone. Riding in the no zone is an invitation for a truck to pull over on top of you.

Sure, you have the right-of-way and those other drivers are supposed to yield. But, why not just change lanes to get out of the way?

Riding in the no zone is an invitation for a truck to pull over on top of you.

Either pull ahead of the truck or drop back far enough that if the trucker changes lanes, you won't be in the way.

When a truck is passing you, make it easier for the trucker to get on by. Maintain your speed so the driver has a better idea of where you are. And when the trailer clears you, it's polite to wink your high beam once or twice to signal to the trucker that he or she is clear to move over. That's especially important when riding after dark.

Either pull ahead of the cab or drop back to avoid a truck's no zone.

Dropping back farther behind another vehicle has obvious advantages to avoiding collisions, but more importantly, dropping back can provide a better view ahead. The novice who follows a truck closely and rides in the center of the lane

Dropping back and moving to the left side of the lane provides a better view of what's happening ahead and also makes you more visible to other drivers.

has a limited view of traffic and surface hazards. If you're trapped in a situation in which you can't pass, you can open up your view by dropping back and moving around in the lane. For instance, the view behind a dump truck is limited. Not only is your view of the situation ahead severely limited but other drivers may not realize a motorcycle is occupying the space behind the truck. Dropping back one or two additional seconds improves the view. Moving over to the left side of the lane opens up the view even more.

Remember that the wheels of cars and trucks tend to kick debris out of the wheel tracks, either toward the center of the lane or to the sides. So when riding in

Drop back far enough behind larger vehicles so surface hazards and debris are visible.

traffic, staying in the wheel tracks helps avoid striking debris that suddenly pops out from under vehicles ahead. That's another reason to drop back far enough behind the vehicle ahead.

While we can't prevent other drivers from swerving into us, we can help them realize we're there by being more visible. Mixed into a line of cars, a motorcycle is easier to see when closer to the left side of the lane and no closer than three seconds behind the vehicle ahead. But there may be times when it's smarter to move over to the right-wheel track.

Let's say you are stuck behind a slow van and waiting for an opportunity to pass. You see an oncoming truck, followed by a driver who also seems anxious to pass. There's a risk that that driver doesn't see you behind the van and will pull out to pass as soon as the van goes by. Moving over to the right creates additional separation should the driver suddenly pull out to pass.

It's critically important to drop back when following larger vehicles through an intersection. Opposing drivers waiting to make a left turn may see the space behind a truck or bus as a gap in traffic. It's never a smart idea to follow a larger vehicle through an intersection, but if you can't avoid following a truck or bus, drop back far enough to give other drivers a better chance to see you.

Maximizing Traction

A motorcyclist must constantly manage available traction to avoid punching through the envelope. Often, a simple adjustment in lane position can do much to maximize traction. Left turn lanes are notorious for collecting a heavy grease strip down the center. We would prefer to avoid the right track, but the left track is dangerously close to opposing traffic. However, by positioning our tires precisely between the grease strip and the left-wheel track, we can maintain traffic separation and also keep our tires out of the greasy goo.

The science of cornering involves constant adjustment of lane position to conserve inertia, tire traction, and cornering clearance. The best lines follow smooth arcs that use the entire lane. Away from cities, grease strips and debris are much less of a problem. Novices who ride through curves following one wheel track or in the center of the lane throw away a lot of traction unnecessarily.

David L. Hough

Negotiating Surface Problems

There are many surface hazards that can cause a motorcycle to lose control while causing other vehicles only to wiggle around. The best tactics for negotiating surface hazards such as loose gravel, edge traps, and V-traps are to change lane position to avoid the most hazardous area or to cross the hazard at the most advantageous angle. For instance, when you spot a rain-slick arrow in the middle of a freeway exit, you can adjust lane position just enough to put your tires to one side of the arrow. If you see a railroad track ahead, avoid the V- and X-traps formed where two rails cross.

The proficient rider uses good positioning tactics for a variety of purposes. What may seem like wandering around in a lane often is intelligent positioning to manage the risks.

Passing

If all drivers moved along at reasonable speeds, followed sensible lane discipline, and loaded their vehicles responsibly, there would be few reasons to pass. But we are faced with a confusing mix of vehicles that create different hazards, and passing is one way to separate ourselves from other vehicles.

For example, let's say you come up on a gaggle of frustrated drivers behind a slow-moving motor home on a narrow, twisting road. Such a scenario is ripe for an accident, triggered by an infuriated driver whose patience finally snaps. The crafty motorcyclist takes action to get away from such situations, either dropping back or quickly passing the gaggle.

Passing ought to follow the same rules worldwide, but it doesn't. There are different laws in different countries and different local customs and taboos. For example, in England it is not only legal but expected that a motorcyclist squeeze by another vehicle within the same lane. In the U.S., such tactics are almost always illegal or socially unacceptable, with a few notable exceptions. In the Los Angeles and San Francisco areas of California, lane splitting (white lining) is tolerated on a jammed freeway.

Elsewhere in the U.S., most drivers consider it offensive for a motorcyclist to elbow by in the same lane. And in many states it's illegal for two vehicles to share the same lane side-by-side. Let's consider the tactics for being passed and for passing, with an emphasis on typical North American laws and customs.

Lane Discipline

One of the frustrating problems in North America is that drivers are peculiarly undisciplined about how speed relates to lane position on multiple lane highways. In the civilized European countries, it is expected that a passing vehicle will accelerate, move into the inside lane, pass the slower vehicle, and then move back to the outside lane again. This tactic leaves the fast lane open for passing and discourages anyone from passing on the off side (the slow side).

On superslabs in the U.S., the outside (right) lanes are for slower traffic. The inside (left) lanes are supposed to be passing lanes, not cruising lanes. Aggressive drivers in other countries bend the laws by passing continuously in the left lane at superlegal speeds, but that's not dangerous so long as slower drivers don't get in the way. Even more dangerous are drivers cruising slowly in the passing lane.

It's somewhat more confusing where there are high occupancy vehicle (HOV, also known as diamond or carpool) lanes to the extreme left, because a slow-moving HOV commuter encourages others to dodge over the white line and pass to the right.

The lack of lane discipline causes traffic to bog down in the passing lanes, which encourages frustrated drivers to make an end run to the right. Some aggressive drivers even dodge over to the exit lane, pass, and dodge left just as the lane comes to an end. This sort of vehicular anarchy jacks up the risks of collisions.

Traffic Speed

If you're passing everyone else on the road, you're probably being too aggressive for the situation. If you're riding at the average speed of traffic or slightly above, you should expect to get passed by a few aggressive drivers. That's just folks in a hurry to get to the radar trap first. But if everyone else on the road is passing you, it's a clue that you ought to roll on the throttle and get up to speed.

On today's roads, the average speed of traffic is typically 5 or 10 miles over the posted limit. Police generally ignore reasonable excesses, but if everyone is actually exceeding the limit, then the police can pick off any driver they choose.

So, should I cruise at a nice, legal 55 and expect most of the other drivers to pass me? Or should I turn up the wick and roll along with local traffic? The lowest-risk

Confusing laws and customs in North America often create hazardous passing scenarios.

situation is when 85 percent or more of the vehicles on the road are moving at the same relative speed. So, in terms of accidents, the least risky choice is to increase speed to match traffic.

Getting Passed

Until just a few years ago, it was assumed that motorcycles pass other vehicles most of the time. A motorcycle could easily zip around a heavily loaded commercial truck bogging down on an upgrade. A bike could easily out-accelerate the typical passenger car. But these days, automobiles and commercial trucks have much more horsepower, and that has jacked up highway speeds to an aggressive level. Even with enough power to cruise at warp speeds, turbulent air, debris, and rain affect motorcyclists more than they affect car drivers. So these days, motorcyclists may get passed more often than not, especially on the super-slabs near big cities.

Our main concern when being passed by another vehicle is staying out of the way. When we're riding aggressively ourselves, we pay most of our attention to what's ahead. One danger is that an aggressive driver zipping around us on the right might not be expected, and we could change lanes directly into the path of a passing car. Here in the U.S., we need to look behind both left and right to spot aggressive drivers moving up through the pack.

Getting passed can be an irritating business. Other drivers typically don't understand (or may not care) how much turbulent air and road grit is stirred up by a close pass. And if a truck is passing, add the insult of a nauseating cloud of diesel soot.

When you suddenly realize you're being passed, the tendency is to speed up, but it's too late for that. If you attempt to accelerate when you realize a truck is passing you,

Drivers of cars and trucks may not appreciate how much turbulent air, road grit, and diesel soot is stirred up by a close pass.

the truck driver may take that as a challenge. Running you off the road might seem justified, and it's going to be a lot less of a problem for the trucker than for the biker.

If you weren't paying enough attention to the traffic behind you to realize another vehicle was gaining on you, it's a little late in the game to speed up just as the other vehicle is passing. It's also illegal in most states. Let the other guy pass, take your lumps, and figure out what you could have done better to avoid the situation.

David L. Hough

Passing Others

On narrow secondary highways with limited visibility and sharp curves, a motorcycle can often maintain speed better than most cars or trucks, so we're tempted to pass frequently. The point to remember is that those narrow roads also have more potential hazards. When passing another vehicle on a two-lane highway, we know that it's important to plan the pass to avoid collisions with either the vehicle we're passing or other traffic that enters the scene. It's not smart to depend on other drivers to brake or swerve to miss us. Since we'll be borrowing the opposing lane for a few moments, we need to choose a section of pavement no one else is likely to use at the same time.

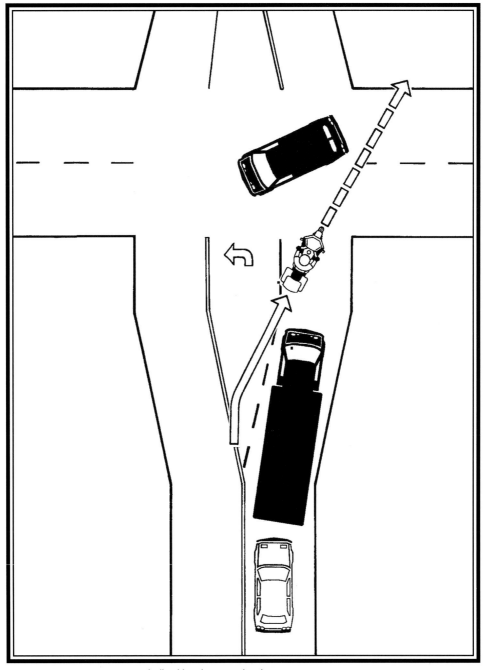

Passing at intersections is not only illegal but also extremely risky.

Even if it's a passing zone, be aware of any roads or driveways ahead.

There are a number of locations where we might be tempted to pass but we should always reject. We don't pass on bridges because there's no escape path, except into concrete or steel. We don't pass on hills or in blind corners because we can't see enough of the opposite lane to know for certain that there isn't another vehicle speeding head-on toward us. We don't pass at intersections because traffic can quickly pull out of a side road into our path. In most states it is illegal to pass in such locations, and there is good reason to obey the law.

Passing accidents occur when someone does something unexpected in the critical moments when the passer is hanging out in the wrong lane. For instance, when a motorcyclist pulls out to pass a truck, and just as the rider

Just before gassing it to make the pass, take one last "lifesaver" look behind.

David L. Hough

gets up to speed, the truck driver turns left into an unmarked driveway. Quick decisions and high speeds can suddenly degrade into panic situations.

One way to avoid such scenarios is to scrutinize the road ahead well enough to spot any place where the other vehicle could make a sudden turn and avoid passing at that point. Another way to avoid tangling with a vehicle being passed is to sound the horn as you come up abreast. Sounding the horn when passing is required by law in many states, but beeping seems rude, so most of us ignore the law.

Here's a place where we could benefit from the British System, which includes the horn as part of the drill. As the metro police remind us, never using the horn is as bad as beeping too much. One polite beep when passing might be a smart tactic.

Look Before You Leap

Remember the final steps in the British System before accelerating? Just before gassing it to make the pass, take one last look behind. The metro cops call it the lifesaver for good reason. I can still remember the time I pulled out into the opposing lane to pass a creeper and an instant later heard the screeching of tires of a van that was silently trying to pass us both in the corner in spite of the double yellow lines. I had forgotten to glance in the mirror one last time before pulling out to pass. The other driver managed to miss me, but the embarrassment lingers on to remind me to always take that one last look before leaping.

When in Doubt, Don't Pass

Once the decision has been made to get around a slower-moving vehicle, we're likely to keep the throttle open even if the situation begins to go wrong. But the smart rider analyzes the situation as it unfolds and is prepared to abort the pass. If that oncoming car is closing up the distance a lot faster than you predicted, the smart decision is to brake and pull back in line. The rule of thumb here is, "When in doubt, don't do it." There's always another place to pass somewhere down the road.

Groups

A group ride doesn't change the passing rules. Riding in a group does not confer the privilege to hold up traffic or to expect other drivers to get out of our way. Even if the group is following the posted speed limit, other drivers may perceive that they are being held up. If an aggressive driver is attempting to pass a big group of motorcycles, open up space as needed to let him or her in. If the group is using radio communication, announce that a car is coming through for the benefit of leading riders.

When a group of motorcycles needs to pass a slow vehicle, each rider is responsible for a safe pass. The temptation is for one more rider to squeeze on by, even in the face of oncoming traffic. It may be that there is space for two bikes to pass but not three. If the third rider doesn't evaluate the situation and make an independent decision to hold back, that rider could be trapped in the wrong lane with nowhere to go. To avoid such surprises, each rider in a group must make the passing decision independently.

It's also tempting to offer hand signals or radio messages to following riders to help them decide when to pass. But if you misjudge the situation, you're endangering the other riders. For instance, you might think the road ahead is clear, wave the next rider to bring it on by, then notice a deer about to leap out just as the other rider gets up to speed. So, the best advice is not to signal other riders. Passing should be their decision, not yours. And if a rider ahead of you waves you to bring it on by, you'd be wise to disregard the signal. Remember, passing is your own decision, based on what you can see.

Politeness

Be aware that passing another driver has the psychological implications of a put-down. The driver being passed can become angered at what he or she perceives as aggressive behavior. It is especially rude to pass other people with obnoxiously loud exhaust pipes, pass too close, or pull back in line too closely in front of the other vehicle.

The slower driver may react to your pass by blasting the horn, waving nasty digits, speeding up, tailgating, or even pulling out a handgun. And there have been more than a few incidents of road rage in which people were shot at or run off the road.

You can help disarm the situation by not tailgating, by signaling your intention to pass well in advance, and by staying well away from the vehicle you're passing. Always allow a minimum space of two seconds in front of another vehicle before pulling back in line, and then maintain a speed that doesn't hold up the other driver. If the other driver takes your pass as a put-down, he or she might speed up to teach you a lesson, and that creates a dangerous situation. Before you decide to pass, consider whether you're willing to speed up to keep in front of an aggressive driver. If you're not willing to stay ahead, you should decide not to do it.

Every rider in a group should make the passing decision independently.

David L. Hough

Traveling

TRAVELING

Tactics

TACTICS

CHAPTER 9
TRAVELING TACTICS

The Flagstaff Travel School

few years ago my eleven-year-old grandson and I took a cross-country trip to participate in a big motorcycle rally in Flagstaff, Arizona. But like many motorcycle journeys, the rally was more an excuse to get out on the road and travel. Sure, a long motorcycle trip would be an adventure, but it would also provide a setting for grandfather and grandson to learn something about each other.

But years after the Flagstaff trip was over, I realized that it had given us both some valuable lessons about travel and life; lessons that only became clear in the context of hundreds of other journeys. I no longer think of a motorcycle trip as merely a way to get from point A to point B. Every trip is like a school, where important lessons are offered. Let me share some of my education with you.

Lesson 1: The Travel Pace
Heading across the wide-open spaces of Nevada, I had become impatient with our progress. We didn't seem to be getting to the horizon as fast as I had expected, and I kept

jacking up the speed higher and higher. It wasn't a schedule problem; it was more of a mental attitude about not feeling comfortable with an unknown area. And the faster we rode, the more frustrated I felt. I finally realized what the problem was. I was trying to be somewhere else, and I wasn't experiencing where I was at the moment. If I didn't want to be out on a lonely highway in the desert, why had I headed out on a motorcycle trip to the Southwest? The solution was not to go faster; the solution was to go slower.

I slowed way down, found a break in the fence where we could get off the pavement, and rode out into the desert far enough to get away from the highway. At first, I heard only the tink, tink of the engine cooling down. But as I opened my senses, I gradually began to take in where we were, not where we'd come from or where we were going. I kicked my boot in the sandy dirt, breathed in the dry sage-tainted air, listened to the whistles of a circling hawk, and scrutinized the bare sandstone cliffs. When the desert had melted away my impatience, I was ready to continue our journey.

That first lesson is good advice for any traveler. The whole point of traveling is to experience what's out there, not to rush so fast across the countryside that you can't absorb any of it.

Lesson 2: Self-Confidence

One evening, just a couple of days into the trip, Jake had confided in me that he didn't like how people looked at him as he rode along in the sidecar. Of course, Jake didn't appreciate that sidecars attract attention or that the people staring at him were spinning an adventure in their minds, not poking fun at him. *Look at that old guy on*

David L. Hough

the bike and that young boy in the sidecar, off to see the world. Doesn't that look like a fun way to travel? I wish I could have done that when I was a kid.

But of course Jake hadn't experienced enough of life to learn to cope with curious stares. Perhaps being exposed to the world on a motorcycle was the start of learning that how you view yourself is what's really important, not how others see you. If you're going to travel far and wide on a motorcycle, it's important to develop confidence in your own choices and your own abilities.

It's not only a matter of feeling good but also generating respect from others. When you're on a bike, you're more vulnerable to nasty characters and prejudice. Your best defense is being self-confident, because your attitude shows. If you appear to be a victim, you're likely to be victimized. If you are confident, purposeful, and direct, you're more likely to be left alone by the nasty characters and given a fair shake by everyone else.

Lesson 3: Food

When you're traveling, food becomes a big part of the journey. Yes, you can stick to what's familiar, but if you don't try the local food, you may miss out on some great meals. More importantly, you'll miss opportunities to learn more about the country you're traveling through and the people who inhabit the area.

After the Flagstaff rally, we motored along the south rim of the Grand Canyon, arriving hungry at the Cameron Trading Post about sunset. Other motorcyclists were passing through, and a rider just leaving the restaurant offered one simple piece of advice:

Don't order the full taco.

Why? I asked. *Is it that bad?*

No, the tacos are fantastic. You just won't be able to finish one.

I didn't believe him. Here we were at the Navajo taco center of the world. A Navajo taco is a concoction of tender meat, tomatoes, lettuce, avocados, cheese, and peppers over tasty fry bread. Out on the reservations, the tacos are small. I was hungry and I wanted a big one. Jake surprised me by ordering a taco instead of a hamburger and fries. My friend was right: an hour later, we were both stuffed and neither of us had finished our giant Navajo tacos. It was a memorable meal.

A few days later, after several hours of fighting a storm, we found ourselves wet, cold, tired, and hungry, just wanting a quick lunch and a chance to warm up. A truck stop looked inviting. While we waited, I observed the food going by, and it all looked greasy and overcooked. Then I realized the silverware wasn't clean, the coffee cup had a crack, and the cleanup guy used the same dirty rag to wipe the seats and then the tabletops. I made a decision to leave without ordering and told my confused grandson to put his riding gear back on.

The lesson is not to be afraid to try local food, but never be too timid to get up and walk out if you don't like what you see or the way you are being treated. There are a lot of restaurants in the world, and there's no point in wasting time on bad service or risking the effects of bad food.

Lesson 4: The Environment

Leaving Arizona, my grandson and I had ridden north through the Painted Desert to Marble Canyon, then west along the Vermillion Cliffs, and back south again, climbing the Kaibab Plateau toward the north rim of the Grand Canyon. After the obligatory stop at the lodge, we rode out to Cape Royal, a spectacular cliff that juts out over the canyon. We arrived at the end of the road just as the afternoon thunderheads began to boil and crackle with lightning.

Running out to the overlook to stay ahead of the rain, we looked down thousands of feet into the majestic canyon. Suddenly we felt the steel railing tingle and our hair begin to rise from the electrical charge, so we beat a hasty retreat downhill and away from the impending lightning strikes.

Over the years, I've come to accept the environmental challenges as part of the journey and a big part of the education of travel. On a motorcycle, you know exactly what the weather is doing, whether it's hot or cold, wet or dry. Most of the time you're in a hostile environment, and you have to learn to deal with it. There's no air conditioner to turn on, no windows to crank up. You don't just watch rain pounding against a windshield; you feel it on your body. When you smash into a june bug, it's a direct and personal reminder that you are traveling through a real ecosystem, not watching a movie.

But the payoff is that at the end of the day you know you've experienced something special, something real, something meaningful. I guess that's a big part of what makes motorcycle journeys so worthwhile. If you stay home to avoid the possibility of uncomfortable weather, you'll miss a big part of the adventure.

Lesson 5: Traveling Companions

In my pretrip imagination, Jake, my grandson, would be asking about how motorcycles work and learning how to read maps and wondering what it was like to travel in Africa or Switzerland or England. And I would be asking what he was studying in school and who his friends were and what he wanted to be when he grew up. But his eleven-year-old concerns centered on toys, junk food, and the hope that our next motel would have a swimming pool.

When I dropped Jake off in San Francisco, I got the impression he was glad it was over. Maybe it was too boring riding cross-country 500 or 600 miles a day with no TV available. Maybe it was too exhausting cruising through the high desert heat in an open vehicle. Maybe we were just on different wavelengths.

More than a few riders have had similar disappointments with their traveling companions. A lot of people dream about hitting the open road on a bike but are afraid of doing it alone. What if the bike breaks down miles from civilization? What if the weather gets nasty? What if there are bad guys in some remote campground? A riding buddy helps cure the fear. After all, there's safety in numbers.

But the reality is that the social connections are usually more of the crisis than the breakdowns, weather, or bad guys. We may think we know someone well enough to travel with him or her, but out on the road slightly different habits or dislikes can turn into major disagreements. One rider wants to stop at a steak house, the other wants to stop at the Golden Arches. One rider wants to get rolling by 8:00 A.M. The other isn't ready until 8:30. A lot of riding buddies have parted company after a week's worth of smoldering resentment.

So, the important lesson is that it's harder to travel with others than alone. If you choose to travel with companions, be aware of the potential for disagreements, be flexible, and be prepared to compromise.

David L. Hough

Lesson 6: Engine Problems

After dropping off my grandson in San Francisco, I continued northward up the California coast, and the next morning into Oregon. Halfway up the Oregon coast, the engine started to complain. The exhaust valves had stopped clattering, and the engine didn't want to idle when I stopped. On the old BMW, this meant the exhaust valves had lost clearance. Two days of spirited riding up the coast had eroded the valve seats. I'd hoped to make it all the way home without any roadside maintenance, but thinking back, I realized I hadn't set the valves in more than 2,000 miles. I could just cool down the engine with water, adjust the valves, and keep going. But I'd need to stop one more night on the way home anyway, and it might as well be here. I checked into a motel, and wandered around town looking for a suitable restaurant.

I was glad it wasn't something serious. I've had a variety of bike problems on the road over the years, from flat tires to blown engines. When you have a bike problem, the first thing to adjust is your schedule. If I'm a day or two late getting home or if the bike comes home in a rental truck, that's the way it will be. There's no point in losing sleep over situations you can't change. This time, I let the bike cool down, let the schedule slide, and planned to solve the problem in the morning.

When you ride long distances, you have to assume that you'll need to do some maintenance, and even repairs, on the road. The lesson for the traveler is that it's not a matter of if you have a breakdown but how to manage the panic when it happens.

Lesson 7: Choosing the Road

My original plan was to turn inland at Lincoln City and head for the superslab. But somehow the idea of merging back into freeway traffic seemed distasteful, while the idea of continuing north up the coast seemed much better. I stopped to review the map and confirmed that the twisty coast route added a lot more miles.

Yes, the twisty road would add several more hours to the trip, but those hours would be enjoyable. The Coast Highway carves around swamps and sleepy coastal towns and climbs up steep cliffs with views of the thundering ocean thousands of feet below. At Tillamook, I stopped for coffee and ice cream. At Astoria, I rode uphill for a quick visit to the Astor tower before heading across the Columbia River to Washington.

The lesson is, if you want to have a memorable journey, you need to get away from the superhighways and big cities, and head for the twistiest roads running through the smallest little towns. Yes, if you need to make a fast transit from one end of the country to the other, the superslabs allow you to cover maximum distance in minimum time. Just put your head down and go. But if you want to experience the country, you've got to visit the small towns. I've found that to be true anywhere in the world.

Lesson 8: Each Trip Stands Alone

As the miles ticked by, I wondered whether the Flagstaff trip would start a tradition of motorcycle travel by grandfather and grandson or if that adventure was just a brief window of opportunity through which we would never pass again. Even if the social connections weren't as ideal as my dreams, my grandson and I had shared an adventure together. We'd crossed the wide-open spaces of Washington, Oregon, Idaho, and Nevada. We'd marveled at the Canyonlands of Utah, sweltered in the heat of Monument Valley, and felt the tingle of lightning on the edge of the Grand Canyon. We'd visited strange ghost towns, marveled at red sandstone cliffs, tasted unfamiliar food, and shopped for a Navajo blanket.

Would we remember the soaring vistas of Cape Royal, the amazing sandstone formations of Bryce Canyon, and the awesome carvings of the Colorado River? Or would we remember the windburn and fatigue, the aggressive traffic through Reno and Sacramento, and the quick-fingered gas station attendant in Nevada who turned a $50 bill into a $20 bill in the blink of an eye?

As it happened, my grandson and I have never done another trip together: he headed off into skateboards and body piercing, I headed off onto other motorcycle journeys. The lesson is, whatever the memories, every journey stands alone. You can't go back later to repeat a trip and expect to encounter the same experiences. Even if I could go back in time and do that same trip over again, it wouldn't turn out the same way. Every trip involves different people, different weather conditions, different food, and different bike problems. Yet I can't think of a single trip I regret taking and I can remember valuable lessons from every one.

You can take your own lessons from the "Flagstaff Travel School." Better yet, pack up your bike and hit the road. Don't wait around for your friends to find the time. Just head off across the landscape, exposing yourself to the possibilities of great adventures and personal lessons.

Moto-Psychology

Handling Breakdowns on the Road

The potential for having bike problems on the road is a big concern for many riders. Actually, the good news is that today's motorcycles are reliable, so the fear of mechanical problems shouldn't keep anyone from getting on a bike and heading off across the country. The bad news is that all machines fail. Sooner or later every bike will have a problem.

A couple of years ago, my primary bike had a serious failure half a day from home. I thought a low-speed misfire on one cylinder indicated a bad spark plug cap. But before I could get to a motorcycle shop to buy a new plug cap, the engine suddenly exploded with an exhaust valve punched halfway through the piston. The low-speed miss was actually a symptom of the valve head breaking off.

Such incidents are a rarity these days because today's motorcycles are a lot more reliable than they used to be. If you've taken up motorcycling within the past ten years or so, you may never have had a roadside breakdown. You may even wonder why some of us old codger bikers are concerned about the contents of a new bike's tool kit or whether the valves are adjusted by screws or whether the bike has a centerstand or how much trouble it is to get the battery out.

Back in the 1970s, the most likely failure on a motorcycle was a flat or blowout. Today, tire failures are rare, unless the tire has been abused by overloading or underinflating. And with tubeless tires, you can usually get back to civilization with a repair plug and a few bottles of carbon dioxide (CO_2). Engines and transmissions seldom fail on contemporary bikes, but we should expect minor electrical gremlins from time to time.

The problem with breakdowns isn't so much getting the problem fixed as it is controlling the panic when the bike fails. A panicked rider might try something stupid or dangerous—say, pushing a dead bike across a freeway—that a calmer rider would instantly recognize as poor judgment. Let's think through the process of handling a roadside breakdown to help you prepare for whatever problems you might happen to encounter in your travels. The following three riders all encountered mechanical problems on the road, with different levels of success in solving their difficulties.

Panicky Paul

Paul finally found a late model, low-mileage bike that he'd been lusting after and bought it from a gent who wasn't riding much anymore. But on the way home, the engine started coughing and sputtering, and then it died. Paul couldn't believe it. He hadn't even owned it for an hour and already it had broken down. He coasted to a stop alongside the freeway and sat in the saddle trying to control his panic as traffic roared by. All he could think to do was to keep trying to start the engine. He pushed the button again and again until the battery finally got too weak to crank any more. Paul cursed his bad luck, abandoned the bike where it sat, and headed home on foot to get his pickup truck.

Moto Mack

Mack had just crested the mountain pass when his V-twin lost power. Mack kept it limping along for a mile or two until he found a safe location to pull off the road, away from traffic. Mack was enough of a mechanic to isolate the problem by a few straightforward tests. Loosening the carburetor float bowls helped him determine that fuel was not the problem. Cranking the starter with the spark plugs removed showed fat blue sparks, so it wasn't ignition. He then felt for compression by holding his thumb over the spark plug holes while cranking the engine. One cylinder didn't even have enough compression to pop his thumb off the hole, which he knew from experience was most likely a burned exhaust valve. The engine was capable of limping to the next town, where hopefully Mack could fix it himself.

Beemer Bill

Bill was on his way home from a rally. Just as he crested a long upgrade against a headwind, the engine suddenly started struggling, followed immediately by a horrible clanking. At the side of the road, the engine complained with loud clanks if Bill tried to increase power above a fast idle. He checked to make sure that the oil level was okay, then he started the engine to locate the knocking, which was deep in the engine, down where the crankshaft turns. It was obvious to Bill that this bike wasn't going home under its own power.

Different Problems

The different riders had vastly different problems and dealt with them in different ways. When Panicky Paul finally retrieved his bike and hauled it to the shop, the mechanic found the fuel tank almost empty. He turned the gas valve to reserve, and the engine immediately started, even with the almost dead battery. Paul had merely run out of gas. In his panic, he had failed to realize all he needed to do was turn the fuel valve to reserve. There was nothing wrong with the bike.

Moto Mack is a pretty fair backyard mechanic, and he decided to try fixing the problem on the road. First, he limped his ailing bike to the nearest telephone, called his parts man, and talked him into shipping a new exhaust valve and head gasket overnight to the bus depot at the next town. The following morning, Mack chuffed the bike around on one cylinder to find a place to work, and located a parking lot next to an auto machine shop. After a short trip to pick up the new valve, he disassembled the ailing head and had the machinist next door fit the new valve. By noon, Mack had the engine back together and was continuing his trip.

Beemer Bill knew he had a seriously damaged engine that wasn't fixable by the side of the road. He decided to transport it home by rental truck. Thumbing a ride to the nearest town, he rented a truck, drove back to the bike, used the clanking engine to pull it up a loading ramp, and completed the homeward journey as a trucker.

Different Reactions

The three riders reacted to their emergencies in different ways. Panicky Paul could have saved himself a lot of time, energy, and money if he had managed to calm down and use the resources he had with him. There wasn't even anything broken. The owner's manual, which was in the toolbox under the seat, would have explained exactly how to operate the fuel valve. Paul was lucky he wasn't struck by a wandering driver as he walked along the freeway shoulder and fortunate his bike was still there and in one piece when he returned to pick it up. What Paul suffered was not so much a mechanical breakdown as a psychological breakdown.

Moto Mack had a potentially serious engine problem that could have ended his trip, but he was calm enough to diagnose it and figure out that it could probably be fixed. He correctly diagnosed the problem as a burned exhaust valve. His decisions involved getting the parts shipped to him, finding a place to do the repairs, and locating a machine shop. It helped that Mack had the necessary tools in his kit and the knowledge to do the work.

Beemer Bill had a more serious engine failure, probably a crankshaft or connecting rod bearing, which couldn't be fixed on the road. There was nothing Bill could do to get his bike home under its own power. He had to decide how to transport himself and his load of gear home, and get the bike to a repair shop.

When the Whatsisframus Snaps

The lesson from these stories is that handling emergencies depends upon keeping a level head after the whatsisframus snaps and leaves you stranded. Before a breakdown, you are dicing with traffic, focusing on the route, and maintaining your schedule. Suddenly, all that changes, and it's easy to panic. To help avoid the panic, take a deep breath, calm down, and temporarily switch off your travel plans. For the moment, ignore getting home in time for dinner or getting to the motel where you have a reservation or getting back to work by the next morning. Those are all lower priorities now. The first priority is getting yourself off the road and into a safe zone where you won't get run over.

If at all possible, coast over to the shoulder while the bike is still moving. Don't stop in traffic. Then push the bike away from the traffic lanes, preferably behind a building or telephone booth where the air is calmer and quieter. If you absolutely can't move the bike away from the road, at least push it to the outside edge of the shoulder. And while you're pushing, keep an eye peeled for cars zooming toward you. It's more common than you may think for drivers to gawk at vehicles parked on the shoulder and accidentally wander over to smash into them.

The next priority, once you've got the bike in a safe zone, is to focus on the problem. If the failure is obvious, such as a flat tire or a broken drive chain, you won't need to do any diagnosis. But if the problem is not obvious—say the engine suddenly quits or refuses to start for no apparent reason—get out your owner's manual and see if it has a troubleshooting guide. Or remember the saying, "The king is a FINK." Use the letters F.I.N.K. (fuel, ignition, neutral, and kill switch) to help you remember what to check.

Fuel: Extinguish any lit cigarettes, open the fuel filler cap, and rock the bike from side to side to be sure there really is fuel sloshing around in there. If fuel is low, select Reserve or Prime, and see if the engine starts. If the fuel valve is opened by a vacuum device, check that the vacuum line is still connected. If the engine still won't start, don't just keep cranking. You need to save your battery. Turn the key to the off position, get out a screwdriver, and open a drain screw in the bottom of a carburetor. You want to see clean fuel dribbling out, not dirty water or diesel oil. If you tanked up with diesel oil at the last station, you'll need to drain the tank and refill it with gasoline. If your bike has a fuel pump, check the fuse on the fuel pump circuit and make sure the pump electrical plug is connected.

Ignition: Turn on the switch and make sure that the headlight is glowing brightly. If you can't get any lights, turn the switch to the off position and check that both battery terminals are clean and tight. If it's not a sealed battery, see if the electrolyte covers the plates. You may be able to see the level through a translucent battery case. If not, unscrew the caps on the two end cells and look inside. Don't stick your finger down into the battery: the electrolyte is acid. If you can't see any electrolyte covering the plates, it's worth a try to add plain water to the cells.

Make sure the big ground wire from the battery terminal to the frame is secure at the engine end as well as the battery terminal. If the connector looks rusty or corroded, remove the fastener, scrape the metal clean, and reconnect it. If you disconnect the battery cables, always remove the ground (black) cable first and reconnect the ground cable last to avoid a short circuit.

If the battery is good, check that each spark plug wire is connected to the plug cap on one end and to the coil on the other end. To check for a spark, remove a spark plug, reconnect the wire to the plug, turn on the ignition, hold the metal part of the spark plug touching bare metal on the engine, and crank the starter for two or three seconds. If you don't see a series of blue sparks zapping between the electrodes on the plug, you could have an ignition failure or simply a switch problem.

When you're cranking the engine to check for sparks, either hold the base of the spark plug firmly against bare metal, or lay the plug on the engine. If you're concerned about a shock, use an insulated screwdriver to hold the plug in contact with the engine. The spark is high voltage, but low current, and very brief. With the plug cap connected, that end of the spark plug is protected. Even if you hold the threaded end of the plug in your hand, you won't get electrocuted, but you'll quickly know if the ignition is working.

Neutral: Shift the transmission to neutral, retract the sidestand, squeeze the clutch lever, turn on the key, and try to start the engine. Interlock switches at the clutch or sidestand may be interrupting the ignition. Some machines are wired so that the starter will crank the engine without firing the ignition if the sidestand isn't retracted. Check that wires to the safety switches at these locations are not unplugged or cut. It's possible that a blob of asphalt or a stone has lodged in the sidestand switch or that a wire to the neutral switch has unplugged itself.

Kill Switch: Don't forget to check that the engine shutoff switch (the kill switch) is in the run position. You'd be amazed how many bikes are hauled in to repair shops simply because the shutoff switch on the handlebar was nudged out of the run position. Check your kill switch and save the embarrassment. In the event the shutoff switch contacts are dirty, click the kill switch between Off and Run several times.

What's the Problem, Anyway?

The point of all this detail stuff is to figure out what has failed. What is the problem, anyway? Don't get too complex here; just try to identify the basic problem. Did you run out of gas or did the engine clank and grind to a stop? Did the battery actually fail internally, or is it just discharged? If the engine runs but won't pull the bike, does the clutch cable have some slack? Is the drive chain still there? Is the rear wheel still bolted to the drive?

Such questions may sound silly here, but a panicked rider may overlook an obvious problem. Panicked riders have been known to keep blipping the throttle, trying to make the bike move without realizing the drive chain has fallen off half a mile back. If emergencies absolutely panic you, it's important to be as logical as possible. Get out a pencil and paper, and write down your thoughts. Record what you have checked and how. If you have a phone handy, try calling a dealer's service manager for advice. Even if the person is 1,000 miles away, the service technician may be able to talk you through diagnosing the problem.

If you can figure out the basic problem, you're well on the way to solving it. There's no point in transporting the bike if all you need is fuel or a charged battery. More than a few riders have limped home on a cheap auto battery in a saddlebag after an alternator or regulator failed.

Don't forget that owner's manual (rider's manual) under the seat. It may have suggestions for troubleshooting.

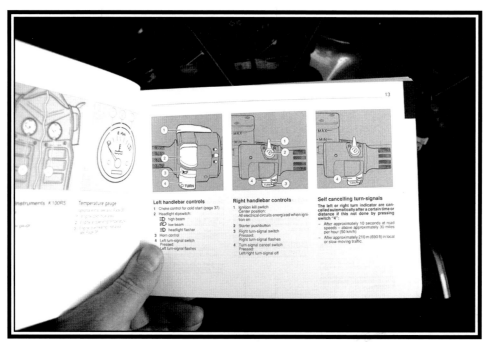

Your owner's manual may have a troubleshooting chart to help you figure out a problem.

David L. Hough

The Options

Once you've figured out the basic problem, you have a few options:

Stay with the bike and get help to come to you. If you have a phone, see if you can arrange for someone to pick up the bike or bring fuel or parts. If you have emergency road service, your call should set in motion a rescue-and-repair mission. Or, if you belong to a volunteer emergency network, you can try calling local riders for help.

You can try flagging down another motorist, but the sad fact is that few motorists will stop to help anyone these days, and that includes motorcyclists. If you have a bike problem, the universal *I need help* signal for other riders is placing your helmet upright on the shoulder, a few feet behind the bike.

Fix it yourself. Assuming you have the necessary know-how, parts, and tools, you may be able to do a little shade-tree mechanical work and fix the problem yourself. Maybe all you need to do is replace a blown fuse, drain water from your carburetors, or clean a ground connection. But if you aren't mechanically inclined, it's not smart to start taking things apart without a plan. It's awfully easy to lose some tiny but important part in the desert sand. If you don't have anything else to collect parts in, take off your T-shirt and spread it on the ground.

Push. If it's only a mile to the next exit, you might be able to push your bike to help. Just remember that a motorcycle isn't worth the risk of heat exhaustion, a heart attack, or an accident. Pushing a heavyweight machine is exhausting. It's a lot easier to walk, buy a fuel can, and bring fuel back to the bike (if that's the problem). And if your bike has a flat tire, forget pushing more than a few feet to get it off the road.

You should also forget towing, even if someone offers a tow and a rope. It's difficult to balance a motorcycle while it's being towed, and you're exposing yourself to a serious accident attempting to tow in traffic. You're also exposing yourself to a ticket in those states where it's illegal for a vehicle to tow a motorcycle.

Abandon the bike and go for help. You can abandon the bike and go to find the help, parts, fuel, etc. needed to return and fix it or transport it. If all you need is fuel, buy a cheap gas can at the next station and call a taxi to get back to the bike.

If the bike has a serious problem that requires transporting it to a repair shop, call the shop and see if it has a truck or trailer, or if there is a nearby car rental office. If you'll be transporting the bike all by yourself, remember that it's practically impossible for one person to push an inoperative road bike up into a rental truck or high trailer even with a ramp. A low trailer towed by a rental car is tough enough. If you're going to have to push an inoperative bike up a ramp into a truck, you're going to need extra help.

Don't forget to pick up some tie-down straps on the return trip back to the bike. You'll need at least four straps, preferably six or eight. When securing a bike in a truck or trailer, it's normal to use two straps at the front, attached to the handlebars or triple clamps; two at the rear; and two more to prevent the bottom of the front wheel from sliding sideways.

Suggestions

Take a few extra precautions prior to leaving home, especially a long trip:

★ **Check your tool kit while you're still close to the hardware store.** The side of the road 50 miles from civilization is a poor place to find out that you don't have the wrench needed to tighten the axle nut. See if the wrenches in the kit are adequate to reach the spark plugs, axle pinch bolts, handlebar clamps, and other obvious fasteners. Maybe you need an extension handle for your spark plug wrench, two 13 mm open-ended wrenches to remove a wheel, a smaller screwdriver bit to remove the drain screws from your carburetors, or a small hex bit to remove a fairing panel.

★ **Read your manuals while you are still close to your refrigerator.** It's a lot more comfortable to be sitting in a soft chair with a cold beverage while you're trying to figure out how everything works. Out on the road, it's a hostile environment, and you're not likely to spend the time to read the book. Once you've memorized everything in the owner's manual, get a shop manual, which is a detailed guide for service and repair, for your machine. The shop manual is too big to carry along with you, but you can study it when the snow is blowing outside. Most shop manuals include general information about tools, fasteners, torque values, lubricants, sealers, and other details before getting into the nitty-gritty about the specific machine. The more familiar you are with the workings of your motorcycle, the less panic you'll have when trouble does come along.

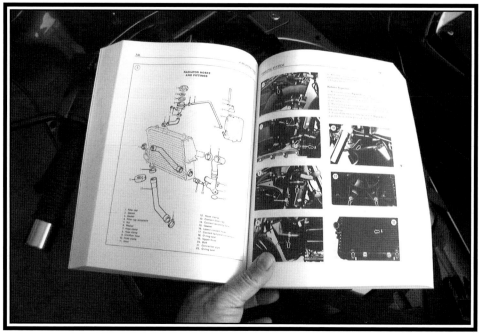

The shop manual is too big to carry along with you, but you can learn a lot about your bike by studying it between rides.

★ **Carry a few common spares and tools tucked away in the fairing or taped inside a saddlebag lid.** Spare fuses, light bulbs, and small fasteners can be stuffed in foam inside a 35 mm film canister. A small 12 volt test light is handy for checking electrical continuity, and it can also serve as a light. A few crimp-on electrical splices can be lifesavers for reconnecting broken wires. If your bike has spoked wheels with inner tubes, consider carrying a spare tube, wrapped in several layers of plastic for protection, or at least a patch kit. Hide spare keys somewhere on the bike.

★ **If you have a roadside assistance plan or belong to a volunteer plan such as the International Help 'N Hands, write the phone number and your membership number on a decal and stick it on the bike where you can't miss it a year or two from now.** In a panic, some riders forget all about their emergency coverage or can't remember the toll-free number. It's fine to have a card in your wallet, but it's much better to put the numbers out in the open.

If you do experience a breakdown, here are some suggestions for reducing the hassles:

⭐ **If your machine starts bucking, clanking, or wheezing, pick a comfortable place to check it out, rather than just continuing to ride on, hoping the problem will go away.** Consider stopping by a motorcycle shop or at least near a telephone booth while you fiddle with the problem. If you do need to make some repairs, it's a lot less frustrating with help, communication, and food nearby.

⭐ **If you must abandon your machine to go for help, try to secure it against thieves and vandals.** Move it out of sight behind a building, bridge abutment, or haystack. Lock it, and take the keys with you. Leaving your loaded bike perched on the sidestand, right next to a busy freeway lane is an invitation to having it struck by a wandering motorist, blown over by the windblasts of passing trucks, or stripped by strangers.

⭐ **After you've hidden your motorcycle, write down where you left it (mile markers, crossroads, business signs, etc.).** It's a lot easier to lose track of where you leave your bike than you might think. Some riders have even lost their bikes by going to the wrong parking garage in the same shopping center. Out on a strange highway, it can be even more confusing. Was that mile 95 on I-15 or exit 15 on I-95? Did you hide it behind a white billboard with red letters or a red billboard with white letters? Really, use your map, gum wrapper, T-shirt, or forearm, but write down the specifics before you leave the scene.

When You're Stranded

Help 'N Hands

The International Help 'N Hands emergency organization (started by John and Bonnie Burnside back in the 1970s) has grown so large that it is now sponsored by the AMA. Participation is voluntary. You list your willingness to help others, and International Help 'N Hands provides you with a special emergency phone number. The operator has current listings of other International Help 'N Hands volunteers based on location. The organization provides phone numbers but not names, to keep things confidential. For information, contact the AMA at (614) 856-1900 or ama@ama-cycle.org.

Club anonymous directories are a way to get in touch with fellow riders when you have a problem on the road.

Anonymous Directories

Various motorcycle clubs and associations also have emergency (or anonymous) directories. For instance, the Harley Owners Group (H.O.G), the BMW Motorcycle Owners of America, and the BMW Riders Association have directories that list phone numbers of volunteers by area. Members receive a pocket-sized directory at no additional expense. It isn't a hard-and-fast rule, but it is assumed you are calling fellow BMW volunteers about a BMW motorcycle, or H.O.G volunteers about a Harley. You should also limit your help calls to genuine emergencies and not use the directory just to score a free room for the night. For more information about owners groups and associations for your brand of motorcycle, ask your dealer.

While volunteers generally bend over backward to help stranded club members, you can't assume they will be available 24-7. You might not find anyone home when you call, or you might have to wait until after working hours for someone to come to your aid. On the other hand, you might find someone just down the road with a trailer handy, working tools in the garage, and spare parts on the shelf. The potential for assistance is certainly worth carrying an anonymous book with you.

Motorcycle Emergency Road Service

For the most comprehensive assistance, you can purchase emergency road service from commercial companies if you and your motorcycle qualify. The obvious advantage of commercial plans is twenty-four-hour, full-time roadside help, but extra benefits may include trip routing, maps, emergency messages, cellular phone rental, and discounts on car rentals and lodging. Commercial plans may exclude certain brands or machines older than a specified age. Motorcycle groups such as H.O.G and the Honda Riders Club of America (HRCA) have various forms of emergency road service. Since the services change from year to year, check with your dealer or the membership representatives of your club to see if you and your machine qualify for a roadside assistance policy and for the current fee.

Another big advantage of commercial roadside assistance plans for motorcyclists is that they are likely to have towing firms with motorcycle-friendly equipment. Auto towing companies generally are not equipped to transport a motorcycle without risk of damage. Imagine your shiny bike supported by chains, banging back and forth on the back of a tow truck, and you'll appreciate having someone who has the proper equipment to transport motorcycles.

New Bike Road Service

Some motorcycle brands include emergency road service on new bikes for a specified number of months or years. If roadside assistance is high on your list of priorities, check with the dealer's finance representative while you're looking at new models. Roadside service might be the determining factor in which brand you buy.

One final note about roadside breakdowns: At the time, a breakdown will tax your sanity and your ingenuity. But later on, after you have survived the problem, it will become the highlight of your trip, the tale getting taller at each telling. It's all part of the great motorcycle adventure.

When in Rome. . .

There's an old saying, "When in Rome, do as the Romans do." Riding out of state isn't quite as confusing as riding in a different country, but you still have to assume that the rules change whenever you cross a border.

California Calvin is on a trip north to Canada on the bike he calls the rat patrol. Cal is a bit of a maverick and enjoys the notoriety of a ratty-looking bike, with its black primer paint job, straight-pipes and a front wheel sticking way out there without a fender. He'd sort of assumed that traffic would thin out as he headed north, but passing through Seattle during the afternoon rush hour, he runs into the same sort of jugged-up traffic he had left behind in Southern California.

As cars slow to a crawl on the I-5, Cal eyes the white line between the lanes, and decides to split traffic just as he does back home. Snaking his machine between the cars, he gets a lot of nasty stares. And then a pickup truck actually cuts him off. The driver looks him right in the eye and eases over into Cal's bike until the saddlebags are rubbing against the tires of an 18-wheeler on the other side.

Cal rolls off the gas to extricate himself and pulls back in line. He is furious at the nerve of the pickup truck driver and is thinking seriously about some retaliatory action when the blue and red lights of the Washington State Patrol start flashing. Sergeant Friendly wants to have a little chat with Cal.

The trooper asks Cal for his license and registration, and he immediately starts a short lecture: *We frown on lane splitting up here. You're lucky you aren't a grease spot now.* Cal can't just shut up and take the lecture. He protests that he splits lanes all the time back home. That attitude pushes the conversation into a more confrontational mode. The officer says, *I notice you have some vehicle discrepancies. Washington requires a front fender on a motorcycle, the headlight and taillight illuminated whenever the motorcycle is in motion, a mirror on both sides of the handlebars, and approved eye protection. Your exhaust pipes don't appear to have legal mufflers, your insurance card is out-of-date, and I suspect your beanie helmet isn't DOT approved. But since you're from out of state, I'm going to cut you some slack and only write you up for an improper lane change. I suggest you take care of those equipment violations as soon as you can. By the way, have you noticed that your license expires tomorrow? Have a nice day.*

In my travels, I've encountered a lot of riders like Cal who get into trouble because of the mental baggage they are carrying. The common misconception is that whatever they do back home will be fine elsewhere. It's easy to forget about important differences as we travel from one state to another because the changes are usually subtle. We just ride across a state line without having to show a passport or change money, so there's no reminder to make any mental adjustments. The point is that even though the interstate signs and restaurant menus may be familiar from coast to coast, local laws, drivers' attitudes, and regional booby traps can be much different from what you've come to expect back home.

Rome, Italy

Legal vs. Acceptable

What's acceptable in a certain part of the world doesn't necessarily mirror what's legal. For instance, the Revised Code of Washington may require all loads on trucks to be secured, but over in Waterville during the haying season you'd just get a good snicker from the Douglas County Sheriff for reporting a hay truck scattering straw into the air. Speed signs in southern Nevada might read 55 mph, but local drivers, including the Nye County Sheriff, the Warm Springs Baptist minister, and the mayor of Duckwater, are more likely to be cruising along at warp speeds. That doesn't mean speeding is legal, just that speed enforcement isn't a high priority out in those wide-open spaces.

The moral is that you need to be aware of local customs, habits, and tolerances, as well as what's legal. The best clue to local customs is to watch the natives, especially the local motorcyclists. Check the license plates. In Rome, Georgia, watch what the Georgia and Alabama riders are doing. If the Pennsylvania riders aren't splitting lanes in Altoona, take a hint. Will you risk a ticket by parking your scoot on the sidewalk in South Bend? Well, are all the Indiana bikes parked on the sidewalk or are they on the street, one to a meter?

Laws

Like it or not, laws are selectively enforced. You shouldn't be amazed that certain laws are policed more aggressively for motorcyclists than for other motorists. That should be obvious when you see a specific sign about motorcycle helmets, radar detectors, or turning lights on as you cross a state line. There are thousands of other laws that don't get posted, so that's a good hint about what they are enforcing. Sometimes the signs are humorous, but the intent of the legal eagles is serious.

Remember, each state has a different set of motorcycle laws. The key is that you are required to obey the laws of the state you are riding

You might find some signs humorous, but when the state puts up a sign, you'd be smart to figure out what it means.

If you happen to pass a licensing office in your travels, pick up a copy of that state's operator manual, which includes the primary laws affecting motorcycles.

in, not just your home state. All fifty states (and many foreign countries) accept your motorcycle license or endorsement from your home state but for only a temporary time period. In other words, your Texas license is okay in Louisiana or Germany, and your British license will do for riding across the U.S., although there may be time limits. For travel in foreign countries, you can get an international driver's

David L. Hough

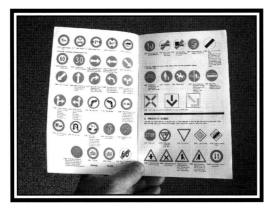

If you're headed for a foreign country, make a point of picking up a booklet on the traffic laws, such as this little volume from the Swiss Motoring Club.

license through American Automobile Association (AAA) offices. The primary use of an international license is to document your licensing status in several different languages, to make it easier for foreign officials who don't speak English.

The AMA provides a periodically updated list of common motorcycle laws, state by state, to give you some clue about what's legal or not as you cruise toward the horizon. Since laws change from year to year, it's worthwhile to check prior to a long trip. You can access this list on the Internet or by calling the AMA. If you are planning a big trip, this information could save you some legal snarls.

Most states provide a motorcycle operator manual, which you can pick up free of charge at driver licensing offices. If you happen to notice a licensing office in your travels, consider stopping to pick up a copy of that state's operator manual, which includes the primary laws affecting motorcycles.

If your travel plans are going to take you to a foreign country, you're advised to obtain a copy of the traffic rules to help you understand the road markings and signs, which may be considerably different from those of any state in the U.S. For instance, in Europe, a white sign with a gray slash means the previous limitation ends. A motorcycle symbol inside a red circle doesn't mean here's where to park your bike; it means no motorcycles allowed. Foreign governments may not provide such information to tourists, but it is often available from other sources, such as tourist agencies or motoring clubs.

The Europeans don't waste time on silly details such as whether you should ride with your wrist up or down. They get right to the important stuff such as warning and regulatory signs.

Insurance

Insurance is a different can of worms. Different states (countries, provinces, districts, etc.) have different insurance requirements. Most states (as well as Mexico and most other countries) require liability, or third party, insurance for motorcyclists. Even if your state doesn't require liability insurance, you'll need to obtain it if you are riding to a state that requires liability insurance. Most U.S. underwriters include Canada at no additional premium but not Mexico or European countries. The smart tactic is to buy insurance prior to crossing a border.

If you are planning a long-distance trip, it might be a good idea to have a chat with your insurance agent before you depart to make sure you are covered wherever you are headed. I can recall only one time I was stopped at a roadblock in the U.S. and asked for license, registration, and insurance card, but it does happen. And if you get stopped for speeding, the first thing the guy with the gun will ask for is your documentation.

The Motorcycle Industry Council (MIC) tracks common motorcycle laws, including insurance requirements. If your local insurance agent is stumped about requirements for a different state, the MIC Government Relations office may be able to provide the information. Be aware that the AMA and MIC track only common state laws applicable to two-wheeled motorcycles. They don't make much of an effort to determine laws relating to three-wheeled motorcycles.

Stock Is Good

If you ride an extensively modified machine, there's an additional risk of being snagged for equipment violations. Basically, a stock-looking bike probably won't draw attention, even if it isn't strictly legal. Be careful about adding or modifying lights, because equipment laws very carefully control lighting, and questionable lights give the police a reason to stop you. For instance, you might think that blue dot taillights would look neat on the back of your bike, but laws requiring taillights to be red are rigidly enforced in some areas.

Yes, you can poke fun at the laws by seeing how far over the line you can go without being cuffed and hauled off to the pokey. Back home, you may know the Danville Chief of Police as Cousin Dan, but in Natchitoches or Plaquemine, the officers probably won't see the humor in illegal or aggressive actions. When you're traveling far from home, it's not too clever to advertise for confrontations. My suggestion is to focus on beating the road hazards and avoid attracting the attention of the legal eagles. Keep it stock-looking, keep it quiet, and keep it under control.

Regional Booby Traps

Adapting to local riding customs isn't just a matter of ducking tickets, it has a lot to do with whether you keep on traveling or spend the rest of your trip munching hospital food. On a trip away from your home turf, you should be aware of different regional booby traps. I assume you have already figured out the weather patterns, know that temperature drops as you gain altitude, and realize that different state maps have different scales. But have you considered that different highway maintenance departments use vastly different repair techniques? For example, in one state, highway maintenance crews may glue down strips of slick white plastic for surface markings such as directional arrows, while a different state may use a gritty plasterlike material that has much better traction.

Big shiny steel plates bouncing around in the streets are a way of life in cities such as San Francisco and New York. And while it would be rare to have a wild deer jump out in front of you in Brooklyn, Seattle, or San Jose, that's an everyday road hazard in West Virginia and Pennsylvania. In Wyoming, you can expect antelope. In

When the highway department erects a big billboard about some hazard, you really ought to pay attention to the problem.

the Northwest and Northeast, you'll see moose signs (and they aren't referring to the fraternal lodge, either). Up on the Alcan Highway in Canada, expect Caribou.

If you're sightseeing in San Francisco, pay close attention to those cable car tracks with the extra slot between the rails.

I've never heard of a motorcyclist ever knocking down a moose. That's not to say that a number of motorcyclists haven't tried. An adult moose is a large and sturdy animal, weighing 1,200 pounds or more. When the highway department goes to all the trouble of putting up huge billboards warning of animal crossings (hence the potential for collisions with animals), you'd be smart to pay attention.

In the Washington and Oregon forests, one of the big motorcycle hazards is when logging trucks drop big chunks of bark or clods of mud into your path. And the truck drivers are always in a rush. Give 'em a lot of room. In North Carolina, the hazards are aggressive truck traffic in the east and gawking tourists in the mountains. In West Virginia, it's coal trucks. In Nevada, Arizona, and New Mexico, it's the heat, punctuated by flash floods. In Oklahoma and Kansas, it's tornados.

The list could go on and on, but the point is that the traveler needs to adjust riding style to regional hazards, whatever the situation may be. If you hail from the big city, you're probably used to dodging cars and trucks at high velocities and close proximities, so when the road is clear of traffic your instinct is to crank up the wick. But you may observe that in forested areas, local riders seem to ride at a much more sedate pace at certain times of the day. They slow down during the early morning hours and during the hour on either side of sunset. So, before you zip on around the locals and show 'em your big-city riding skills, snap your left fingers in front of your eyes and remember that business about mental baggage. Ease up on that riding style you brought from home, and focus on the local situation.

Surface Hazards

You're probably familiar with the road surface problems in your home area. But remember that there are different hazards over the horizon. For example, if you're sightseeing in San Francisco for the first time, have a lot of respect for those cable car tracks with the extra slot between the rails for the cable-grabber. San Francisco streets also seem to be constantly under construction, with temporary steel plates covering the holes. That's a lot of shiny steel in the street, and some of those streets are on steep hills. Take special care to keep your tires out of the grooves and avoid any dramatic takeoffs or stoppies while you're crossing the shiny steel.

Grated Bridge Decks

Have you encountered grated bridge decks yet? If you haven't, you're in for a thrill. Grated decks are made up of vertical steel strips with open spaces in between. The thrill comes from your tires nervously dancing around on the steel edges.

The narrow Bridge of the Gods between Washington and Oregon is a special thrill ride when the winds are howling up the Gorge, which means almost every summer

Have you encountered grated bridge decks yet? The thrill comes from your tires nervously dancing around on the shiny edges of those vertical steel strips.

afternoon. The Mackinac Bridge from northern to southern Michigan is even scarier, longer, and higher. Grated bridge decks are often used on lift spans, which open to allow boats to go through, because the steel is much lighter than a comparable concrete deck. Yes, there are a lot of motorcycle accidents on grated bridge decks, usually the result of a rider attempting some sudden maneuver, such as a quick slowdown or lane change.

Good news, bad news. The good news is that today's wide, oval tires don't wiggle around as much on grooves and ridges. The bad news is that today's powerful engines and brakes can easily punch through the traction envelope on slick surfaces. The tactic for riding on grated decks is to maintain a steady speed, concentrate on pointing the front end in the direction you want to go, ignore whatever the rear end is doing, and have faith you'll get to the other side.

The point of all this is to adopt the local attitude when you travel away from home. With a little planning and a lot of observation, you should be able to have a good time without suffering the indignity of receiving a hard-luck trophy. Now, get out those maps and start planning a long-distance journey.

Know When to Fold 'Em

I should have realized the Kenny Rogers concert at Billings was a premonition about how my trip was going to end. I'd been invited to do some seminars at a big Gold Wing rally. Kenny was giving a concert, and a benevolent Gold Wing rider had given me a ticket. When Rogers got to his famous gambler piece, I should have taken the advice personally.

I didn't want to cancel my big trip just because of a little back pain.

An old back problem had resurfaced just a couple of days before the cross-country trip that included rallies in both Montana and Michigan. I didn't want to cancel the trip because I had obligations to give seminars at both events.

On the road, the riding position on my BMW K1 didn't seem to increase the pain. But at the rallies, I was on my feet way too much. By the end of the second rally in Michigan, the message was making itself clear: my back was refusing to cooperate with riding the bike 2,500 miles home. Fortunately for me, a fellow BMW rider volunteered to store my bike in Chicago and got me on a flight home.

This episode reminded me of how difficult it is to abandon the original travel plan and come up with a new one. Usually, we ride our bikes out and ride them back home. Once in a while, a crisis comes along that delays the trip or even ends the journey out on the road somewhere. The crisis may be weather, mechanical, financial, social, or medical.

Motorcycling travelers are tough and independent, and we tend to keep motoring toward the horizon as long as the bike still runs and we can hang in the saddle.

Whatever the crisis, the biggest problem is just coming to grips with the idea that we may have to interrupt the trip or that we aren't going to be riding the bike home.

Let's say you are making a fast transit homeward and run into a bad storm two days out. Even if it's a tornado or a blizzard coating the road with ice, the urge is to just get back on the bike and keep rolling. It's hard to make the decision to hole up in Nowhereville for a couple of days, waiting for a storm to pass on by. Maybe it's just that riders like to push the envelope. Or maybe it's a fear of failing to complete what we set out to do. But most of the veteran riders I know have scars, broken bones, frostbitten fingers, and photos of totaled bikes to prove we have a problem with knowing when to quit.

When I say "we" need to get a little smarter about knowing our limits, I'm including myself. In Chicago, even with considerable back pain, I was still debating whether to fly home or get back in the saddle and see how far I could ride the bike. We obviously need to make smarter decisions about dealing with trip interruptions.

Weather

Because we're more exposed to the elements than car drivers, we need to be a bit more clever than the average motorist about dealing with changing weather conditions.

On my eastbound leg across Montana and the Dakotas, there were several storm fronts blowing through. The night before departing

Motorcyclists need to be a bit more clever than the average motorist about dealing with changing weather conditions

from Billings, the Weather Channel showed severe thunderstorms over the border of Montana and South Dakota, with reports of baseball-sized hail. The storms were moving rapidly eastward across the Dakotas, and I gambled that I'd be several hours behind them if I took a more northern route across North Dakota. The gamble paid off. I was able to synchronize my progress with a bubble of blue sky for the next couple of days, thanks to the Weather Channel.

On the flip side, I was once making an all-night transit from Seattle down to central Oregon that had me ascending the slopes of Mount Hood a little after midnight. It started to rain, which turned to sleet then snow, as I gained altitude, and I was still 1,000 feet (in elevation) short of the summit. I turned around, paused for a few minutes to warm my freezing fingers on the cylinder head, and retreated back to lower elevations. The alternate route was east through the Columbia River Gorge, then south over a lower pass, perhaps 200 miles farther than my original plan.

When I finally pulled in at the rally site Saturday afternoon, I mentioned the sleet and snow to the other riders. Those who had come over the mountain later that morning reported blue sky and dry pavement. If I had just holed up in some all-night restaurant for a few hours, I could have continued over the pass in the sunshine and saved myself 200 extra miles and a lot of discomfort. Yes, it was a good idea to turn around and get off the mountain. But it might have been a better idea to wait for daylight hours to go over the mountain pass.

There is no single answer for weather problems. What's important is to think clearly about what's happening and be willing to adjust your travel plan to reduce the risks. For instance, if you are suddenly surrounded by a thunderstorm, it's not smart to keep riding nor is it wise to park under a tall tree. Your rubber tires are not going to insulate you from a lightning strike. If you have a choice, get yourself inside a building until the storm passes. If you can't get inside a building, stop under an overpass. If a storm is bearing down on you and you can't find any other shelter, consider hunkering down in a dry ditch.

The trick is to be willing to change your route or your schedule without a major psychological hang-up. If your habit is to navigate by just following freeway signs rather than by studying maps or using a Global Positioning System (GPS), the tendency will be to just keep motoring ahead into a storm, hoping it won't get too bad. It's a lot easier to revise your plans if you've got a map in your tank bag and you're in the habit of thinking about alternate routes.

Mechanical Breakdowns

As with weather problems, the biggest hang-up with a bike problem is often psychological. When you're suddenly stranded, it's easy to panic and make strange decisions such as attempting to push your loaded bike toward the next town 20 miles away. Take a deep breath, put your original plan on hold, and think as calmly and logically as you can. Roll the bike away from traffic, take off your helmet, and calm down. If it's hot, take a drink of water and try to find or erect some shade.

It's a sad sign of the times, but stranded motorcyclists have been ignored by passing bikers as well as by car drivers. We'd like to think that motorcyclists would be willing to help a stranded rider, but there are apparently more and more self-centered bikers out there. If you see a motorcyclist stopped by the side of the road, do us both a favor and see if you can help, regardless of the brand of motorcycle. After all, what goes around comes around.

Find Someone to Lean On

When you're panicked, lean on others for advice, but use a little common sense when sharing your dilemma. The police may be able to suggest what to do next. If you have an emergency roadside assistance policy, call the number and explain the situation. Even if it isn't a mechanical emergency, the person on the other end of the line may be able to offer advice about what to do next or forward a message for you. Some plans provide emergency cash or medical payments. Your bike insurance company may be able to help too. Writing down the telephone number of your insurance companies on a sticker that's in plain view is helpful when you're panicked. The point is, calm down and deal with the situation. Don't just keep motoring toward the horizon, burning up the last of your fuel.

Financial

Sometimes the problem is financial. You reach into your pocket to pay for gas, and your wallet isn't there. Or you slide a credit card in the machine at the gas pump, and it won't work any more. It's panic time, unless you have a backup plan. Most veteran riders stash emergency cash somewhere on their bikes or in a jacket pocket. A $20 bill wrapped in a plastic bag survives for years in a toolkit.

If you lose your wallet, don't lose your cool. The trip isn't necessarily over. Think back to where you stopped last. If you keep your wallet in a pocket inside your riding gear, it's unlikely you lost it to a pickpocket. The odds are that you dropped your wallet or left it at the cash register when you last paid for food or fuel. When I gas up or pay for a meal, I keep the receipt and stuff it in a jacket pocket. That's one way to figure out where you gassed up or had lunch. Someone might be holding your wallet and just waiting for you to call.

If you think a thief has ripped you off, it's important to take action to limit your responsibility for credit card charges. Contact the local police, who can help you through the process. At least you'll want to notify your credit card companies and initiate action to get your driver's license replaced. It's helpful to have your credit card numbers and your bank's telephone number recorded somewhere, say in your address book.

Credit card problems are relatively easy to solve. Let's say your credit card refuses to work at the gas pump (after you made the mistake of parking your wallet on top of the TV the night before). First, try a different pump to see if it's a problem with the card reader. If it still doesn't work, take the card inside and let the attendant fill out a charge slip manually.

And even if you can't access a cash machine, your credit cards will probably be accepted at a bank, where the teller can read the numbers. Yes, it may cost you extra to get a cash advance from your account, but it's better than finding yourself hungry and out of gas with no cash in hand.

You can also telephone home or call your bank or credit union and have cash wired to you. A bank may even let you use the telephone. If you don't have the coins for a long-distance call, make a collect call or have the call charged to your home phone number.

Debit or Credit?

Some words of advice about charge cards: when using plastic for purchases such as motel rooms and meals, use it as a credit card, not as a debit card. A credit transaction has much more fraud protection. A debit is usually required for cash withdrawals but offers almost no protection against fraud. If a crooked waiter or motel clerk steals your card number and purchases a few thousand dollars worth of merchandise over the phone as debits, that person can drain your account while you're sleeping, and the bank doesn't have to share the responsibility when you discover the loss.

With a credit charge, take steps to reduce the chances of someone finding your numbers in a trash can. After the cashier fills out the charge slip, cross out the last four digits of your card number on the original and any of the copies. When the actual charge is electronic, your personal account numbers are not needed for any records, and it's legal for you to do this. This won't prevent a crooked waiter from downloading your card data on a pocket reader in the back room, but it will help keep your private data more secure as the charge slips circulate around the accounting office.

Social Crisis

If you're not having fun on a group ride, that's a clue that it's time to fold your participation and continue the trip alone. First, try announcing your decision to the other riders or to the group leader. Don't feel obliged to explain your reasons. Just say that you have decided to travel on your own starting tomorrow. Don't get sucked into an argument about the situation; just make it clear that you are splitting.

David L. Hough

If you're not having fun on a group ride, that's a clue that it's time to fold your participation and continue the trip alone.

If the other riders won't easily accept your decision, back off, but keep in mind how easy it is to get "lost" on a group ride. Get up early and depart on your own. Or, drop back a few miles and take a different road. If you've already explained your feelings, the others should get the message not to waste any time looking for you. Yes, leaving the group will probably cause hard feelings, but if it's the group that's the problem, you're probably better off severing your relationship with these people.

Medical Problems

If the crisis is an accident or serious injury, the decision is automatic. For instance, if you end up in a hospital, plugged into life support, no one needs to convince you the ride is over. The hospital staff will probably take over the process of notifying your relatives, the police will arrange to have your bike hauled away, and your relatives will start making decisions for you.

The problem is when we're still mobile and still undecided about whether to keep going or to hang it up. On my Montana to Michigan trip, I was in pain, but I wasn't bleeding. I could still get dressed, hold the bike up, and keep food down. It wasn't a problem, such as a heart attack or broken leg, that demanded immediate medical attention. But I could have been a lot smarter about seeking help. I could have stopped at a fire station and asked the EMTs for advice. I could have located a medical clinic or chiropractor for some assistance.

I could have canceled my trip at the beginning and notified the rally folks I wouldn't be doing any seminars. On the other hand, I'd had back problems before, and the pain would usually subside after a week or so. In retrospect, the decision to head out wasn't wrong, but I'm glad I decided to fold the motorcycle trip at the halfway point when the pain flared up. That decision was a lot easier because a fellow rider stepped in with assistance. We should all be so lucky.

Hopefully, thinking through these things in advance will help you avoid the panic when you encounter your next crisis out on the road somewhere. As Kenny Rogers sings, "You gotta know when to fold 'em."

The Bottom Line

CHAPTER 10
THE BOTTOM LINE

Ten Tips That Can Save Your Life

Most of us understand that mastering the ride takes a lot of study plus years of skill practice. We need to explore both the concepts of managing risk and the riding exercises that help build proficient control skills. That's why I've gone into considerable detail about both the mental and physical skills in *Proficient Motorcycling* and *More Proficient Motorcycling*. But if you want the short course, here are ten tactics that sum it all up.

1. **Anticipate what's going to happen.** Accidents may seem to occur suddenly, but there is almost always an advance warning for riders who are looking and thinking about what's happening ahead. By observing the flow of traffic around, behind, and especially in front of you, you can often spot a potential collision several seconds before it becomes an immediate crisis. Are you prepared for an oncoming car to turn left in front of you or for the vehicles ahead to suddenly come to a stop?

    The more time you have to anticipate problems, the less often those problems will seem to occur suddenly, and the more time you'll have to react.

Anticipate what's going to happen.

Two ways to increase your anticipation time are looking farther ahead and reducing speed in busy situations. Continuously scan the situation you are riding into, and then anticipate what will happen as the next few seconds unfold. Reducing speed reduces the distance you will travel over the same time, and that results in fewer potential hazards to observe.

Most importantly, expect the unexpected. Why do the majority of motorcycle accidents happen on familiar streets, within a few miles of home, and in perfect daytime weather? Because that's where local riders get complacent. Far away from home, a traveler must negotiate strange traffic that demands full attention. Close to home, familiar streets seem to be predictable, and local riders assume they know what's happening. Keep your head in the ride, especially when you're close to home.

2. **Never ride under the influence.** Alcohol is often implicated in motorcycle accidents, and it isn't just a matter of drunk car drivers running into innocent motorcyclists. Motorcyclists involved in accidents tend to have higher BACs than operators of any other types of vehicles.

Anticipating what's happening ahead depends upon good vision and clear thinking. And avoiding collisions depends upon good judgment, quick reactions, and accurate control skills. Consuming even one ounce of alcohol starts to degrade vision, judgment, reactions, and motor skills for most adults. A couple of beers don't sound like much, but even a small amount of alcohol can mean the difference between life and death. The obvious tactic for avoiding alcohol-precipitated crashes is to avoid riding after drinking. And that's a decision you have to make before your judgment is impaired.

3. **If you're going to ride fast, get serious.** Excessive speed is

The obvious tactic for avoiding alcohol-precipitated crashes is to avoid riding after drinking.

Riding fast on public roads involves not only good control skills but also the knowledge and judgment to avoid hazards such as a left-turning farm tractor in a blind corner.

often implicated in single-vehicle motorcycle crashes. The real culprit is not simply speed but rather punching through the envelope defined by the rider's skill level and the situation. Riding fast on the public roads involves not only good control skills but also the knowledge and judgment to avoid hazards such as a left-turning farm tractor in a blind corner.

So, if you are going to ride fast on public roads, get serious about tactics and control skills for riding fast. One primary tactic is to adjust speed for sight distance. The edge of the speed envelope should be dictated by the view ahead, not by memory or prediction. As the view expands, speed can increase. But when the view contracts, immediately reduce speed so that you can always come to a complete stop within the roadway you can see ahead. The more you must predict what the road is doing beyond your view, the greater the risk.

4. **Countersteer.** Practice countersteering to control lean angle and direction. A common single-vehicle motorcycle accident is running out of road in a curve,

Make a habit of countersteering to control lean angle and direction, not just simply thinking *lean*.

most often in a downhill, left-hand turn. In urban traffic, crashes have occurred when the motorcycle crossed the centerline in a decreasing radius turn or the rider could not change direction quickly enough to avoid a collision with another vehicle that suddenly got in the way.

Two-wheelers are controlled accurately by pushing on the grips, rather than by merely shifting weight. Turns are initiated by momentarily steering the front wheel opposite to the direction of lean. That is, to turn right, push on the right grip. To turn left, push on the left grip. Because the handlebars are initially turned opposite, or counter, to the direction of lean, this is called countersteering.

The reason it is better to control a motorcycle by consciously countersteering rather than allowing the brain to do it automatically is that habits tend to limit lean angles and roll rates. If you fall into the habit of steering around corners by just thinking *lean*, your habits may prevent you from making quick evasive maneuvers when needed. Worse yet, the rider who does not understand or practice countersteering may panic in a crisis and steer the bike in the wrong direction. The key is to consciously use countersteering on every ride.

5. **Get in the habit of using the front brake.** Quick stops are the primary tactic for avoiding a collision with hazards such as a left-turning car or a deer in the roadway. Yet many accidents occur when the rider either doesn't get on the brakes at all or applies too much rear brake, causing the bike to slide out. When you need to reduce speed quickly or stop in the shortest possible distance, the correct technique is to get the bike vertical in a straight line and brake harder on the front as weight transfers to the front tire. Shortest stops are made with both brakes applied firmly but just short of a skid. And that requires not only skill but good habits.

In a crisis situation, habits determine reactions. A rider who consistently uses the front brake effectively in normal riding will use the front brake during a crisis. Quick stops depend upon good habits, even on machines with integrat-

In a crisis situation, habits determine reactions. A rider who consistently uses the front brake effectively in normal riding will use the front brake during a crisis.

ed systems or ABS. Braking in corners is a skill that can be improved through practice and is especially important for riders of machines with these systems. When it is necessary to make a quick stop while in a turn, the primary technique is to straighten the bike to vertical and then make a maximum-effort, straight-line stop. But the faster you ride, the more important it is to be able to brake hard while still rounding a curve.

6. **Get some training when you get a new motorcycle.** A new motorcyclist can significantly reduce the risks of riding that first machine by taking a rider training course taught by professional instructors, rather than by learning from friends or family. Motorcyclists trained by certified instructors have about half the accident rate of self-taught riders.

    But even if you've been riding for years, you're a lot more likely to have an accident on a bike you're not familiar with. It might seem that once you have learned to ride, it would be easy to transfer those riding skills to a different motorcycle, but the statistics hint that the risks double with a new or different machine.

    The Hurt Report calls the motorcycle on which the rider crashed the "accident motorcycle." According to the Hurt Report, motorcyclists who have been riding the accident motorcycle for less than six months have twice the accident frequency of those with twelve month's experience on the same machine. The accident

Even if you're an experienced rider, take a training course when you buy a new machine.

David L. Hough

risk for those with forty-eight month's experience on the same motorcycle is reduced to one-fourth of the six-month rate.

So, if you're an experienced rider who buys a new motorcycle, you would be smart to take a rider training course on that new machine. Training exercises such as tight turns, cornering speed selection, and stopping in curves will quickly familiarize you with the controls and characteristics of the different motorcycle.

7. **Wear an approved helmet.** Use your head, protect your brain. The human brain wasn't designed to survive bouncing down a road at motorcycle speeds. A helmet is no cure-all for stupid riding, but an approved helmet can help prevent brain injury during a crash. The average crash speed of 20 mph is fast enough to produce a 1,000 g head impact with the pavement. (That's an instantaneous 1,000 times the force of gravity.) A 400 g impact is enough to cause a brain concussion.

A helmet is no cure-all for stupid riding, but an approved helmet can help prevent brain injury during a crash.

Impartial experts who have studied helmet effectiveness in real-life motorcycle crashes confirm that even a cheap DOT-approved helmet can reduce brain injuries. Even the cheapest DOT-approved fiberglass helmet can reduce a 1,000 g impact to 150 g. The more coverage the helmet offers, the greater the protection. Remember the most likely impact area of a motorcyclist is the chin.

Some bikers wear costume helmets. You know, those flimsy plastic shells that look sort of like a helmet, but aren't made to protect your brain. Perhaps it's a personal statement about risk acceptance or a protest against mandatory helmet laws. But a pretend helmet without an energy-absorbing liner transfers the full impact of a crash directly to the brain.

8. **Get a license.** More than one-fourth of motorcyclists involved in fatal accidents are not licensed to ride a motorcycle or have previous license suspensions.

A motorcycle license or endorsement is more than a legal formality. The knowledge and riding tests provide an objective evaluation of skills. A rider may learn of deficiencies in braking or steering, or that person may find that his or her vision needs correcting. Perhaps the most important reason for getting a license is that submitting to a test helps a rider develop the attitude that motorcycling is serious business, not a lark. Getting a license revoked should be a wake-up call about a dangerous attitude or poor riding skills. What's more, in those states in which licensing fees finance rider training, the unlicensed rider is avoiding his or her fair share of the costs, even while the training program is providing the benefits of fewer accidents and reduced insurance premiums. If you're serious about motorcycling, you'll get a motorcycle endorsement.

9. **Stay home on Friday night.** There are more motor vehicle accidents on weekdays than on weekends, but weekday collisions tend to be fender benders. Weekend crashes are typically more deadly. Friday and Saturday night crashes are three times more likely to be high-impact collisions with more fatalities.

Fatal accidents are most likely between 9:00 P.M. Friday night and 3:00 A.M. Saturday morning, with the peak risk at 1:00 A.M. Saturday (when drunks head

If you're serious about motorcycling, you'll have a motorcycle license.

home from the taverns). As you might suspect, the risks are also high Saturday night, peaking at 1:00 A.M. Sunday.

The bottom line is that riding around on a motorcycle in traffic late Friday or Saturday night seriously increases your risks of a fatal accident, even if you haven't been drinking. If you're going to be out in traffic during the dangerous hours, you'd be better off in a vehicle that offers greater protection than a motorcycle in a crash.

10. **Learn to read the road surface.** One of the reasons two-wheelers have a higher accident rate than automobiles is that motorcycles require traction just to stay upright. Where a car might slide sideways on loose gravel or spilled diesel oil, a motorcycle is more likely to fall down. The important key to keeping the rubber side down is predicting the surface traction of the road ahead before you get there. Since you have a good idea of the relative traction of the surface you're already on, look for differences in color or texture of the surface ahead.

When you observe that the road surface ahead is different, reduce your traction needs until you determine whether the different pavement has more traction or less traction. For exam-

Riding around on a motorcycle in traffic late Friday or Saturday night seriously increases your risks of a fatal accident, even if you haven't been drinking.

The important key to keeping the rubber side down is predicting the surface traction of the road ahead.

ple, the white color of a plastic directional arrow on the pavement makes you suspect it of being slicker than the surrounding asphalt. The rougher texture of the surface in the corner ahead could be loose gravel or it could be tractable concrete.

Some road surfaces that are especially hazardous to two-wheelers. Long, hard edges such as railroad tracks, curbs, grooves, steel plates, and sunken pavement become traps from which the unwary motorcyclist cannot escape. When such edge traps run parallel to the motorcycle's path, they must be avoided or crossed at the widest possible angle.

Between Rides

Ten Tips plus a Free One

I had to take a month off from writing toward the end of 1997. I just couldn't type with a big bandage on my throbbing finger. I'd mangled my "switch to channel 1" finger on my left hand when the bike toppled off the jack while I was changing the knobby desert tire back to the street tire. It's always a bit of a shock to feel pain and see blood dripping off an appendage. The finger has healed nicely—just a little scar, thank you. But the event reminded me that there are risks involved in bike maintenance as well as in riding. I'd like to share some personal discoveries I've made over the years.

1. **Give gasoline a little more respect.** We tend to get complacent about gasoline. Fill up the tank. Ride the bike. Fill up the tank. Ride the bike. Gasoline does its job so well that we tend to forget how much energy it contains. Consider how many miles 1 gallon will push your bike down the road at freeway speeds. Think about the muscle power it would take to push your bike along the shoulder for

the same distance, and multiply that by 50 or so. A gallon of gas can be converted into a lot of energy.

What's really amazing about gasoline is that as a liquid it burns, but as a vapor it explodes. Remember Molotov cocktails used against Russian tanks in the Balkans? They were made from just an empty wine bottle, a couple ounces of gasoline, and a rag. Tip the bottle to soak the rag, light it, and throw. When the bottle shatters, the flaming rag ignites the vapor, and KA-WHOOM!

Keep that image in mind as you fuel your motorcycle. All it takes is one little spark to ignite the fuel vapors pouring out of your tank as you pump it full. It used to make me nervous to see someone smoking a cigarette around a gas station. It doesn't make me nervous any more because if I see someone smoking near the pumps when I pull up, I keep rolling right out the other side. Getting seriously burned is bad enough without also getting punctured by shrapnel from exploding car bodies.

When filling portable containers, the smart precaution is to set them on the ground to encourage any static charge to bleed off.

At a previous residence, my motorcycles used to reside in a garage under the living room. One night after dinner I went down to work on my commuter bike, and in the seconds between opening the door and flipping on the light switch, I smelled gasoline vapor. I yanked my hand away from the switch and opened an outside door to dilute the vapor, and then I looked for the source. A throttle cable had rubbed a hole through the back of a fuel valve, and it had been dripping gas on the floor for a couple of hours. I'll leave it to your imagination what could have happened if I had applied a 115-volt spark to a switchbox full of gas vapor.

There have been a number of explosions of gas cans that were being refilled while resting on plastic truck bed liners or trunk mats. The problem is that portable cans build up a static charge. The fuel nozzle at the pump is grounded, but a portable container isn't. Sometimes the can discharges a spark to the nozzle, igniting the fuel vapor. And, yes, plastic fuel jugs do build up static charges, just like knit sweaters on a cold day. When filling portable containers, the smart precaution is to set them on the ground to encourage any static charge to bleed off. It's also not a bad idea to ground the filler nozzle to the outside of the container before unscrewing the cap.

You should also be aware that today's fuels are relatively hazardous to your health. You know, liver damage, skin cancer, and all that. It's not a good idea to breathe gasoline vapor or dip your skin in liquid gasoline. I can remember using raw gas as a chain-cleaning solvent or paintbrush cleaner when I was an optimistic youth, and even siphoning gas by sucking on the hose, but I don't do that any more. If I knew I was going to last this long, I would have taken better care of myself.

2. **Don't start it in the stall.** When it comes time to tune up your engine in the spring, it's tempting to fire up the bike inside the garage. You're only going to run it for a couple of minutes, right? Well, it only takes a few minutes of

David L. Hough

breathing exhaust vapors for your eyes to be staring up at the coroner. Remember, one of the by-products of burning gas is carbon monoxide (CO). What's really insidious about CO is that it's clear, odorless, and quiet. You won't see it or smell it, and it goes right to the bloodstream, displacing oxygen. If your blood absorbs very much CO, your oxygen-starved brain will conk out. Carbon monoxide is nasty stuff, and if all you get is a headache, you're lucky.

Do yourself a big favor and never, ever start an engine in a closed space. If it's too cold outside, at least roll the bike back toward the open garage door and point the mufflers toward the open air. Cold is better than dead.

Do yourself a big favor and never, ever start an engine in a closed space.

3. **Pulling is good; pushing is bad.** How many times have you skinned a knuckle when a wrench slipped? The hot tip is to pull rather than push. In other words, position the wrench so you are pulling toward you rather than pushing away. If you are pushing on the tool when the bolt shears off or the socket slips, you'll punch your knuckles into those sharp cylinder fins or whatever before you can say, *Ow!* If you are pulling when the part breaks free or the wrench slips, your hand just jerks back toward your body, with much softer results. Yeah, it sounds too simple, but your knuckles will be thanking me next time your wrench slips while you are trying to break loose that big nut on the steering head or tighten that footpeg bolt.

Position the wrench so you are pulling toward you rather than pushing away.

4. **Chamfer those cutting edges.** Motorcycle factories can't afford to spend time smoothing out the sharp edges of machined parts. Even expensive bikes have parts with razor-sharp edges. Maybe it's just a sharp fin on a cylinder casting or the edge of a stamped plate on the back of the frame, but if you slide your finger

across it while washing the bike, you can draw blood. When I notice a sharp edge, I smooth it out. Little blobs of weld splatter can be knocked down with a sharp cold chisel and then touched up with a dab of paint.

Aluminum castings, such as cylinder heads and valve covers, often have sharp edges on the machined surfaces. Whenever I have an engine apart, I spend a few minutes with an oval file or scraper, chamfering the sharp edges. A few minutes with a scraper now can save a lot of blood later.

5. **Watch your welding.** If you need any critical welding done, do yourself a favor and take it to a professional welder, who can either do it right or explain to you why you shouldn't weld that part at all. More than a few serious motorcycle accidents have occurred because someone did an uncritical weld on a critical part. For example, a well-known East Coast rider was seriously injured when the front forks on his vintage BMW collapsed at speed. It's not inconceivable that a thirty-year-old metal tube might have fatigued or rusted away inside. But subsequent reports hinted that the fork tubes had been cut and welded to modify steering geometry and those welds had broken. The rider survived, but at the cost of both legs—a steep price to pay for a poorly engineered or uncritical weld job.

Yes, in the good old days I fearlessly heated up steel with a torch and melted it together. But in spite of my training and good intentions, some of my welds broke. Eventually, I learned to keep my torch away from critical parts such as fasteners, fork tubes, axles, frames, swing arms, and any other highly stressed items. These days I take the critical stuff to a professional welder who has the right equipment and know-how to do the best welding possible.

A few minutes chamfering those sharp edges now will save a lot of cut fingers later.

Take your cutting and welding outside the shop. And for serious welding jobs, take them to a professional who has the right equipment and know-how.

Those of us who do our own welding, cutting, or grinding at home need to remember that hot sparks have ignited a lot of fires, even when a professional welder was involved. I take any spark-generating tasks outside the shop, and make sure the sparks aren't directed toward anything of value. And yes, I keep a fire extinguisher handy.

6. **Don't sprong your springs.** Use a little caution when you're taking apart any assembly that has springs. I'm talking shock absorbers, clutches, cylinder heads, and especially any torsion springs in drive shafts or transmissions. Springs usually need a compression tool to allow a controlled release of tension. If you happen to release a compressed spring suddenly, it can sprong across the room like a bullet. If you don't have the right tools to compress springs safely, take the parts to a mechanic who does.

7. **Pop the bead, not the rim.** Some of us do our own tire mounting. But even tire-mounting veterans should remember that the most dangerous part of the operation is getting the tire seated on the rim. With today's rim configuration, the tire bead has to stretch over a hump to pop into place. If the bead is reluctant to seat, the temptation is to keep pumping up the pressure until it does pop. The potential disaster is that a cracked or dinged wheel rim can suddenly let go, or a flawed tire cord can rip apart. The resulting shrapnel can be serious, even at pressures of 50 or 60 pounds per square inch (psi), and deadly at pressures of 80 or 90 psi. That's one reason serious riders check their wheels carefully and don't attempt to repair a bent or damaged rim.

If you don't have the right tools to compress springs safely, take the parts to a mechanic who does.

When popping the bead, hold the wheel upright, point the side of the wheel away from you, and don't exceed the recommended pressures.

For the home motorcycle mechanic, the best advice for popping the bead is to hold the wheel upright, point the side of the wheel away from you, and don't exceed the recommended pressures. For example, BMW recommends a maximum of 56 psi. If the bead doesn't pop onto a BMW rim by 56 psi, let the air out, clean the rim, smear the contact surfaces again with tire mounting lube or soapy water, and try again. If it's a tube-type wheel, be sure the inner tube or rim strap isn't trapped under the bead somewhere.

8. **Be benevolent to batteries.** Batteries are getting more sophisticated these days, but there are still plenty of lead-acid batteries around that need periodic topping up. One of my battery cases developed some ozone cracks a few years ago. I didn't realize that acid was slowly oozing out of the fine cracks and migrating down the side of the battery. I topped up the electrolyte and wiped the case down with a shop rag. A day or two later the skin started peeling off my fingers. I must have wiped my hands on my pants, too. They came out of the dryer ventilated above the knees.

When you are connecting or disconnecting a battery, the hot tip is to disconnect the negative (ground) cable first when removing the battery; connect the negative cable last when installing.

It was a reminder that battery acid isn't kind to skin or clothing. When you're working around a battery, at least wear eyeglasses or, preferably, safety goggles. When adding distilled water to a lead-acid battery, use a squeeze bottle with a small spout that enables you to dribble water into the cells without splashing. And if you think the battery case might be leaking, remove the battery before it dribbles corrosive acid down onto your frame and running gear.

When you've got the cells topped up, screw the caps in, wash the battery with soapy water, and then wash your hands. A water and baking soda solution neutralizes battery acid, whether it's on your skin or on bike parts. The solution mix isn't critical. Just dump some baking soda in a container of water until most of it dissolves, and use the solution to wash down any suspicious corroded areas. If it foams, the soda is neutralizing the acid.

When charging a motorcycle battery, watch the amperage, or the current flowing into the battery. A big automotive charger may be the correct voltage, but the high amperage will quickly fry a motorcycle battery. Use a low-amperage trickle charger, preferably an automatic charger designed for motorcycles.

Remember that charging a battery produces hydrogen gas, which is explosive. Yes, batteries do occasionally explode, blowing corrosive acid in all directions. No, you don't want that to happen, even if you aren't leaning over the battery at the moment. So, don't wave any flames or sparks near a battery that is being charged or has recently been charged.

When you are connecting or disconnecting a battery, the hot tip is always disconnect the negative (ground) cable first when removing the battery; connect the negative cable last when installing. That way, if you do happen to touch the wrench or screwdriver between the positive battery terminal and the frame, it won't cause any sparks, meltdowns, or explosions.

9. **Use a drill vise.**

A drill press is indispensable for making straight holes in parts or for cutting through tough metals such as stainless steel. But if you're trying to hold a

David L. Hough

small part in your hand, the drill bit can snag the part and turn it into a rotary knife before you can say big dog. It took me a few years and a few nasty cuts and bruises to get around to bolting a drill vise on a table. Now I can clamp the part down and keep my fingers out of the way.

10. Goggle yourself.

Years ago, I arrived at work with one eye irritated. After various unsuccessful attempts to wash out whatever was causing the problem, I finally trotted over to the company medical clinic. The doctor discovered a tiny sliver of steel imbedded straight in the cornea. He managed to remove it with a magnet. The night before, I had been cleaning up some exhaust valves with a wire wheel on my grinder without wearing safety goggles.

The free tip: Secure your stands.

Now, let's get down to the problem that triggered this subject: supporting a bike while doing maintenance or repairs. Back home in my shop, I've got nice jacks and stands to support the machines. But in a dark parking garage in Las Vegas, while trying to wiggle the knobby rear tire past the brake shoes, I pushed my bike off the centerstand and got my fingers in the way. The tip that I knew but didn't remember is to tie off the stand to prevent it from retracting. A bike strap secured between the centerstand and the front wheel does the trick. If you push too hard on the bike, it will just skid.

I knew that. I had a strap. I just didn't take the few seconds to use it. The same tactic works for a bike perched on the sidestand. Sure, you can park it in gear. But if you want to run the engine, there's the risk the bike will roll forward and you could find yourself with a lap full of bike. The easy precaution is to tie off the sidestand to the front wheel. If you like to putter around your motorcycles like I do, take a few hints from my experiences. As with riding a motorcycle, there's no point in taking unnecessary risks between rides.

A drill vise holds those small, sharp parts away from your fingers.

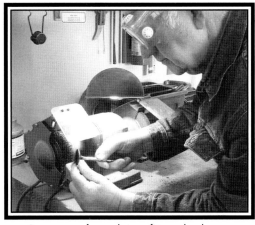

Do your eyes a favor and wear safety goggles whenever you're working around tools that might throw debris into your face.

A tie-down strap keeps a centerstand or sidestand from retracting when you're working on the bike.

Resources

Riding Schools, Courses, and Clinics

Advanced Riding Clinic (Lee Parks)
P.O. Box 1838
Victorville, CA 92393
(800) 943-5638
Web site: www.leeparksdesign.com

California Superbike School
(Keith Code)
940 San Fernando Road
Los Angeles, CA 90065
(323) 224-2734
Web site: www.superbikeschool.com

CLASS Motorcycle Schools
(Reg Pridmore)
320 E. Santa Maria Street, Suite M
Santa Paula, CA 93060-3800
(805) 933-9936
Web site: www.classrides.com

Dennis Pegelow's dp Safety School
DP Enterprises
P.O. Box 1551
Morro Bay, CA 93443-1551
(805) 772-8301
Web site: www.dpsafetyschool.com

Experienced RiderCourse
Call the MSF hotline: (800) 446-9227

Fastrack Riders
P.O. Box 129
San Juan Capistrano, CA 92693-0129
(877) 560-2233
Web site: www.fastrackriders.com

Freddie Spencer's High Performance Riding School (Freddie Spencer)
7055 Speedway Boulevard, Suite E106
Las Vegas, NV 89115
(888) 672-7219
Web site: www.fastfreddie.com

Sidecar/Trike Education Program
Evergreen Safety Council
401 Pontius Avenue N.
Seattle, WA 98109
(206) 382-4090 or (800) 521-0778
Web site: www.esc.org

Stayin' Safe Motorcycle Training School (Larry Grodsky)
P.O. Box 81801
Pittsburg, PA 15217
(412) 421-5711
Email: stayinsafe@earthlink.net

Willow Springs Motorcycle Club New Racer School
P.O. Box 911
Rosamond, CA 93560-0911
(661) 256-1234
Email: wsmcschool@aol.com
Web site:
www.willowspringsraceway.com

Organizations

American Motorcyclist Association
13515 Yarmouth Drive
Pickerington, OH 43147
(614) 856-1900
Web site: www.ama-cycle.org

Bureau of Transportation Statistics
400 7th Street SW, Room 3103
Washington, DC 20590
(800) 853-1351
Web site: www.bts.gov
Email: answers@bts.gov

Insurance Institute for Highway Safety
1005 N. Glebe Road, Suite 800
Arlington, VA 22201
(703) 247-1500
Web site: www.iihs.org

Motorcycle Industry Council
2 Jenner Street
Irvine, CA 92618-3806
(949) 727-3227

Motorcycle Safety Foundation
2 Jenner Street, Suite 150
Irvine, CA 92618-3806
(949) 727-3227
Training hotline: (800) 446-9227

National Center for Statistics and Analysis
National Highway Traffic Safety Administration

NRD-30, 400 Seventh Street SW
Washington DC 20590
(800) 934-8517
Web site: NCSAweb@nhtsa.dot.gov

National Safety Council
1121 Spring Lake Drive
Itasca, IL 60143-3201
(630) 285-1121
Web site: www.nsc.org

Books and Papers

Code, Keith. *A Twist of the Wrist: The Motorcycle Racers Handbook* (first edition). Hollywood, Calif.: Acrobat Books, 1983. (818) 841-7019

Hough, David L. *Proficient Motorcycling: The Ultimate Guide to Riding Well.* Irvine, Calif.: BowTie™ Press, 2000. (888) 738-2665

Hough, David L. *Street Strategies: A Survival Guide for Motorcyclists.* Irvine, Calif.: BowTie™ Press, 2001. (888) 738-2665

Hurt, Hugh H. Jr. *Motorcycle Handling and Collision Avoidance: Anatomy of a Turn.* Second International Congress on Automotive Safety, 1973. Available from Head Protection Research Laboratory, 6409 Alondra Boulevard, Paramount, CA 90723-3759 (562) 529-3295; E-mail: info@hprl.org

Motorcycle Safety Foundation Staff. *The Motorcycle Safety Foundation's Guide to Motorcycling Excellence: Skills, Knowledge, and Strategies for Riding Right.* North Conway, N.H.: Whitehorse Press, 1995. (800) 531-1133

Stermer, Bill. *Motorcycle Touring & Travel.* North Conway, N.H.: Whitehorse Press, 1999. (800) 531-1133

Frame measuring and straightening

G.M.D. Computract Network
Atlanta (404) 297-8464
Boston (508) 876-9407
Chicago (847) 763-9900
Ft. Lauderdale (954) 786-2875
Los Angeles (310) 640-2825
Maryland (301) 668-0747
San Jose (800) 734-2639

Motorcycle Periodicals

Motorcycle Consumer News
Subscriptions: P.O. Box 55661
Boulder, CO 80323-5661
(800) 365-4421

Motorcycle Magazine Back Issues

Ian Smith Information
(303) 777-2385

Motorcycle books

Whitehorse Press
P.O. Box 60
North Conway, NH 03860-0060
(800) 531-1133
Web site: www.WhitehorsePress.com

Motorcycle Riding Gear and Travel Equipment

Aerostich
Eight South 18th Ave. West
Duluth, MN 55806-2148
(800) 222-1994
Web site: www.aerostich.com

Videos

Motorcycle Safety Foundation. *Riding Straight*. 12 min. (MSF Item 512). 1995. Video cassette. To order, send $22.50, plus $3.00 S&H, plus sales tax if you're in California to: Motorcycle Safety Foundation, 2 Jenner Street, Suite 150, Irvine, CA 92718-3812 or call (949) 727-3227.

Emergency Services and Owners Associations

BMW Motorcycle Owners of America
P.O. Box 3982
Ballwin, MO 63022
(636) 394-7277
Web site: www.bmwmoa.org

BMW Riders Association International
P.O. Box 120430
West Melbourne, FL 32912-0430
(321) 984-7800
Web site: www.bmwra.org

Gold Wing Road Riders Association
21423 N 11th Avenue
Phoenix, AZ 85027
(800) 843-9460
Web site: www.gwrra.org

Gold Wing Touring Association
P.O. Box 24175
Indianapolis, IN 46224-0175
(800) 960-4982
Web site: www.gwta.org

Harley Owners Group (H.O.G)
National H.O.G Office
P.O. Box 453,
Milwaukee, WI 53201
(800) 258-2464
Web site: www.hog.com

Honda Riders Club of America
1919 Torrance Boulevard,
Torrance CA 90501-2746
(800) 847-4722
Web site: www.hondamotorcycles.com/hrca/

International Help 'N Hands
American Motorcyclist Association
13515 Yarmouth Drive, Pickerington, OH 43147
(614) 856-1900
Web site: www.AMADirectlink.com

List of Abbreviations

AAA: American Automobile Association
ABS: antilock braking system
AC: Assistant Coroner
AMA: American Motorcyclist Association
AWOL: absent without leave
BAC: blood alcohol concentration
BCMA: British Columbia Medical Association
BMWMOA: BMW Motorcycle Owners of America
cc: cubic centimeter
CoG: center of gravity
CO: carbon monoxide
CO$_2$: carbon dioxide
DMV: Department of Motor Vehicles
DOT: Department of Transportation
DUI: driving under the influence
DWI: driving while intoxicated
EMT: emergency medical technician
ERC: Experienced RiderCourse
EVO: BMW integrated power brake system
g-force: the force of gravity
GPS: Global Positioning System (navigation receiver)
hi-viz: high-visibility (color)
H.O.G: Harley Owners Group
HOV: high occupancy vehicle
HRCA: Honda Riders Club of America
MCN: Motorcycle Consumer News
MIC: Motorcycle Industry Council
mph: miles per hour
MSF: Motorcycle Safety Foundation
NCSA: National Center for Statistics and Analysis
NHTSA: National Highway Traffic Safety Administration
OODA: observe, orient, decide, act
psi: pounds per square inch
rpm: revolutions per minute
S/TEP: Sidecar/Trike Education Program
tach: tachometer, used to display engine rpm
TT: Tourist Trophy, an annual race on the Isle of Man
VID: visually identify

Glossary

This book contains various terms, phrases, and slang words, whose meanings may be obvious to some motorcyclists but not to others. Some of these terms are defined in the following glossary to help all readers understand their meanings.

apex: the location on a curve where a motorcyclist comes closest to the edge of the road

barrel roll: rolling over and over sideways like a barrel rolling across the floor

big dog rider: an experienced and aggressive motorcyclist known for feats of daring and skill, such as riding at high speeds on public roads, without apparent fear of accident or arrest

blind curve: a turn in the road that is partially hidden by visual obstructions such as trees or an embankment, making it so that a rider cannot see the road's path or the hazards around the rest of the turn. Same as blind corner or blind turn.

body English: a method motorcycle riders use to help control lean angle or direction independent of the handlebars by moving body position on the motorcycle

bodysteering: a method used by motorcycle riders to control the direction of the motorcycle or to adjust balance by moving body position laterally on the motorcycle

camber: sideways angle or slant of the pavement

centerstand: a ladderlike stand that pivots down from the center of a motorcycle frame to support the motorcycle

vertically with the rear wheel off the ground

chamfer: scraping the knifelike edge of a machined part to round it off

contact patch: the spot in which the tire of a motorcycle is in contact with the road's surface

cornering line: a motorcycle's path of travel through a curve

countersteering: a method of controlling and balancing a bike as it initiates a turn in which the handlebars are momentarily turned in the direction opposite to where the rider intends to go

crashbar: an external structural part, usually a tubular loop on both sides of a bike, positioned to support the bike in the event of a fall and limit damage to the bike or rider

cruiser: a motorcycle designed for less aggressive riding, i.e. cruising

delayed apex: an apex imagined to be farther around the curve than where the rider believes the sharpest part of the curve actually is

dirt donks: off-road motorcyclists

dual sport: a motorcycle designed to be operated both on and off pavement

edge traps: the raised edges of bumps or cracks in a paved surface that can catch a motorcycle's tire and cause the bike to lose balance

fog line: the white line painted on the outside edge of a paved road to help motorists see the direction of the road in low visibility conditions

hanging off: the act of a rider sliding his or her buttocks to one side of the saddle to shift body weight as far as possible toward the curve

high side flip: when a sliding rear tire suddenly regains traction while the motorcycle is leaned over, causing the motorcycle to violently snap from the leaning side to the other side (the high side)

inside: the side of the lane closest to the direction of a curve; the right edge of the pavement in a right-hand curve; the centerline in a left-hand curve

K-bike: A BMW motorcycle powered by the K series engine; a liquid-cooled inline 3 or 4 cylinder with the engine positioned flat in the frame

leading throttle: rolling on just enough throttle for the engine to keep pulling the bike forward

low side: the left side in a left turn or the right side in a right turn

low sides: a crash in which the motorcycle loses traction and falls onto its low side

medevac: a helicopter used for medical evacuation

off-camber: a road that slants in the wrong direction, especially a corner in which the surface slants away from the direction of turn

off side: passing another vehicle on the wrong side—i.e. the right side in countries where traffic drives on the right or the left side in countries where traffic drives on the left

outside: the side of the lane away from the direction of a curve; the centerline in a right-hand curve; the right edge of the pavement in a left-hand curve

out-track: the path of travel of the front contact patch outside of the path of the rear contact patch as the bike leans into a turn

paddle walk: supporting the motorcycle at a very slow speed by sitting in the saddle and paddling the ground alternately with both feet

positive camber curve: a curve where the road surface slants toward the direction of the turn

punching through the envelope: exceeding the physical limits of a situation, typically exceeding traction while cornering or braking

push steering: see *countersteering*

quick stop: an aggressive maximum-effort stop primarily to avoid a collision

rake: slope; the inclination of the steering head leaning back from vertical

road craft: the concept that riding a motorcycle is a craft requiring knowledge and skill

safetycrats: a bureaucrat focused on protecting you from yourself

sight distance: the relative amount of roadway that is visible ahead at a given moment

sportbike: a motorcycle designed for aggressive performance, especially cornering

squid: a cocky motorcyclist who darts very aggressively through traffic

steering input: the physical effort of countersteering and/or shifting body weight to cause the motorcycle to change its course

step-out: when the rear tire loses traction for an instant during a corner, allowing the rear end of the bike to slip sideways

stiction: extra friction or sticking in the front suspension sliders

stoppie: applying sufficient front wheel brake to cause the rear end to rise, balancing the motorcycle on the front wheel

superslab: a generic term for any multilane, high-speed, limited access highway, including a freeway, tollway, motorway, parkway, or superhighway

sweeping turn: a corner with a very large radius (sweeper)

target entry speed: whatever speed allows you to continuously roll on leading throttle through the rest of the turn

throttle: the rotating grip on the handlebar that controls engine power

traction: rolling friction between a tire and the road surface

trail braking: applying either or both brakes while decelerating and leaning into a turn

trailing throttle: decelerating with the throttle closed to apply engine compression braking to the rear wheel

warp speed: any speed that is obviously in excess of the posted limit

wheel track: 1. the path of one wheel of a moving vehicle 2: the width between the contact patches of two wheels of a multitrack vehicle (the width between the contact patches of the two rear wheels of a trike)

woodsing: riding a dirt bike slowly along a path through the woods

Index